PERPETUA'S JOURNEY

FAITH, GENDER, & POWER IN THE ROMAN EMPIRE

JENNIFER A. REA

LIZ CLARKE

New York   Oxford
OXFORD UNIVERSITY PRESS

Oxford University Press is a department of the University of Oxford. It furthers the
University's objective of excellence in research, scholarship, and education by publishing
worldwide. Oxford is a registered trade mark of Oxford University Press in the UK and
certain other countries.

Published in the United States of America by Oxford University Press
198 Madison Avenue, New York, NY 10016, United States of America.

For titles covered by Section 112 of the US Higher Education
Opportunity Act, please visit www.oup.com/us/he for the
latest information about pricing and alternate formats.

Library of Congress Cataloging-in-Publication Data

Names: Rea, Jennifer A., author. | Clarke, Liz, 1982- illustrator.
Title: Perpetua's journey : faith, gender & power in the Roman Empire /
    Jennifer Rea ; [illustrated by] Liz Clarke.
Other titles: Passio SS. Perpetuae et Felicitatis.
Description: New York, NY : Oxford University Press, 2018.
Identifiers: LCCN 2016059263| ISBN 9780190238711 (paperback) | ISBN
    9780190238728 (instructor paperback)
Subjects: LCSH: Perpetua, Saint, -203. | Perpetua, Saint, -203—Pictorial
    works. | Passio SS. Perpetuae et Felicitatis. | Felicity, Saint, -203. |
    Christian women saints—Rome—Biography. | Christian women
    saints—Tunisia—Carthage (Extinct city)—Biography. | Christian women
    martyrs—Rome—Biography. | Sex role—Rome—History. | Power (Social
    sciences)—Rome—History. | Rome—History—Empire, 30 B.C.-284 A.D.
Classification: LCC BR1720.P42 R43 2018 | DDC 272/.1092 [B] —dc23
LC record available at https://lccn.loc.gov/2016059263

Printing number: 9 8 7 6

Printed by LSC Communications, Inc.

PERPETUA'S JOURNEY

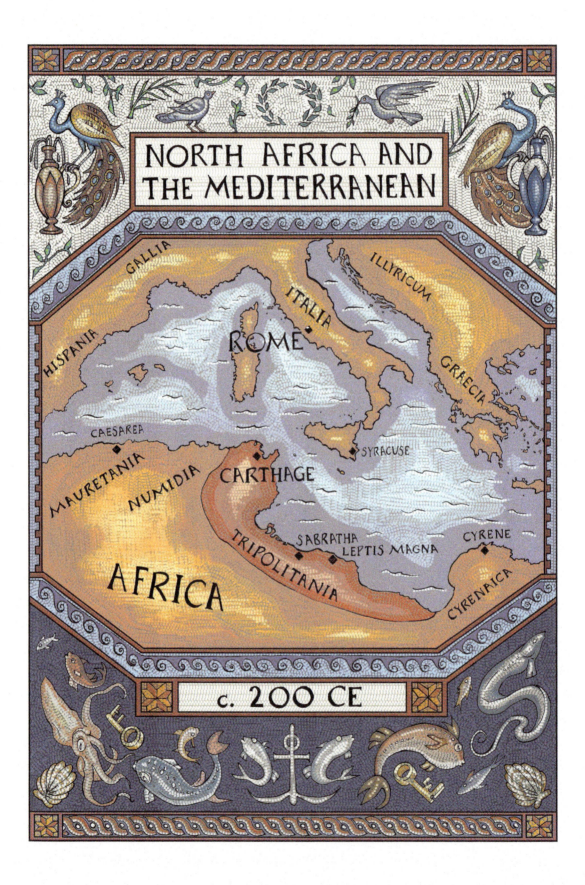

NORTH AFRICA AND THE MEDITERRANEAN

GALLIA

ILLYRICUM

ITALIA

HISPANIA

ROME

GRAECIA

CAESAREA

SYRACUSE

MAURETANIA

NUMIDIA

CARTHAGE

SABRATHA

CYRENE

TRIPOLITANIA

LEPTIS MAGNA

AFRICA

CYRENAICA

c. 200 CE

For A.D.C. and N.D.C.

CONTENTS

MAPS AND FIGURES

MAPS

FIGURES

PREFACE

ABOUT THE *PASSIO*

This is the story of a young mother, Vibia Perpetua, who lived in Roman Africa and, at the age of twenty-two, chose to proclaim publicly her Christian faith. She became a martyr, which meant that she died as a result of her beliefs. She did not die alone: she was part of a group of Christian martyrs, including several slaves, who were imprisoned and then sentenced to die. Perpetua and her fellow Christians died during the birthday games held in Carthage in honor of the Emperor Septimius Severus's son Geta on March 7 in the year 203 CE. Perpetua's diary, known as the *Passio Perpetuae et Felicitatis*, or *The Passion of Perpetua and Felicity*, contains Perpetua's account of the days leading up to her martyrdom.

The *Passio* is the first extant diary authored by a Christian woman. Perpetua's words give us insight into her world. We can look at what kind of education she may have had, what prison life was like from a female perspective, her feelings as she prepared to say goodbye to her baby and family, and many other aspects of her life.

What makes this work unique and worthy of consideration is that it offers us insight into the female perspective on the complex relationship between power and gender in antiquity. From the start of her diary, Perpetua acts as an advocate for her right to be Christian. At that time women could legally act as their own advocates. Later on in the diary, she argues for better conditions for herself and the other Christians in the prison with her, even though it was illegal at that time for women to advocate on behalf of others. Despite her act of civil disobedience, Perpetua earns respect from male authority figures and succeeds in achieving her goals by using rational arguments and even humor.

KEY FEATURES OF *PERPETUA'S JOURNEY*

Perpetua's Journey is a graphic history that occupies a space between (1) the many works designed primarily for specialists and advanced scholars who already know a great deal about Perpetua and the Roman Empire's history and (2) projects about the saints' lives that could be classified as forms of popular media (films, illustrated texts, etc.) made for a more general audience. This work differs from other sources that inform us about Perpetua's life because it contains both a graphic portion and historical and social commentary on the *Passio*. The graphic part of this work strives for an authentic and realistic portrayal of events that happened to the persons in the diary.

But studying and writing about a particular set of events that occurred during a historical period is always complicated, and analysis of past events is never without bias. For this reason, the reader will find diverse and varying critical approaches to Perpetua's story. The work is divided into four parts. First, the graphic history, illustrated by Liz Clarke, tells the story of Perpetua and her fellow Christians. The text that accompanies the sequential art is taken directly from the *Passio*. It is our hope that the inclusion of the graphic portion will inspire readers to engage with the *Passio* and to facilitate new critical thinking and discussion of the text. Second, the essays provide historical and social context for the events described in the *Passio*. Third, a translation of the *Passio* is provided so the reader can see the original text, translated from Latin to English. This allows the reader to assess the interpretative choices made when we transformed the text into illustrated storyboards. As the illustrator and the author of this book, Liz and I became the *Passio*'s interpreters for a modern and diverse audience of believers and nonbelievers alike. And that is why the graphic portion begins not with the introduction from the narrator's viewpoint about ancient examples from the past, but with a brief summary of the *Passio*'s critical information, so that the audience can begin reading Perpetua's words in context. A complete translation is included in this work so that readers can read the longer introduction.

Finally, a conclusion asks crucial questions about the interpretative materials, which include the graphic history and the social and historical commentaries. The conclusion invites the reader to question and assess what they have learned about Perpetua. It also asks the audience to consider what questions have been raised by *Perpetua's Journey*. All documents from the past, including the *Passio*, will leave audiences with some questions unanswered and will raise awareness of new and significant issues to consider. Although there are studies, translations, and commentaries already published on the *Passio* (see "Further Reading"), the purpose in writing this work was to contribute to the ongoing dialogue about Perpetua and the early Christian church in a way that has not been done before.

METHODOLOGY

The approach to this text was not to deconstruct it in order to find one way to read and interpret the *Passio*, but rather to explore why the diary still resonates with audiences today. Regarding the methodology for how readers should interpret the *Passio*, it is important to remember that in antiquity, the ancient audience for the diary would not have been reading or listening to this text and asking themselves whether or not the story was true, or trying to discern what *really* happened versus what was only symbolic within the work. This is a modern approach that scholars sometimes take to texts; the question of whether the text was written as a historically correct account of the events did not concern the *Passio*'s audience because for them, the *Passio* was about faith. And Perpetua was demonstrating how to be faithful to one's convictions.

Reading this document from either solely a spiritual standpoint or solely a secular one would deny the complexity of the text and the social and political conditions that shaped its content. Perpetua's story is about both civil disobedience and her fight for religious freedom. The experiences she recorded in her diary can tell us much about forming a Christian community across social boundaries, enduring when one's faith is tested, and being a martyr.[1] Perpetua's authentic voice, her genuine relationships with her biological family members, and her bond with her Christian family make this work engaging to read.

Modern or personal assumptions about terms such as *religion*,[2] *pagan*,[3] *Christian* or *Christianity*,[4] and *martyr*[5] may influence an individual's reading of this text and understanding of what life was like for persons living

---

1   Farina (2009, 191–92).

2   See the section "Roman Religion and Early Christianity" for how I am defining the term *religion* in this work.

3   Throughout this work, the term *pagan* is used to describe the community and/ or individuals who adopted traditional forms of worship. But the term is problematic, and it would be incorrect to assume that there was a cohesive pagan community in Roman Africa. Maxwell (2012, 853) suggests that "the pagans were people rooted in local customs of an ancient religious landscape" but argues against generalizations that propose pagans had adopted a consistent set of beliefs, rather than a "wide range of local traditions."

4   Christianity, which is based on the life and teachings of Jesus Christ, is a monotheistic religion. Monotheistic religions have only one god, as compared with polytheistic religions, which have multiple gods. Christians believe that Jesus Christ is the Son of God and humanity's savior. Throughout this work, the terms *early Christian* or *Christians* are used to mean the community of believers who existed in Roman North Africa before the First Council of Nicaea (in 325 CE), although sometimes *Christians* will be used in reference to events taking place outside of Carthage.

5   See the section "Martyrs in Antiquity" for a discussion of modern and ancient concepts of martyrdom.

in the Roman Empire during the third century CE. But Perpetua's diary demonstrates that when we use *Christian* and *pagan* to refer to members of the community in Roman Africa, these are complex and fluid categories. It is important to acknowledge that in antiquity, one's identity was shaped not only by religion, but also by one's civic and social obligations. As Rebillard notes, being a Christian "was only one of the many affiliations that mattered in everyday life."[6] Perpetua declared herself to be a Christian in the *Passio*, but her social obligations included being a mother, and Roman officials expected her to perform her civic duty and sacrifice to the Roman emperor.

Within the *Passio*, Perpetua's resistance toward male authority figures and her vision in which she changes gender from female to male raise significant questions about what it meant to transcend limits in antiquity and push social boundaries. But by engaging with these topics we are not anachronistically suggesting that Perpetua's behavior can be seen as feminist in the same way that we might consider a modern person a feminist, nor are we attempting to claim that when she acted as an advocate on behalf of others she was trying to improve the social and political conditions for women in her time. Rather, the discussions of identity and gender are meant to engage the modern audience in thinking about what cultural and social assumptions society in antiquity might have held regarding women, and in particular with regard to women's minds and bodies.

THE GENRE OF THE *PASSIO*

There is no consensus among scholars who attempt to classify this work within a particular genre.[7] Perpetua's text is often called a diary because it appears to be written as if it were a memoir in her own voice. It communicates the immediacy of her death as she recounts the events of the final days of her life until the birthday games arrive at last. Also, she records in her work that she came to her death voluntarily. This kind of autobiographical account of one's own actions and reflections allows the reader to glimpse at a subject's personality. Often, we learn about Perpetua's state of mind. But there are ways in which the *Passio* does not follow the modern conventions of a diary. It is very difficult to gauge the progression of time, for example, as the sequence of events does not contain dates before each activity. The diary is also an unusual document because it is a recording of the legal authority that she assumes during her trial.

---

6   Rebillard (2012, 33).

7   See Ameling (2012, 89) and Bal (2012, 138).

A narrator places Perpetua's work within the frame of a panegyric, which is a text in praise of someone, and in her own clear and straightforward prose, she describes the events that led to the end of her life.[8] It would be hard to say that Perpetua kept a journal solely for her own private use; the work appears to have been written for a Christian audience. The document is unique in that it is the first diary that we have from a Christian woman from this time period and she did not write from the perspective of a theologian.[9]

A NOTE TO THE READER

This text is designed so that Parts I, II, and III can be read independently of one another and in any order. Thus, those who wish to begin with the graphic portion can do so, while others may prefer to read the historical commentary and essays or even the translation of the *Passio* before looking at the sequential art. Readers will find there is some slight overlap in the various sections of this work. There is also some intersection of content in the commentary portion of the text as certain aspects of the diary require viewing through several critical lenses.

Perpetua's Journey is a graphic history because it combines artwork that occurs in a sequence with historical commentary.[10] Sequential art is not just a means by which one creates an imaginary world: graphic images depict the early third-century imperial Roman world that Perpetua inhabited, including the material culture of Roman Africa and Carthage. We chose to tell Perpetua's story in the graphic format because her diary contains a great deal of striking and vivid description of what happened to her, including a detailed account of her visions, her terrifying first impression of prison, and the explicit details of her death. One thing we did not want to do was tell Perpetua's story word-for-word via text boxes within the pictures Liz drew. Doing so would defeat the purpose of having the graphic text accompany the diary. That is why

---

8 LeMoine (1996, 220) notes that Perpetua is different from a female poet who writes "only for herself and her own desires," as the *Passio* was concerned with advocacy. Bal (2012, 138) refers to Perpetua's account as an "autobiographical, testimonial narrative."

9 For the purposes of this text I am assuming Perpetua was a real person and not a literary construct. See Heffernan (2012, 5–8) for a discussion of the authenticity of the text. Ameling (2012, 79) notes that "there is no remotely comparable woman's writing" from this time period and "none at all by a Christian woman."

10 The term *comic* is also used to describe art that occurs in a sequence. According to Duncan and Smith (2009, 3–4), comics are "a particular kind of sequential art" that is "concerned with storytelling"; they do not distinguish between a comic book and a graphic novel.

sometimes readers will see only pictures of what is happening—instead of text boxes plus pictures—to avoid having the graphic portion of the book become too repetitive. The visuals allow the audience to experience the events in a way that is similar to watching social dynamics within a theater performance.

Changes from one narrator to another are signified visually instead of by means of writing. The narrator often appears speaking to the audience. When the diary shifts to Perpetua's own words, then the symbol of a reed pen appears in front of her text. Sometimes words appear in a thought or speech bubble when the people in the story are talking to one another or when someone is thinking.

In addition, many of Perpetua's encounters with authorities take place in public venues such as the forum or the amphitheater, and the onlookers' reactions, which are described in the story, provide another way to think critically about her experience. The crowd plays a very important role in this story, as their reactions can tell us a great deal about the social norms of the time. The inherent drama in Liz's drawings will raise questions for the modern audience that they would not have considered had they only read the written text. The graphic format allowed us, for example, to get at deeper issues of identity formation—for example, how much of Perpetua's identity was shaped by social constructs of the times?

Another reason using both text and image seemed like an ideal way to represent the *Passio* was because of the intersection between the culture of provincial Carthage and the presence of the Roman imperial cult in the city. The Roman Empire's influence on Carthage's architecture, clothing styles, and other aspects of life for the community was strong. Liz's visual representations make manifest the Roman presence in Carthage, through the architectural elements in buildings, the presence of Roman soldiers in scenes, and reminders of Roman rituals.

When Liz and I first sent our proposal off to Oxford University Press, some readers in Oxford's focus group expressed their concerns about whether students who read this book would be more passive in their engagement with the text because it would be accompanied by pictures. This is not the first graphic history published by OUP: prior texts in this series include *Abina and the Important Men* (2011; 2016) and *Inhuman Traffick* (2014). The critical success of *Abina and the Important Men* by Trevor R. Getz and Liz Clarke, which is now in its second edition, is just one example that confirms that a historical commentary with illustrations is not going to encourage passive learning. To those critics we would respond that visual communication has long been established as another way to convey essential information about a text and that it enhances, not replaces, the readers' understanding and their use of imagination.[11] Furthermore, to show prejudice against or reject discussion of a graphic history solely because it interests an audience beyond a select group of scholars would be to deny the broader audience the opportunity to ask critical questions about and engage in a dialogue on why Perpetua's story remains relevant today. The story has the potential to engage a broader audience than the one whose interest lies in studying early Christianity or the history of the Christian church.

Can a graphic representation of events in someone's life be considered historical? The relationship between history and comics is complex. One question that problematizes the issue of making a graphic illustration of Perpetua's diary is whether or not the diary is a historical document. The narrator mentions that Perpetua wrote it in her own hand and that the diary was just as she composed it, suggesting that the narrator did not make any editorial changes to it and that it is a first-person narrative of events that took place in Carthage under Septimius Severus's reign. Scholars still debate the text's authenticity and historicity.[12]

When looking at the diary, one of the more challenging aspects is to let go of modern assumptions and expectations for how a twenty-two-year-old married female would or should act. The diary helps the audience do this because there is a built-in audience that responds to Perpetua's actions. Witnesses to her actions make demands of her, blush in response to her behavior, fly at her as if to pluck out her eyes, pull out a beard, and even jeer at her and her companions at their last meal. Sometimes the audience is angered or startled by her behavior, giving the modern reader clues that her behavior is regarded as shocking and sometimes even monstrous. At the end she stares back at everyone who came to see her die. And then they lower their eyes in shame.[13] Thus, when considering the events of Perpetua's life, modern readers should bring to the story an open mind regarding Perpetua's life choices. The audience may see something that sparks their imagination and raises significant new questions about the text.

---

11 The past several decades of graphic publications have established that sequential art is not just for children's entertainment, as it had been regarded for most of the prior century. Many graphic novels convey sophisticated stories and describe consequential events in history (e.g., *Maus: A Survivor's Tale*, 1980–91; *Persepolis*, 2000–2003). Art Spiegelman won a Pulitzer Prize for *Maus*, which chronicles the experiences of a Holocaust survivor. Marjane Satrapi's *Persepolis* is a coming-of-age memoir about life in Iran for the duration of and after the Islamic Revolution.

12 See Frend (1993, 90), who in particular argues for the authenticity of the prison description. Perkins (2007, 330), however, argues that the text is "rhetorical rather than realistic."

13 Perkins (1994, 845). See also Shaw (1993, 4) and Farina (2009, 13).

ACKNOWLEDGMENTS

I would like to thank the following individuals for lending their expertise and support to this project: John Berneche, University of Massachusetts at Amherst; Neil Bernstein, Ohio University; David Billig, University of Florida; Lidia Buono, Università degli studi di Cassino e del Lazio Meridionale; Nina Caputo, University of Florida; Julian Chambliss, Rollins College; Stamatia Dova, Hellenic College Holy Cross; Don Mariano Dell'Omo, Montecassino Abbey; Linda Fuchs, University of Florida; Adrian Goldsworthy, Newcastle University; Irina Goodman, University of Florida; Thomas J. Heffernan, University of Tennessee; Trevor Luke, Florida State University; Éric Rebillard, Cornell University; David Reis, University of Oregon; Brett Rogers, University of Puget Sound; Karen Ros, University of Illinois at Chicago; Michael A. Speidel, Bern University; Benjamin E. Stevens, Trinity University; and Velvet L. Yates, University of Florida.

I also wish to extend my thanks to the following individuals who served as reviewers for Oxford University Press: Jessica Clark, Florida State University; Nicola Denzey-Lewis, Brown University; and Isabel Moreira, University of Utah. Their enthusiastic endorsement of this project as both a commentary and a graphic history and their expertise on the *Passio* contributed significantly to the end result. Many individuals at OUP contributed to the completion of this book, including Katherine Schnakenberg, Sara Birmingham, and Rowan Wixted, editorial assistants, and Marianne Paul, Senior Project Editor.

My colleagues in the classics department at the University of Florida provided a lively and collegial atmosphere in which to complete this work. They were always available to lend their advice regarding the details of the text and to offer critiques of the text's graphic portion. In particular, Miller Krause and Biagio Santorelli offered many helpful suggestions for my translation of the *Passio*, and special thanks also goes to Father Andreas Kramarz (Legion of Christ College of the Humanities) for his advice on the text. I would also like to thank my department chair, Mary Ann Eaverly, for her support and advice. This project was also supported by the University of Florida Rothman Family Endowment in the form of a Rothman Faculty Summer Fellowship in the Humanities.

Perpetua's story has always fascinated me because of the bravery, honor, and resolve she demonstrated in her account of her final days. I want to thank Charles Cavaliere at Oxford University Press for the opportunity to delve deeply into all aspects of Perpetua's life and to write a book about her that places the *Passio* into the wider context of early Christianity's development. His enthusiasm for this project from the start and his support of it were essential.

I want especially to thank Tom Hart from the Sequential Artists Workshop in Gainesville, Florida. Tom guided me from my starting point of many questions to the moment when I had developed a base of knowledge about how to turn a Latin text into a storyboard. He encouraged me and listened patiently to my ideas. His vision for how to depict the enduring appeal of the *Passio* and Perpetua herself helped in particular to influence the final two pages of this text's graphic portion.

The support and encouragement of my husband, Avery, and my son, Nicholas, were essential for the completion of this work. They were enthusiastic and intrepid participants in treks to catacombs, amphitheaters, and museums; they asked critical questions; and they understood how important this project was to me. Avery especially possessed equal parts patience and curiosity when listening to my ideas for the essays that comprise this work's historical commentary. This book would not exist in this form without both of them.

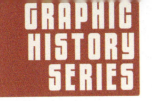

GRAPHIC HISTORY SERIES

GRAPHIC HISTORY SERIES

Widely acclaimed by educators, the award-winning Graphic History Series introduces students to the ways that historians construct the past. Going beyond simply depicting events in the past, each title in the Graphic History Series combines the power of imagery with primary sources, historical essays, and cutting-edge historiography to offer a powerful tool for teaching history and teaching *about* history.

PUBLISHED

Trevor R. Getz and Liz Clarke, *Abina and the Important Men*

Ronald Schechter and Liz Clark, *Mendoza the Jew: Boxing, Manliness, and Nationalism*

Rafe Blaufarb and Liz Clarke, *Inhuman Traffick: The International Struggle Against the Atlantic Slave Trade*

Nina Caputo and Liz Clarke, *Debating Truth: The Barcelona Disputation of 1263*

Andrew Kirk and Kristian Purcell, *Doom Towns: The People and Landscapes of Atomic Testing*

FORTHCOMING

Michael G. Vann and Liz Clarke, *The Great Hanoi Rat Hunt: Empire, Race, and Modernity in French Colonial Vietnam*

Bryan McCann and Gilmar Fraga, *The Black Lancers and the Ragamuffin Revolt*

Maura Elizabeth Cunningham and Liz Clarke, *Wandering Lives: Art and Politics in Twentieth-Century China*

Karlos K. Hill and Dave Dodson, *The Murder of Emmett Till*

PERPETUA'S JOURNEY

PART I
THE GRAPHIC
HISTORY

CHAPTER 1
CARCER ET PRAETORIUM, "THE PRISON AND THE PALACE"

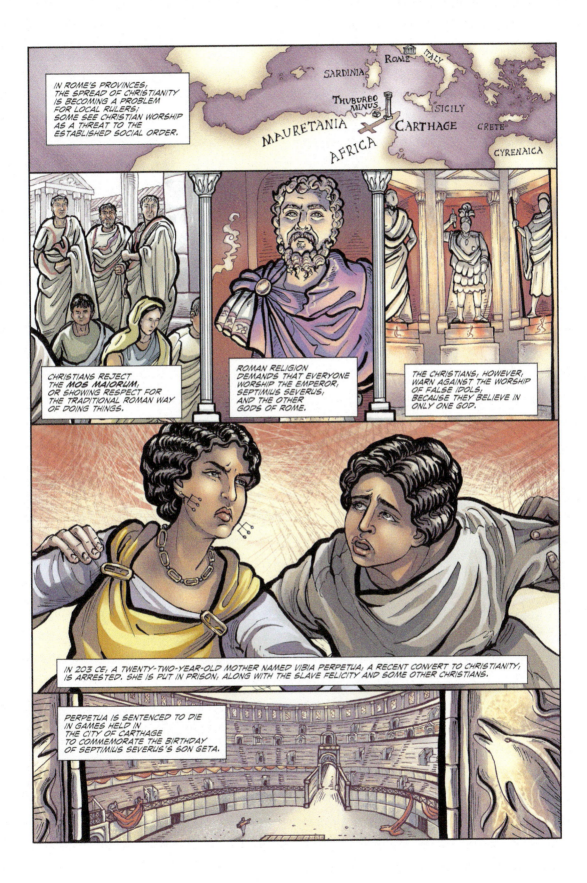

IN ROME'S PROVINCES, THE SPREAD OF CHRISTIANITY IS BECOMING A PROBLEM FOR LOCAL RULERS; SOME SEE CHRISTIAN WORSHIP AS A THREAT TO THE ESTABLISHED SOCIAL ORDER.

ROME ITALY
SARDINIA
THUBURBO MINUS
MAURETANIA CARTHAGE SICILY CRETE
AFRICA CYRENAICA

CHRISTIANS REJECT THE **MOS MAIORUM**, OR SHOWING RESPECT FOR THE TRADITIONAL ROMAN WAY OF DOING THINGS.

ROMAN RELIGION DEMANDS THAT EVERYONE WORSHIP THE EMPEROR, SEPTIMIUS SEVERUS; AND THE OTHER GODS OF ROME.

THE CHRISTIANS, HOWEVER, WARN AGAINST THE WORSHIP OF FALSE IDOLS, BECAUSE THEY BELIEVE IN ONLY ONE GOD.

IN 203 CE, A TWENTY-TWO-YEAR-OLD MOTHER NAMED VIBIA PERPETUA, A RECENT CONVERT TO CHRISTIANITY, IS ARRESTED. SHE IS PUT IN PRISON, ALONG WITH THE SLAVE FELICITY AND SOME OTHER CHRISTIANS.

PERPETUA IS SENTENCED TO DIE IN GAMES HELD IN THE CITY OF CARTHAGE TO COMMEMORATE THE BIRTHDAY OF SEPTIMIUS SEVERUS'S SON GETA.

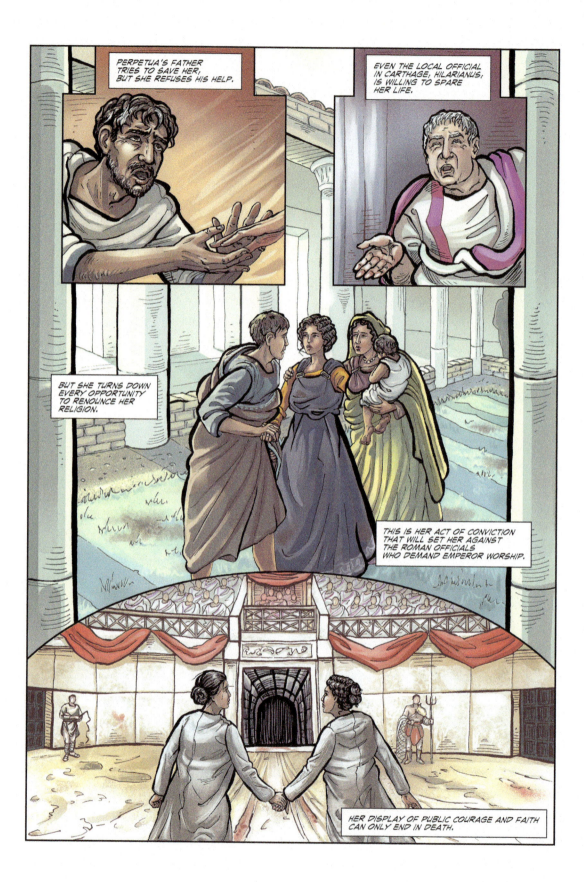

PERPETUA'S FATHER TRIES TO SAVE HER, BUT SHE REFUSES HIS HELP.

EVEN THE LOCAL OFFICIAL IN CARTHAGE, HILARIANUS, IS WILLING TO SPARE HER LIFE.

BUT SHE TURNS DOWN EVERY OPPORTUNITY TO RENOUNCE HER RELIGION.

THIS IS HER ACT OF CONVICTION THAT WILL SET HER AGAINST THE ROMAN OFFICIALS WHO DEMAND EMPEROR WORSHIP.

HER DISPLAY OF PUBLIC COURAGE AND FAITH CAN ONLY END IN DEATH.

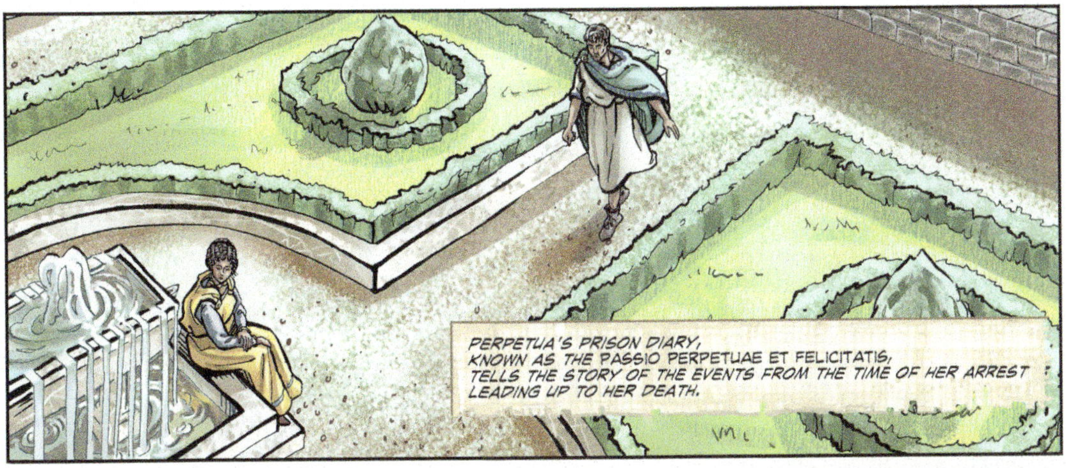
PERPETUA'S PRISON DIARY,
KNOWN AS THE PASSIO PERPETUAE ET FELICITATIS,
TELLS THE STORY OF THE EVENTS FROM THE TIME OF HER ARREST
LEADING UP TO HER DEATH.

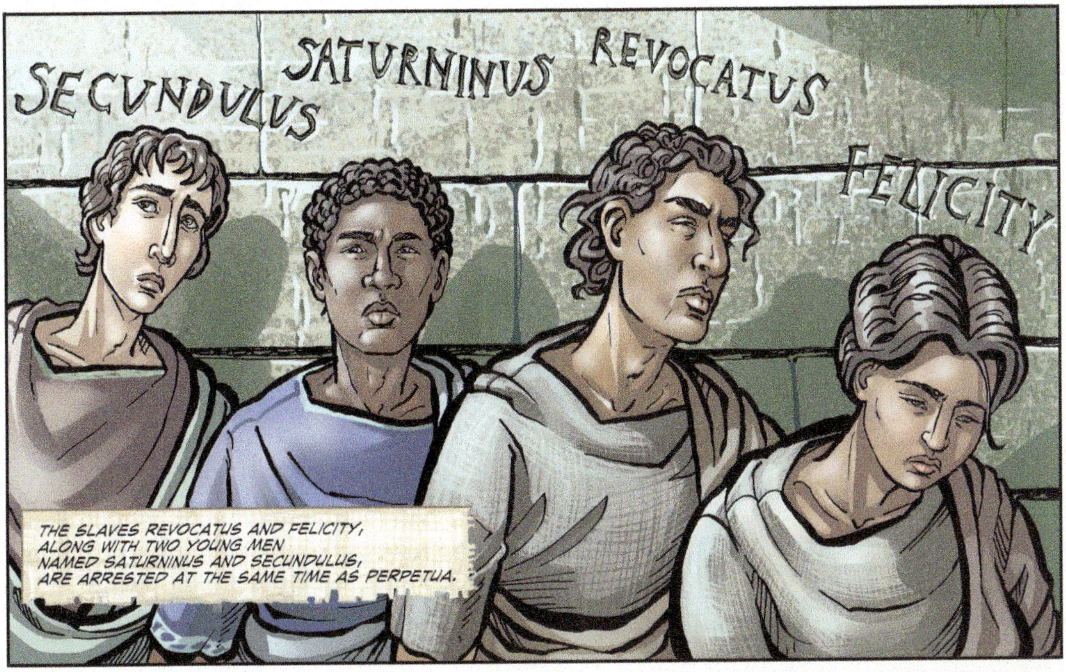
SECUNDULUS
SATURNINUS
REVOCATUS
FELICITY
THE SLAVES REVOCATUS AND FELICITY,
ALONG WITH TWO YOUNG MEN
NAMED SATURNINUS AND SECUNDULUS,
ARE ARRESTED AT THE SAME TIME AS PERPETUA.

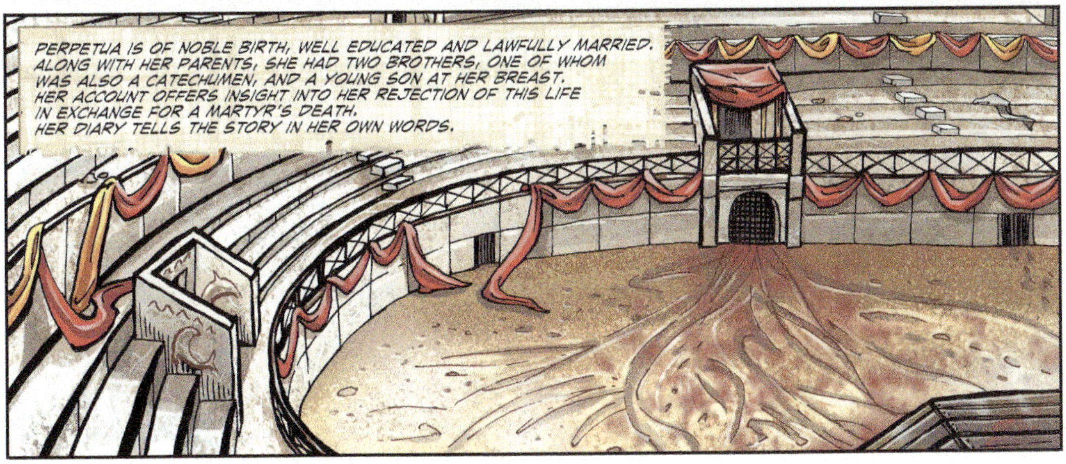
PERPETUA IS OF NOBLE BIRTH, WELL EDUCATED AND LAWFULLY MARRIED.
ALONG WITH HER PARENTS, SHE HAD TWO BROTHERS, ONE OF WHOM
WAS ALSO A CATECHUMEN, AND A YOUNG SON AT HER BREAST.
HER ACCOUNT OFFERS INSIGHT INTO HER REJECTION OF THIS LIFE
IN EXCHANGE FOR A MARTYR'S DEATH.
HER DIARY TELLS THE STORY IN HER OWN WORDS.

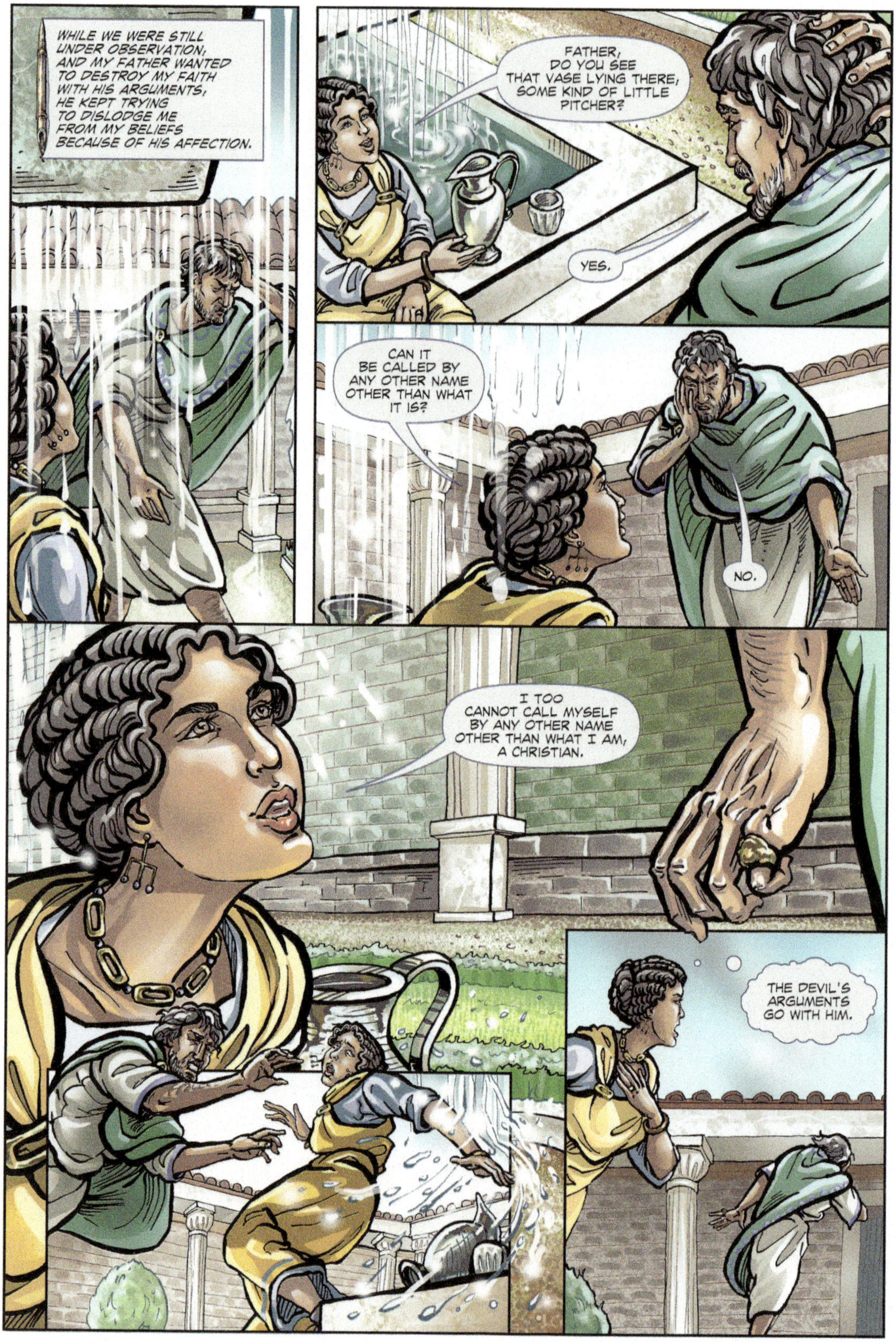
WHILE WE WERE STILL UNDER OBSERVATION, AND MY FATHER WANTED TO DESTROY MY FAITH WITH HIS ARGUMENTS, HE KEPT TRYING TO DISLODGE ME FROM MY BELIEFS BECAUSE OF HIS AFFECTION.
FATHER, DO YOU SEE THAT VASE LYING THERE, SOME KIND OF LITTLE PITCHER?
YES.
CAN IT BE CALLED BY ANY OTHER NAME OTHER THAN WHAT IT IS?
NO.
I TOO CANNOT CALL MYSELF BY ANY OTHER NAME OTHER THAN WHAT I AM, A CHRISTIAN.
THE DEVIL'S ARGUMENTS GO WITH HIM.

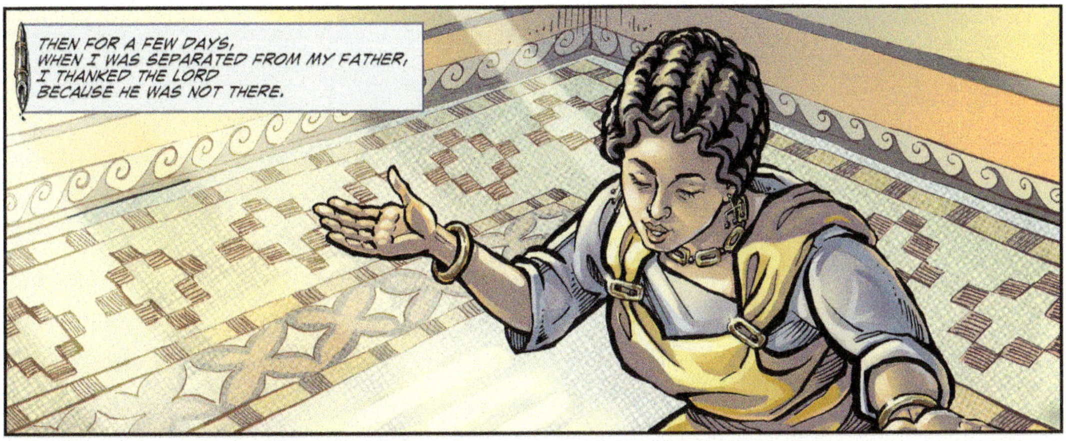
THEN FOR A FEW DAYS, WHEN I WAS SEPARATED FROM MY FATHER, I THANKED THE LORD BECAUSE HE WAS NOT THERE.

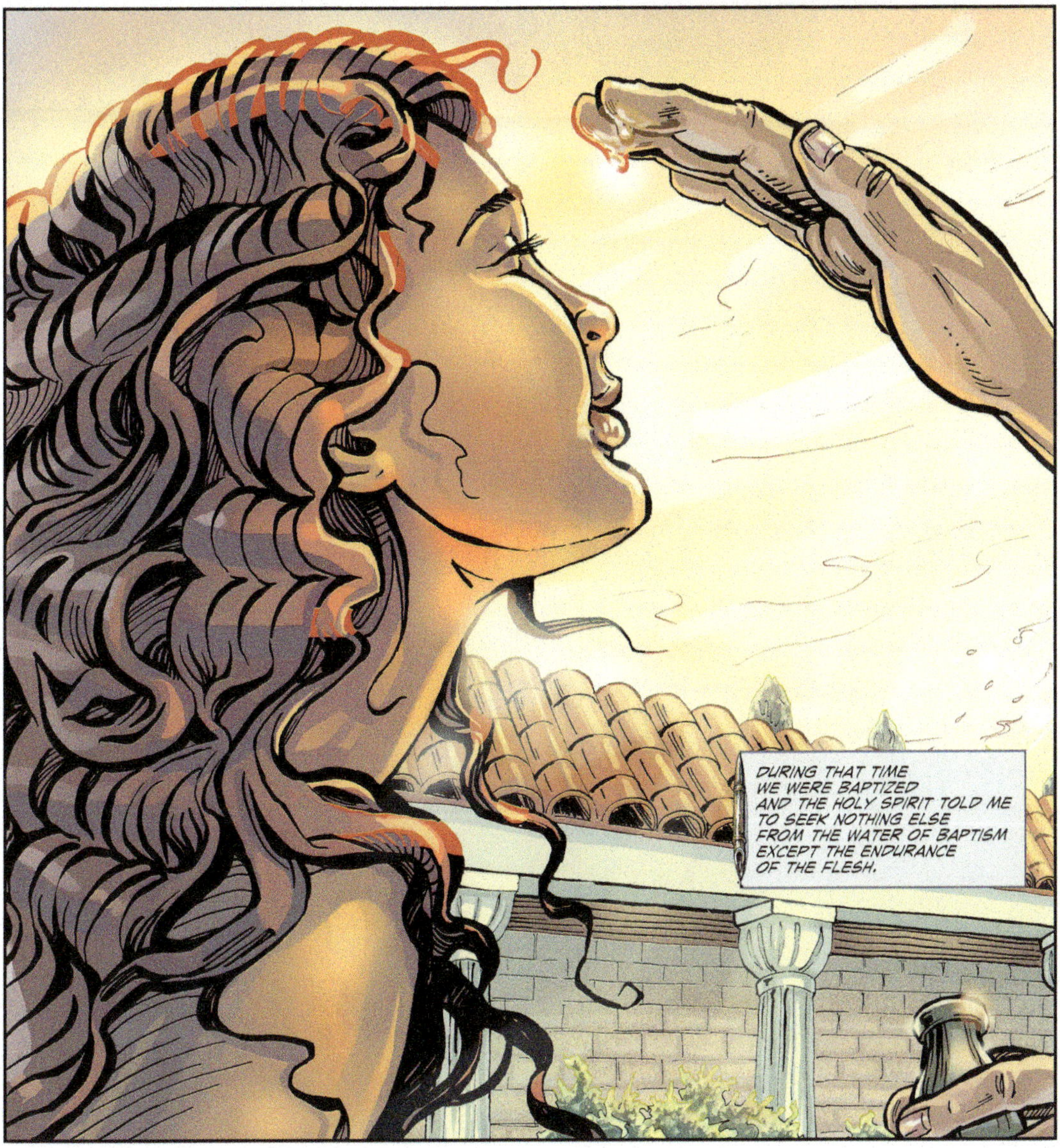
DURING THAT TIME WE WERE BAPTIZED AND THE HOLY SPIRIT TOLD ME TO SEEK NOTHING ELSE FROM THE WATER OF BAPTISM EXCEPT THE ENDURANCE OF THE FLESH.

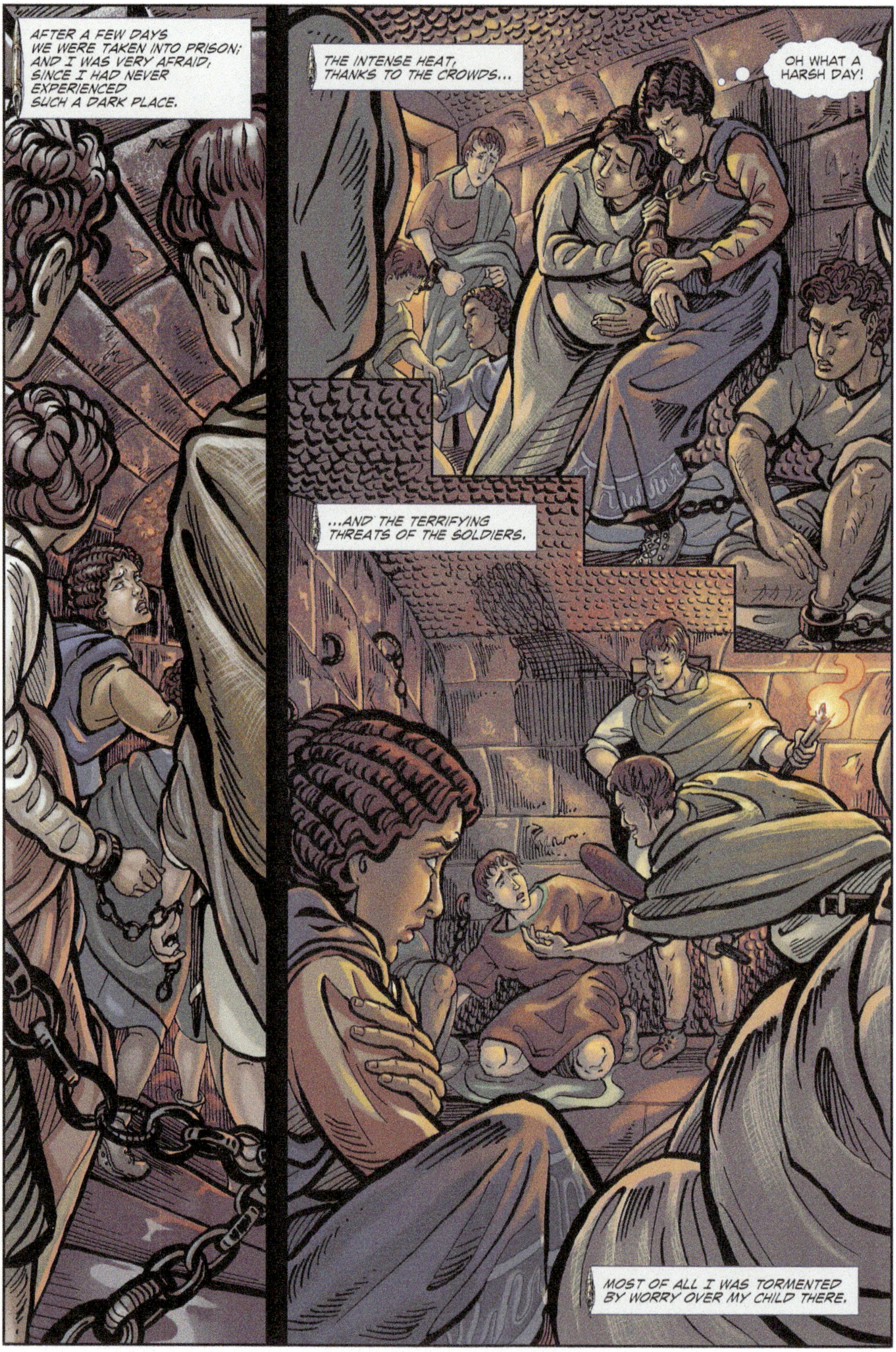
AFTER A FEW DAYS WE WERE TAKEN INTO PRISON; AND I WAS VERY AFRAID, SINCE I HAD NEVER EXPERIENCED SUCH A DARK PLACE.
THE INTENSE HEAT, THANKS TO THE CROWDS...
OH WHAT A HARSH DAY!
...AND THE TERRIFYING THREATS OF THE SOLDIERS.
MOST OF ALL I WAS TORMENTED BY WORRY OVER MY CHILD THERE.

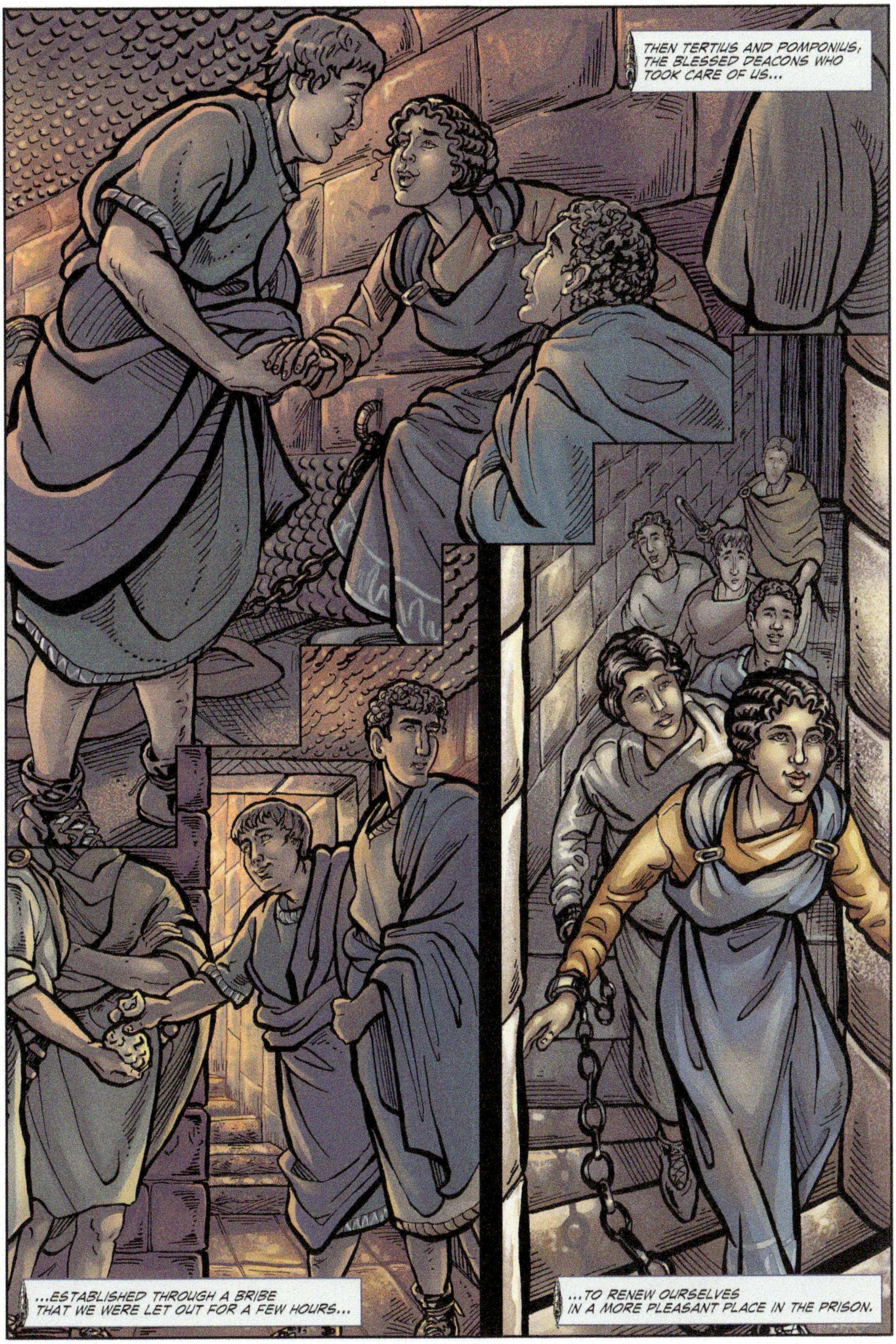
THEN TERTIUS AND POMPONIUS, THE BLESSED DEACONS WHO TOOK CARE OF US...
...ESTABLISHED THROUGH A BRIBE THAT WE WERE LET OUT FOR A FEW HOURS...
...TO RENEW OURSELVES IN A MORE PLEASANT PLACE IN THE PRISON.

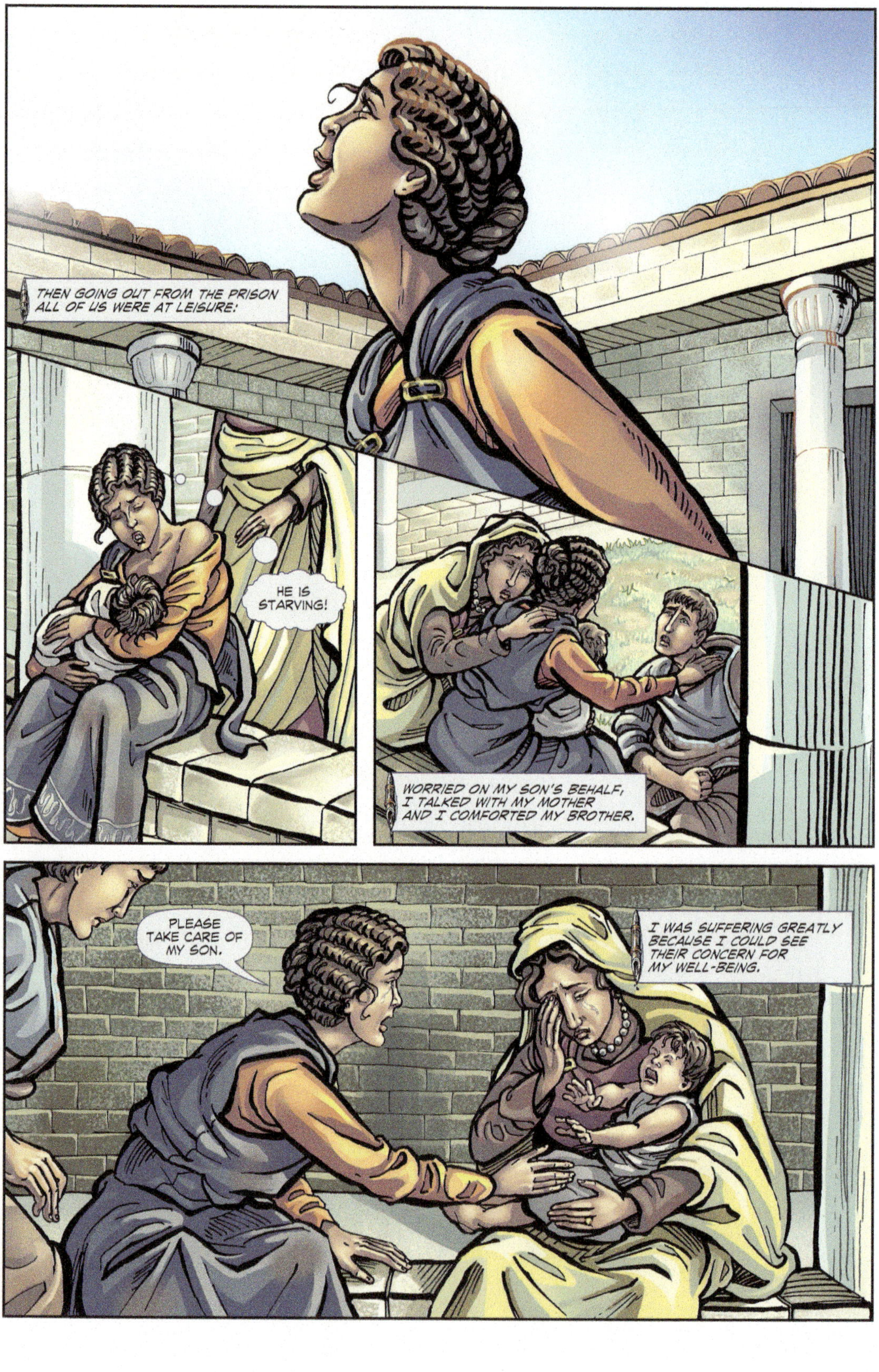
THEN GOING OUT FROM THE PRISON ALL OF US WERE AT LEISURE:
HE IS STARVING!
WORRIED ON MY SON'S BEHALF, I TALKED WITH MY MOTHER AND I COMFORTED MY BROTHER.
PLEASE TAKE CARE OF MY SON.
I WAS SUFFERING GREATLY BECAUSE I COULD SEE THEIR CONCERN FOR MY WELL-BEING.

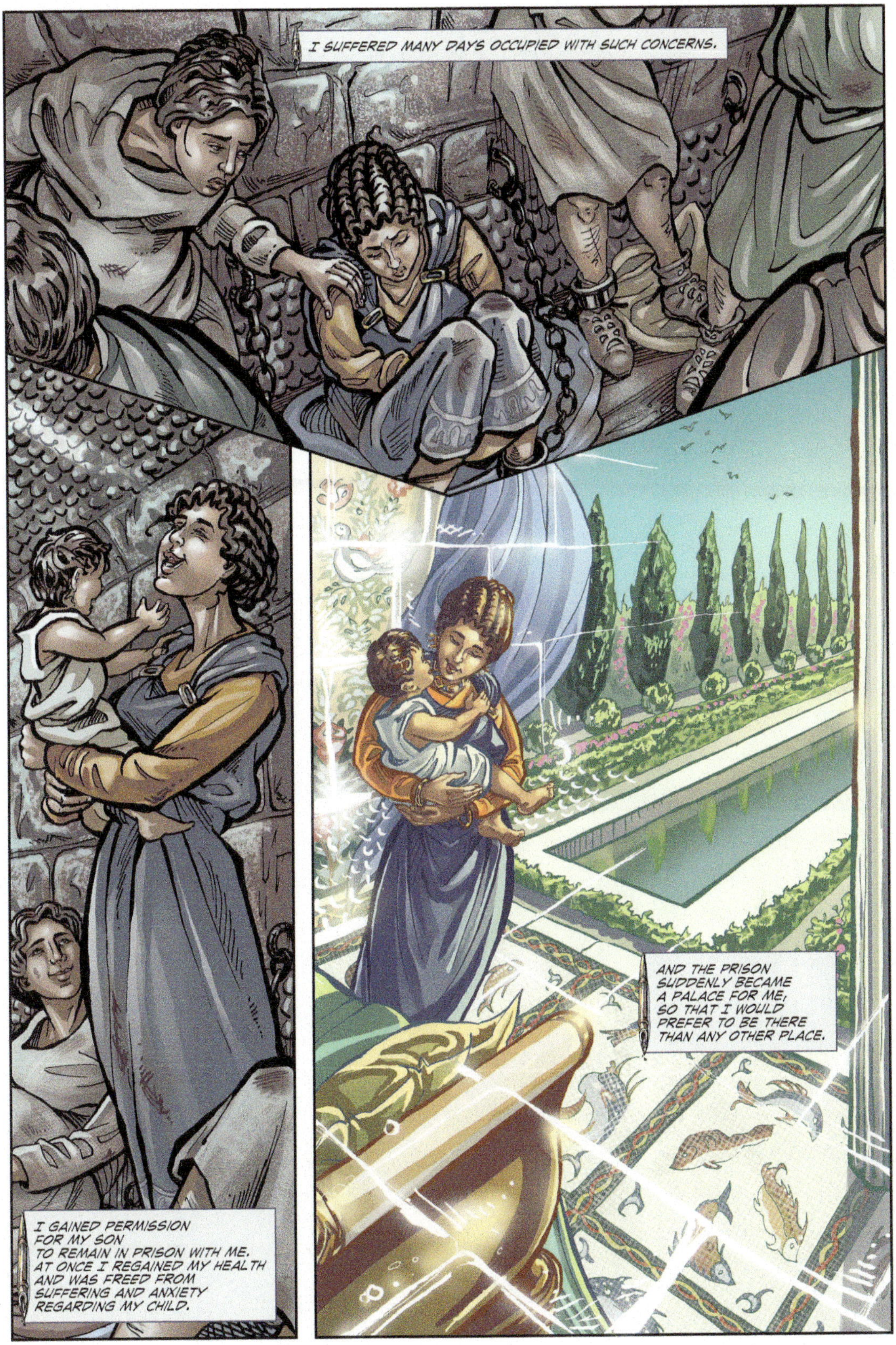
I SUFFERED MANY DAYS OCCUPIED WITH SUCH CONCERNS.
I GAINED PERMISSION FOR MY SON TO REMAIN IN PRISON WITH ME. AT ONCE I REGAINED MY HEALTH AND WAS FREED FROM SUFFERING AND ANXIETY REGARDING MY CHILD.
AND THE PRISON SUDDENLY BECAME A PALACE FOR ME, SO THAT I WOULD PREFER TO BE THERE THAN ANY OTHER PLACE.

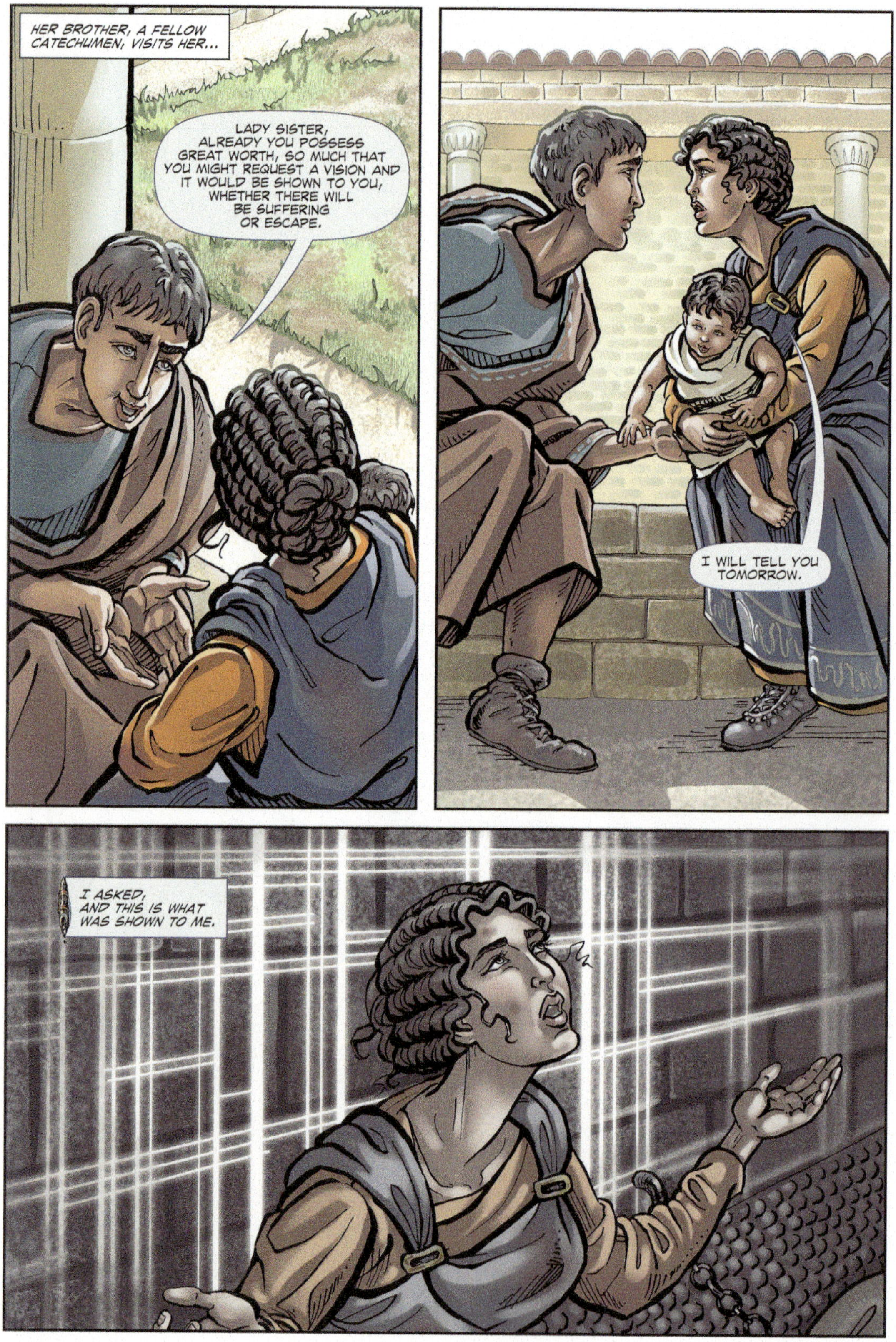
HER BROTHER, A FELLOW CATECHUMEN, VISITS HER...
LADY SISTER, ALREADY YOU POSSESS GREAT WORTH, SO MUCH THAT YOU MIGHT REQUEST A VISION AND IT WOULD BE SHOWN TO YOU, WHETHER THERE WILL BE SUFFERING OR ESCAPE.
I WILL TELL YOU TOMORROW.
I ASKED, AND THIS IS WHAT WAS SHOWN TO ME.

I saw a bronze ladder of amazing length reaching all the way up to heaven, and it was narrow, so that it was only possible to climb it one by one, and on the ladder's sides, every type of iron tool was attached. There were swords, lances, hooks, knives, and darts, so that anyone who would climb negligently, or not looking up, would be cut to pieces, and his flesh would stick to the iron. And there was a serpent of amazing size lying under this ladder ready to ambush the climbers, and he frightened people from climbing. Yet Saturus climbed first. (At that time when we had been led away, he had not been there. Afterward, he had voluntarily surrendered himself on our account, because he had instructed us.) And he arrived at the top of the ladder and he turned and said to me, "Perpetua, I am waiting for you, but take care that the serpent does not bite you." And I said, "In the name of Jesus Christ, he will not harm me."

From below the ladder, as if fearing me, the serpent slowly stuck out its head. As if I was stamping on the first step, I stepped on its head, and I climbed up. And I saw the vast space of a garden and sitting in the middle a white-haired old man dressed as a shepherd, a great man, milking sheep, and many thousands standing around dressed in white. And he lifted his head and looked at me and said to me, "You are welcome, child." And he called me and from the cheese that he was milking, gave to me about a mouthful; and I took it in clasped hands and I chewed it. And everyone standing around said, "Amen."

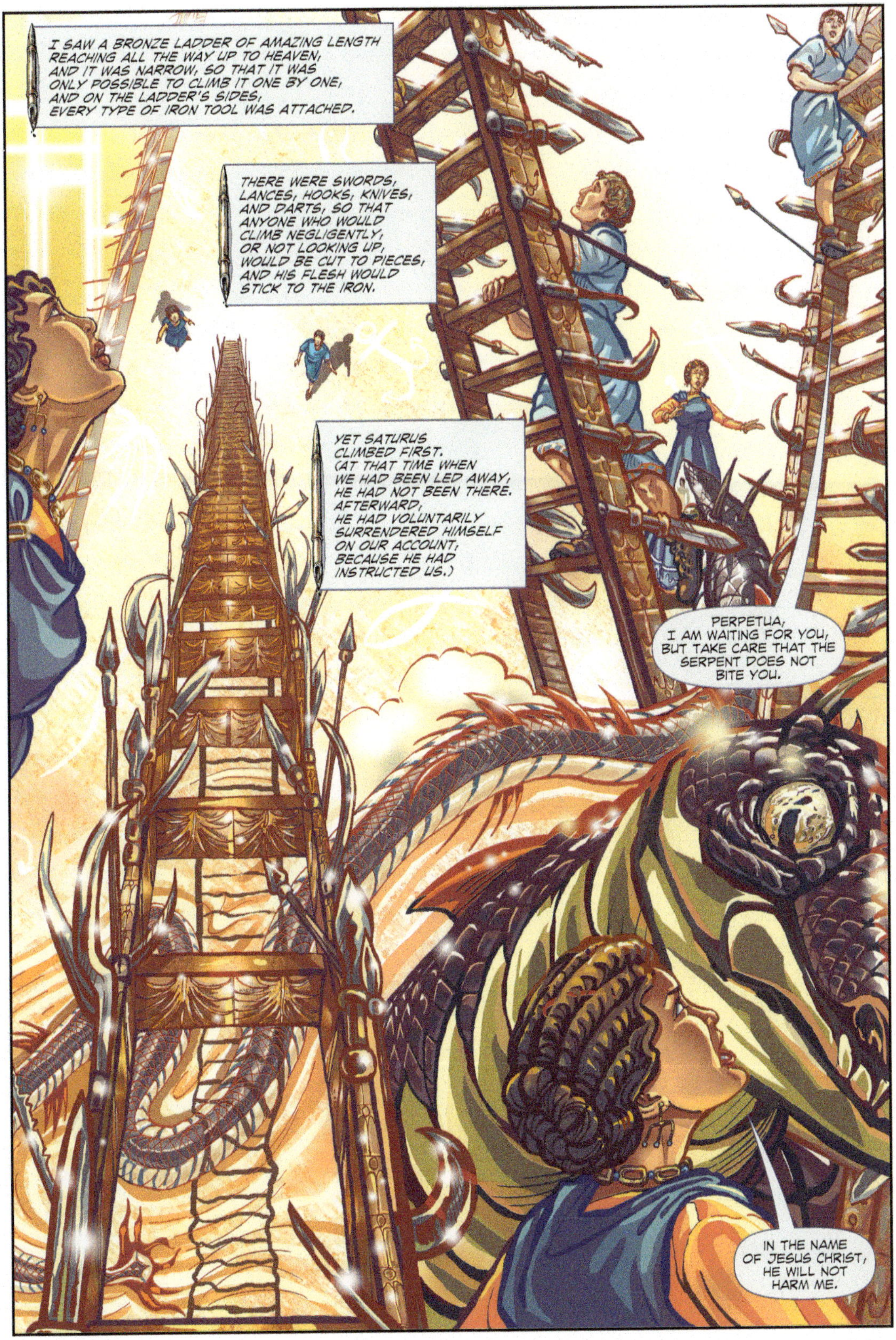
I SAW A BRONZE LADDER OF AMAZING LENGTH REACHING ALL THE WAY UP TO HEAVEN; AND IT WAS NARROW, SO THAT IT WAS ONLY POSSIBLE TO CLIMB IT ONE BY ONE, AND ON THE LADDER'S SIDES, EVERY TYPE OF IRON TOOL WAS ATTACHED.
THERE WERE SWORDS, LANCES, HOOKS, KNIVES, AND DARTS, SO THAT ANYONE WHO WOULD CLIMB NEGLIGENTLY, OR NOT LOOKING UP, WOULD BE CUT TO PIECES, AND HIS FLESH WOULD STICK TO THE IRON.
YET SATURUS CLIMBED FIRST. (AT THAT TIME WHEN WE HAD BEEN LED AWAY, HE HAD NOT BEEN THERE. AFTERWARD, HE HAD VOLUNTARILY SURRENDERED HIMSELF ON OUR ACCOUNT, BECAUSE HE HAD INSTRUCTED US.)
PERPETUA, I AM WAITING FOR YOU, BUT TAKE CARE THAT THE SERPENT DOES NOT BITE YOU.
IN THE NAME OF JESUS CHRIST, HE WILL NOT HARM ME.

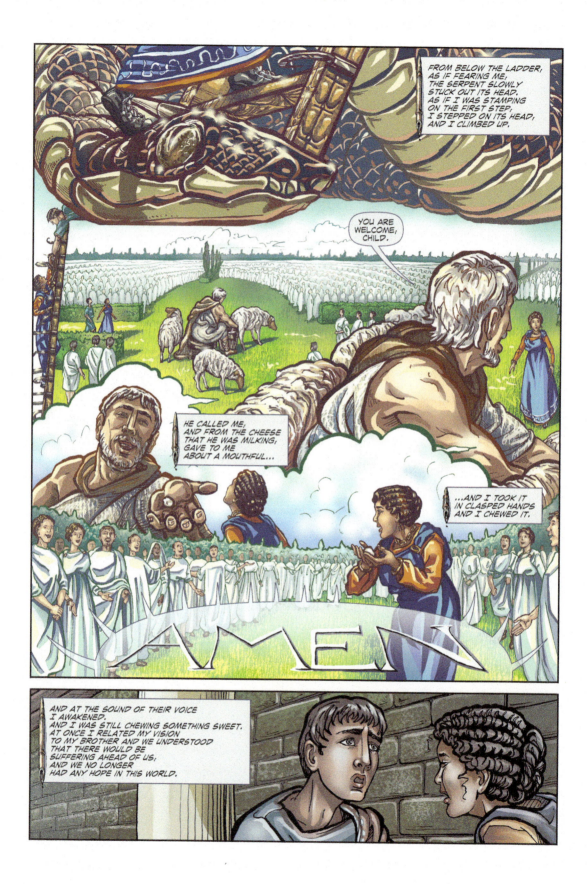

FROM BELOW THE LADDER, AS IF FEARING ME, THE SERPENT SLOWLY STUCK OUT ITS HEAD. AS IF I WAS STAMPING ON THE FIRST STEP, I STEPPED ON ITS HEAD, AND I CLIMBED UP.

YOU ARE WELCOME, CHILD.

HE CALLED ME, AND FROM THE CHEESE THAT HE WAS MILKING, GAVE TO ME ABOUT A MOUTHFUL...

...AND I TOOK IT IN CLASPED HANDS AND I CHEWED IT.

AMEN

AND AT THE SOUND OF THEIR VOICE I AWAKENED. AND I WAS STILL CHEWING SOMETHING SWEET. AT ONCE I RELATED MY VISION TO MY BROTHER AND WE UNDERSTOOD THAT THERE WOULD BE SUFFERING AHEAD OF US, AND WE NO LONGER HAD ANY HOPE IN THIS WORLD.

18

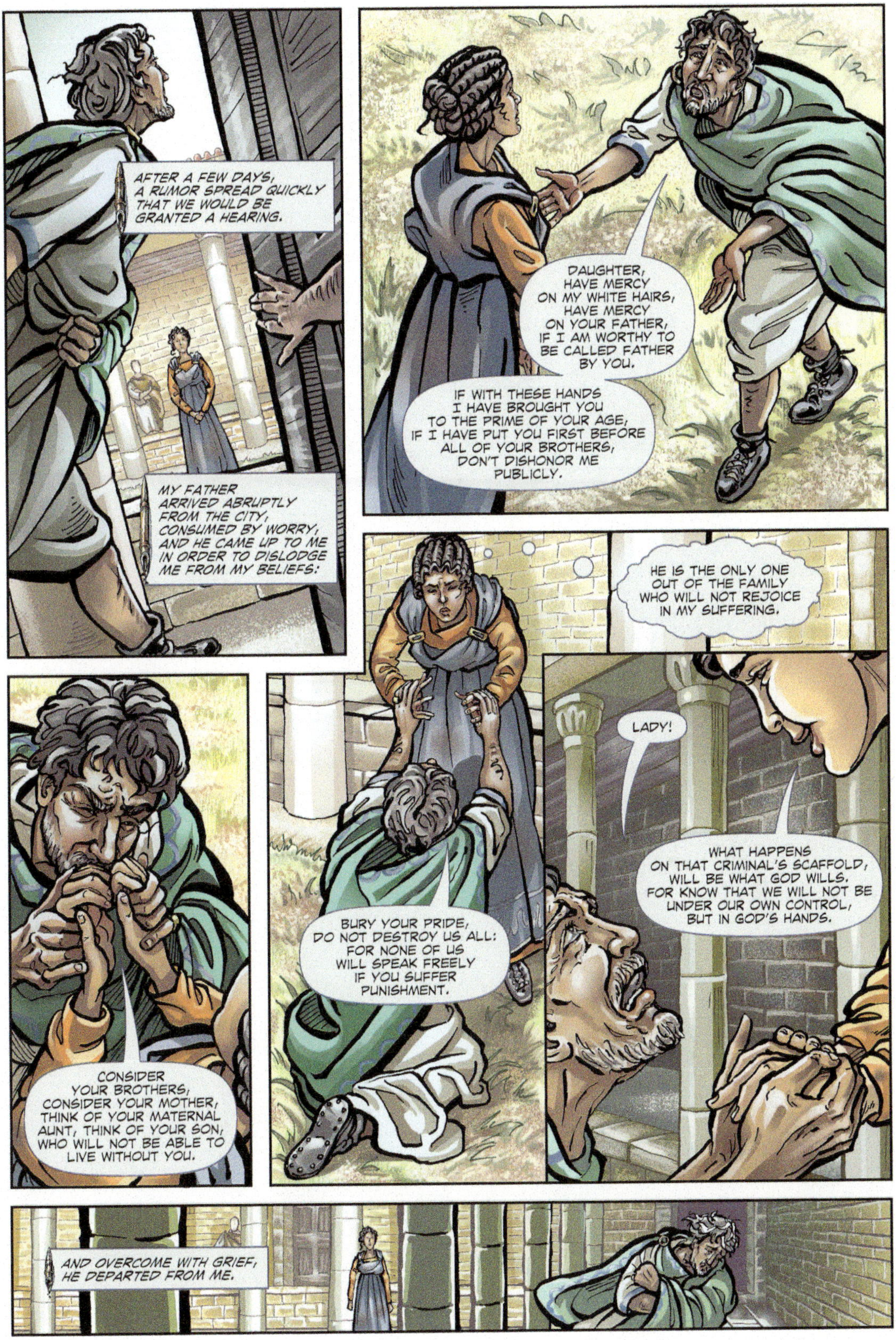
AFTER A FEW DAYS, A RUMOR SPREAD QUICKLY THAT WE WOULD BE GRANTED A HEARING.
MY FATHER ARRIVED ABRUPTLY FROM THE CITY, CONSUMED BY WORRY, AND HE CAME UP TO ME IN ORDER TO DISLODGE ME FROM MY BELIEFS:
DAUGHTER, HAVE MERCY ON MY WHITE HAIRS, HAVE MERCY ON YOUR FATHER, IF I AM WORTHY TO BE CALLED FATHER BY YOU.
IF WITH THESE HANDS I HAVE BROUGHT YOU TO THE PRIME OF YOUR AGE, IF I HAVE PUT YOU FIRST BEFORE ALL OF YOUR BROTHERS, DON'T DISHONOR ME PUBLICLY.
HE IS THE ONLY ONE OUT OF THE FAMILY WHO WILL NOT REJOICE IN MY SUFFERING.
CONSIDER YOUR BROTHERS, CONSIDER YOUR MOTHER, THINK OF YOUR MATERNAL AUNT, THINK OF YOUR SON, WHO WILL NOT BE ABLE TO LIVE WITHOUT YOU.
BURY YOUR PRIDE, DO NOT DESTROY US ALL: FOR NONE OF US WILL SPEAK FREELY IF YOU SUFFER PUNISHMENT.
LADY!
WHAT HAPPENS ON THAT CRIMINAL'S SCAFFOLD, WILL BE WHAT GOD WILLS. FOR KNOW THAT WE WILL NOT BE UNDER OUR OWN CONTROL, BUT IN GOD'S HANDS.
AND OVERCOME WITH GRIEF, HE DEPARTED FROM ME.

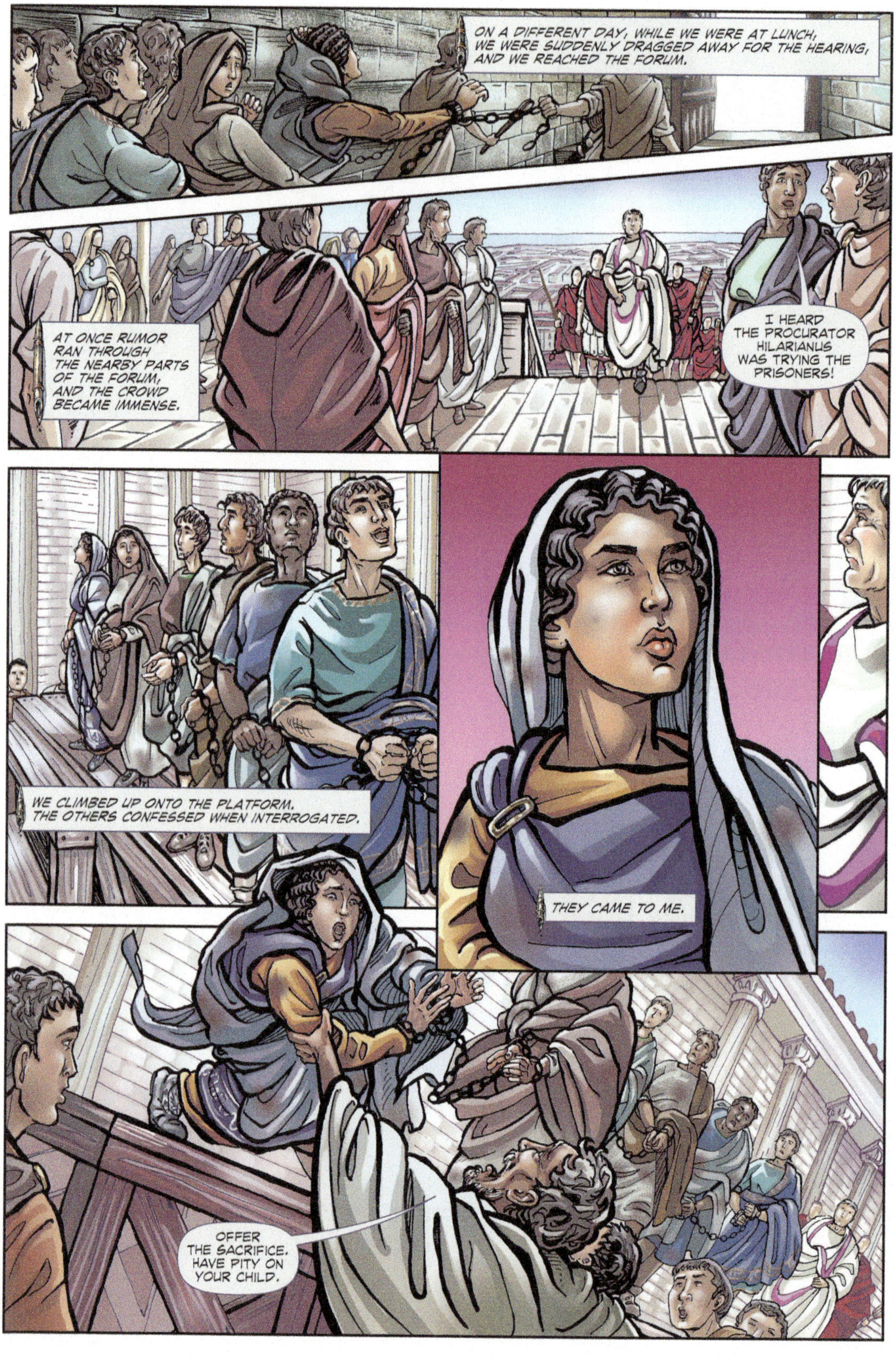

ON A DIFFERENT DAY, WHILE WE WERE AT LUNCH, WE WERE SUDDENLY DRAGGED AWAY FOR THE HEARING, AND WE REACHED THE FORUM.
AT ONCE RUMOR RAN THROUGH THE NEARBY PARTS OF THE FORUM, AND THE CROWD BECAME IMMENSE.
I HEARD THE PROCURATOR HILARIANUS WAS TRYING THE PRISONERS!
WE CLIMBED UP ONTO THE PLATFORM. THE OTHERS CONFESSED WHEN INTERROGATED.
THEY CAME TO ME.
OFFER THE SACRIFICE. HAVE PITY ON YOUR CHILD.

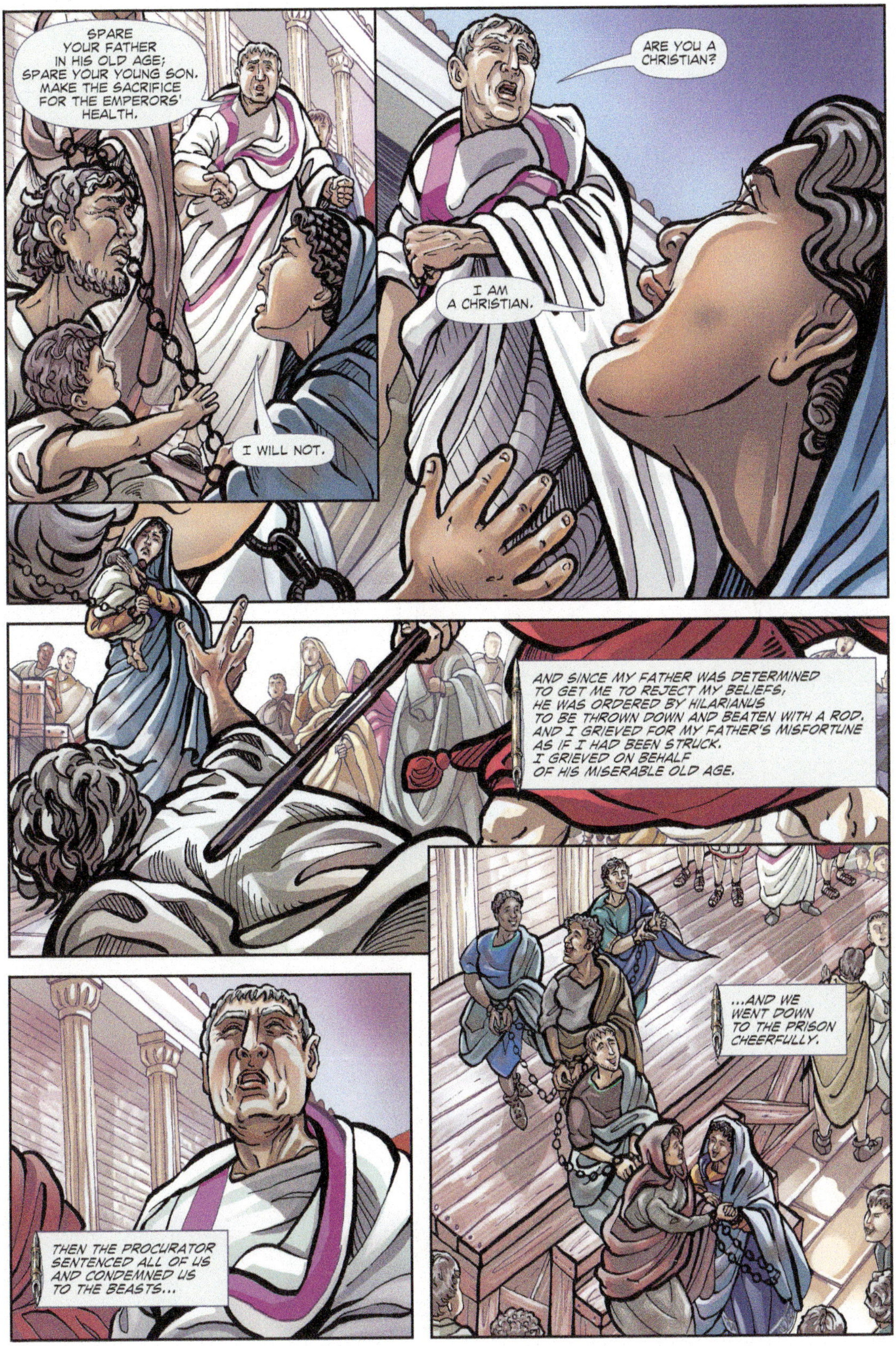
SPARE YOUR FATHER IN HIS OLD AGE; SPARE YOUR YOUNG SON. MAKE THE SACRIFICE FOR THE EMPERORS' HEALTH.
I WILL NOT.
ARE YOU A CHRISTIAN?
I AM A CHRISTIAN.
AND SINCE MY FATHER WAS DETERMINED TO GET ME TO REJECT MY BELIEFS, HE WAS ORDERED BY HILARIANUS TO BE THROWN DOWN AND BEATEN WITH A ROD. AND I GRIEVED FOR MY FATHER'S MISFORTUNE AS IF I HAD BEEN STRUCK. I GRIEVED ON BEHALF OF HIS MISERABLE OLD AGE.
THEN THE PROCURATOR SENTENCED ALL OF US AND CONDEMNED US TO THE BEASTS...
...AND WE WENT DOWN TO THE PRISON CHEERFULLY.

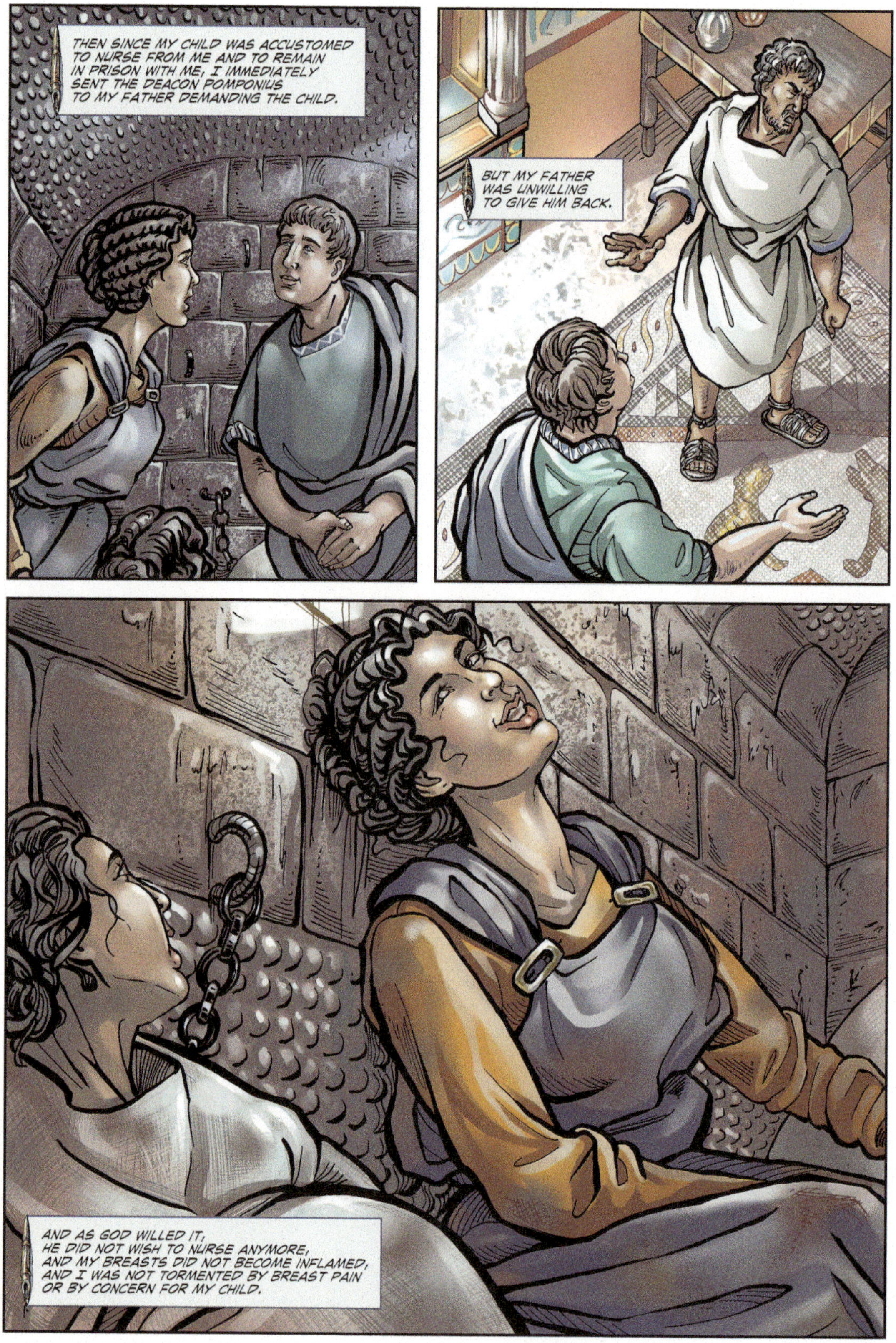

THEN SINCE MY CHILD WAS ACCUSTOMED TO NURSE FROM ME AND TO REMAIN IN PRISON WITH ME, I IMMEDIATELY SENT THE DEACON POMPONIUS TO MY FATHER DEMANDING THE CHILD.
BUT MY FATHER WAS UNWILLING TO GIVE HIM BACK.
AND AS GOD WILLED IT, HE DID NOT WISH TO NURSE ANYMORE, AND MY BREASTS DID NOT BECOME INFLAMED, AND I WAS NOT TORMENTED BY BREAST PAIN OR BY CONCERN FOR MY CHILD.

CHAPTER 2
CHRISTIANA SUM, "I AM A CHRISTIAN"

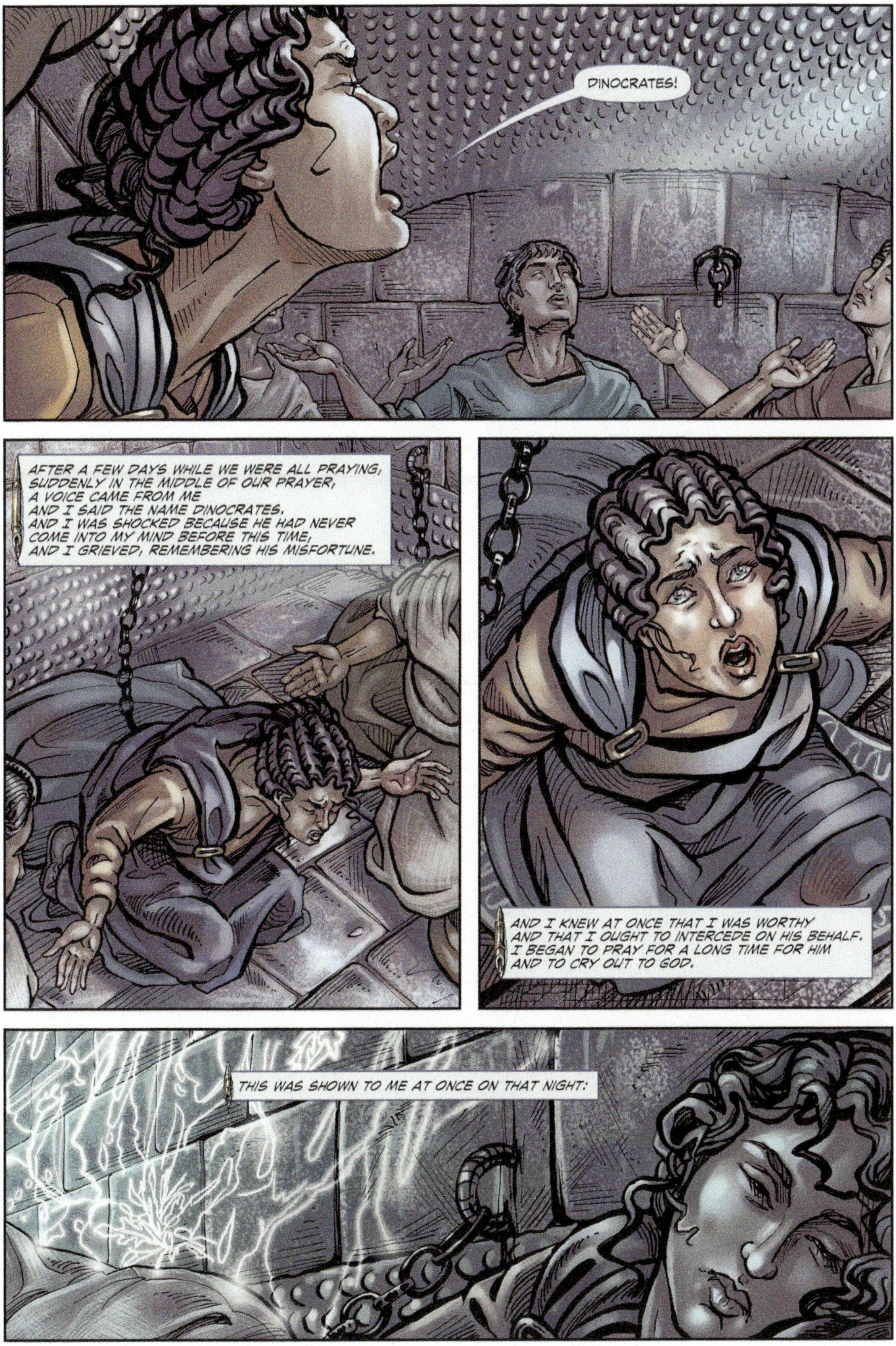
DINOCRATES!
AFTER A FEW DAYS WHILE WE WERE ALL PRAYING, SUDDENLY IN THE MIDDLE OF OUR PRAYER, A VOICE CAME FROM ME AND I SAID THE NAME DINOCRATES. AND I WAS SHOCKED BECAUSE HE HAD NEVER COME INTO MY MIND BEFORE THIS TIME; AND I GRIEVED, REMEMBERING HIS MISFORTUNE.
AND I KNEW AT ONCE THAT I WAS WORTHY AND THAT I OUGHT TO INTERCEDE ON HIS BEHALF. I BEGAN TO PRAY FOR A LONG TIME FOR HIM AND TO CRY OUT TO GOD.
THIS WAS SHOWN TO ME AT ONCE ON THAT NIGHT:

I saw Dinocrates going out from a dark place where there were also many others. He was very hot and thirsty, with a dirty face and a pale complexion, and with the wound in his face which he had when he died. This Dinocrates had been my brother in the flesh, seven years old, whose skin cancer on his face led to his painful demise, so the manner of his death was hateful to all. So I prayed for him. But a great divide existed between him and me, so we were unable to approach each other. There was a pool full of water in that place where Dinocrates was and it had a rim higher than the boy's height. And Dinocrates stretched himself up like he was trying to drink. I was sad, because although the pool held water, due to the height of the rim, he would not be able to drink.

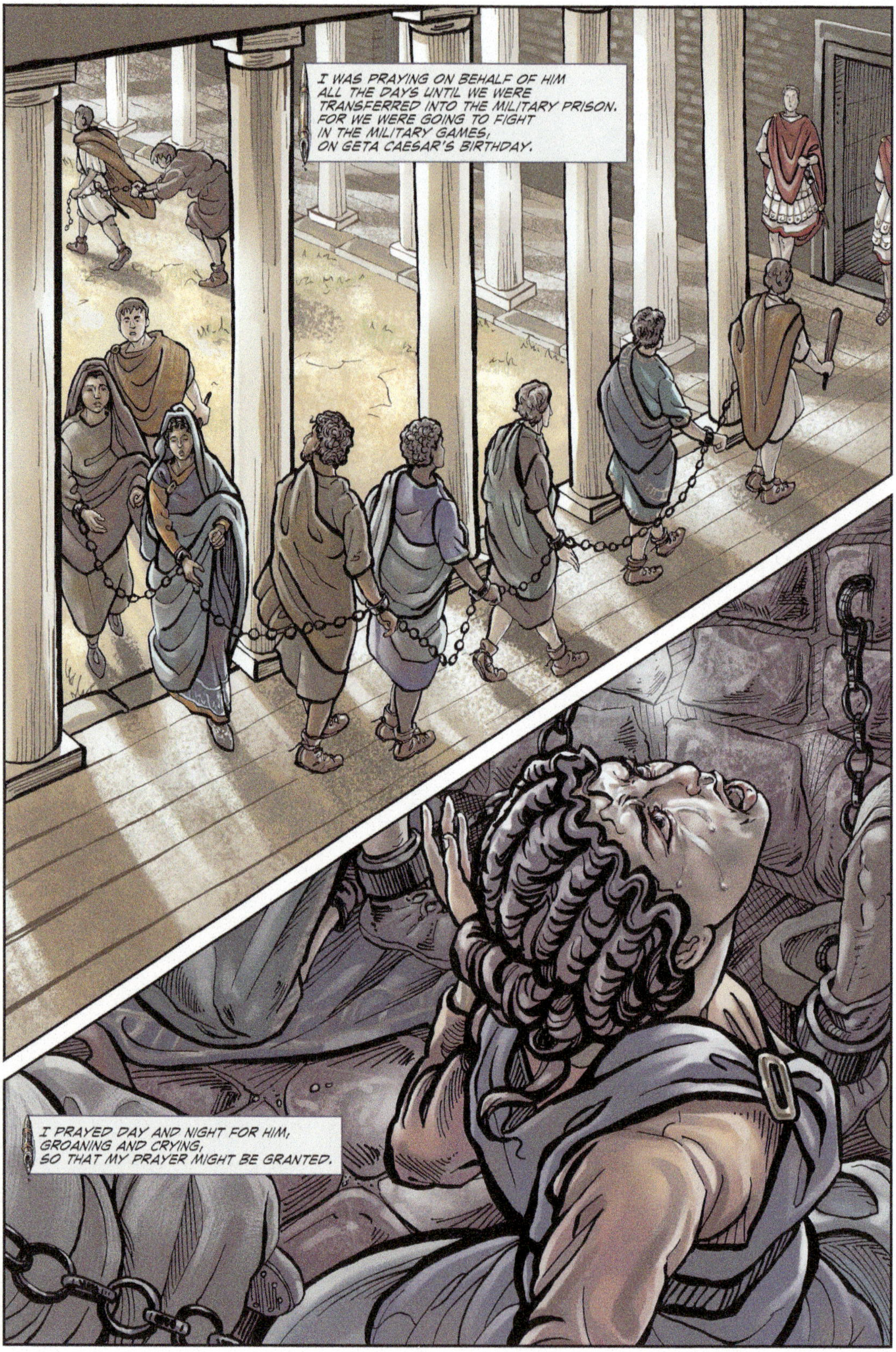
I WAS PRAYING ON BEHALF OF HIM
ALL THE DAYS UNTIL WE WERE
TRANSFERRED INTO THE MILITARY PRISON.
FOR WE WERE GOING TO FIGHT
IN THE MILITARY GAMES,
ON GETA CAESAR'S BIRTHDAY.
I PRAYED DAY AND NIGHT FOR HIM,
GROANING AND CRYING,
SO THAT MY PRAYER MIGHT BE GRANTED.

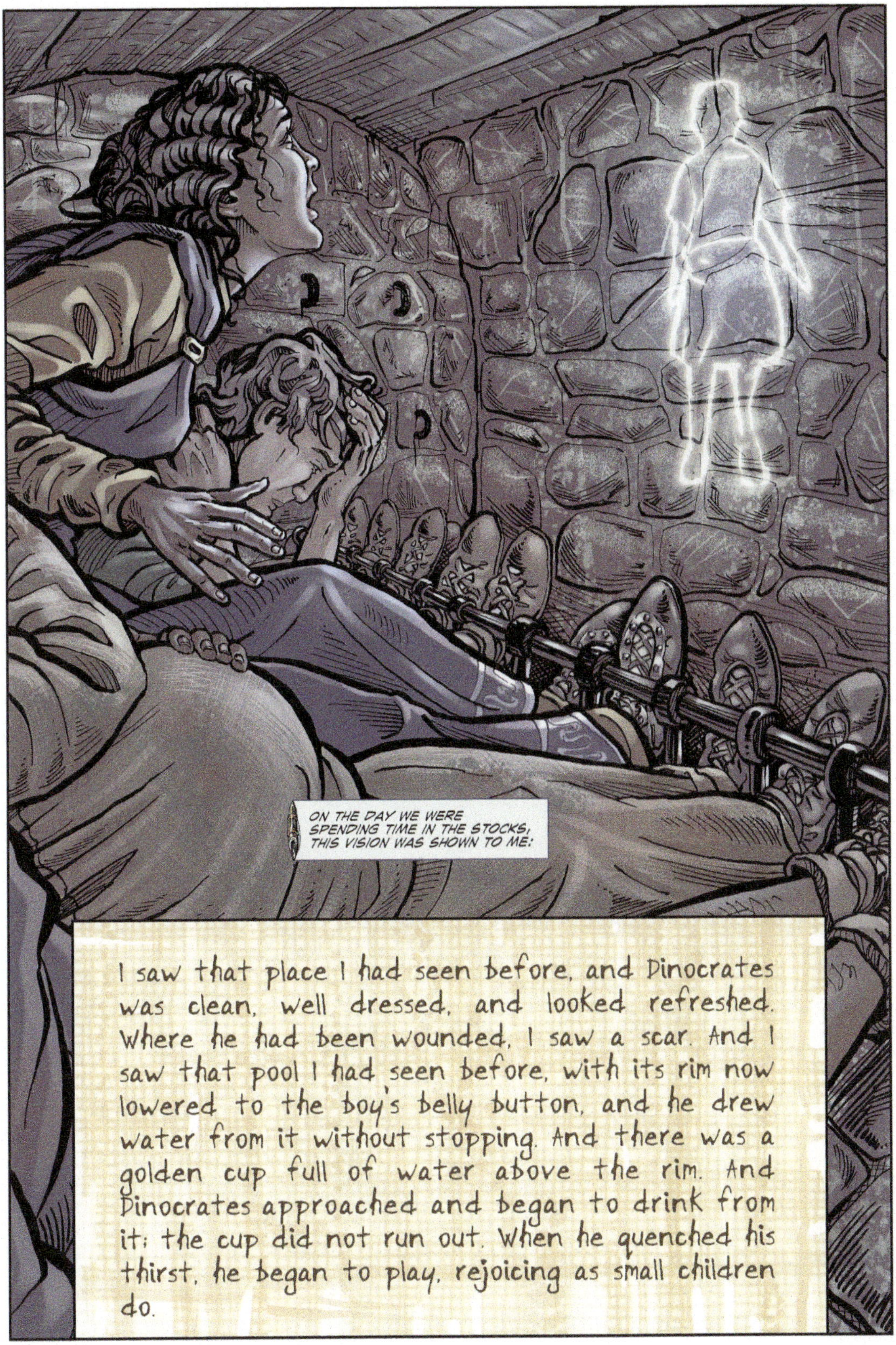
ON THE DAY WE WERE SPENDING TIME IN THE STOCKS, THIS VISION WAS SHOWN TO ME:
I saw that place I had seen before, and Dinocrates was clean, well dressed, and looked refreshed. Where he had been wounded, I saw a scar. And I saw that pool I had seen before, with its rim now lowered to the boy's belly button, and he drew water from it without stopping. And there was a golden cup full of water above the rim. And Dinocrates approached and began to drink from it; the cup did not run out. When he quenched his thirst, he began to play, rejoicing as small children do.

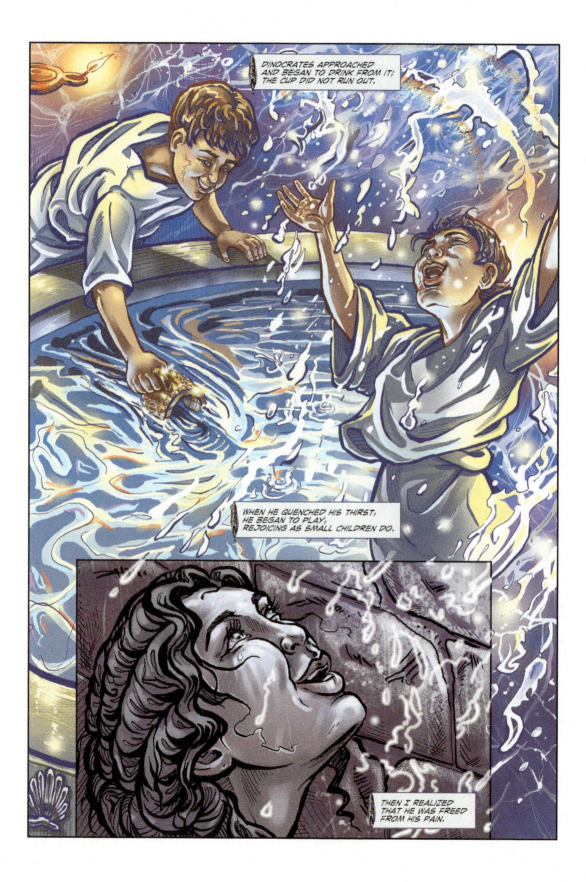

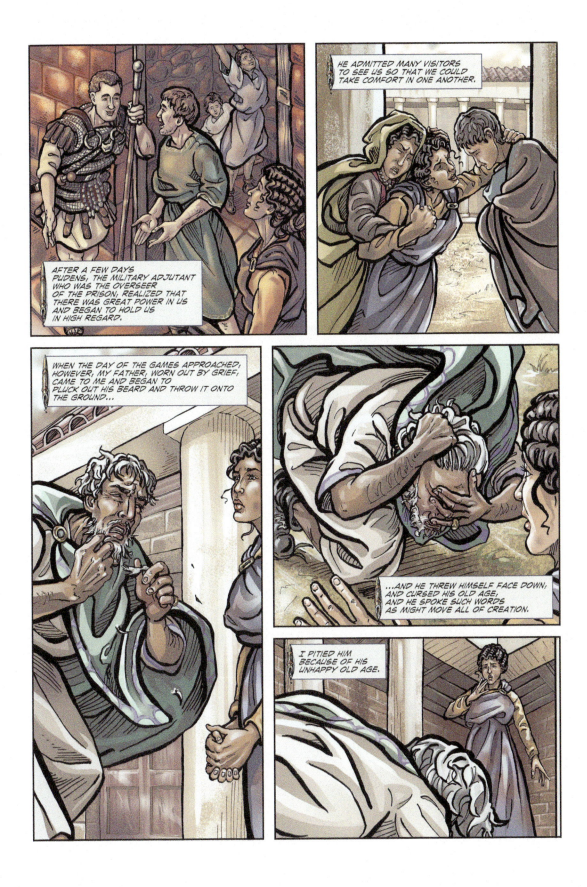

AFTER A FEW DAYS PUDENS, THE MILITARY ADJUTANT WHO WAS THE OVERSEER OF THE PRISON, REALIZED THAT THERE WAS GREAT POWER IN US AND BEGAN TO HOLD US IN HIGH REGARD.

HE ADMITTED MANY VISITORS TO SEE US SO THAT WE COULD TAKE COMFORT IN ONE ANOTHER.

WHEN THE DAY OF THE GAMES APPROACHED, HOWEVER, MY FATHER, WORN OUT BY GRIEF, CAME TO ME AND BEGAN TO PLUCK OUT HIS BEARD AND THROW IT ONTO THE GROUND...

...AND HE THREW HIMSELF FACE DOWN, AND CURSED HIS OLD AGE, AND HE SPOKE SUCH WORDS AS MIGHT MOVE ALL OF CREATION.

I PITIED HIM BECAUSE OF HIS UNHAPPY OLD AGE.

On the day before we were to fight in the arena, I saw this in a vision:

The deacon Pomponius had come to the prison's entrance and was beating on it loudly. I went out and I opened the door for him. He was dressed in an unbelted white tunic and his shoes had elaborate straps. And he said to me, "Perpetua, we are waiting for you; come." He held my hand and we began to go through terrain that was rough and winding. We had just arrived all out of breath at the amphitheater, when he led me into the middle of the arena, and he said to me: "Don't be afraid, for I am here with you and I suffer with you." And then he left. I caught sight of the huge, stunned crowd. Since I knew that I had been condemned to the beasts, I was amazed because the beasts were not being unleashed upon me. A certain Egyptian, who was horrible in appearance and determined to fight with me, came out along with his assistants. Handsome young men came to me as well; they were my supporters and assistants. I was undressed and I became a man. My supporters began to rub me with oil, just as they usually do for an athletic contest. In turn I saw that Egyptian was rolling in the sand.

Then a man came out of such great size that he even rose above the highest point of the amphitheater. He was dressed in an unbelted tunic, a purple one with two stripes extending down the middle of his chest, and intricate sandals decorated with gold and silver. He was carrying a rod as if he were a gladiatorial trainer and a green branch on which there were golden apples. And he called for silence and said, "If the Egyptian is victorious over her, he will kill her with a sword, if she is victorious over him, she will receive this branch." Then he left. We approached one another and we began to throw punches. He wanted to grab my feet; but I began kicking him in the face with my heels. And I was raised up into the air and I began to kick him as if I was not treading on the ground. But when I saw him hesitate, I joined hands so that I interlocked my fingers and I seized hold of his head. Then he fell on his face and I trampled on his head. And the crowd began to shout and my supporters began to sing psalms. And I approached the gladiatorial trainer and I received the branch. He kissed me and he spoke to me: "Daughter, peace be with you." And I began to go with glory to the Gate of Life.

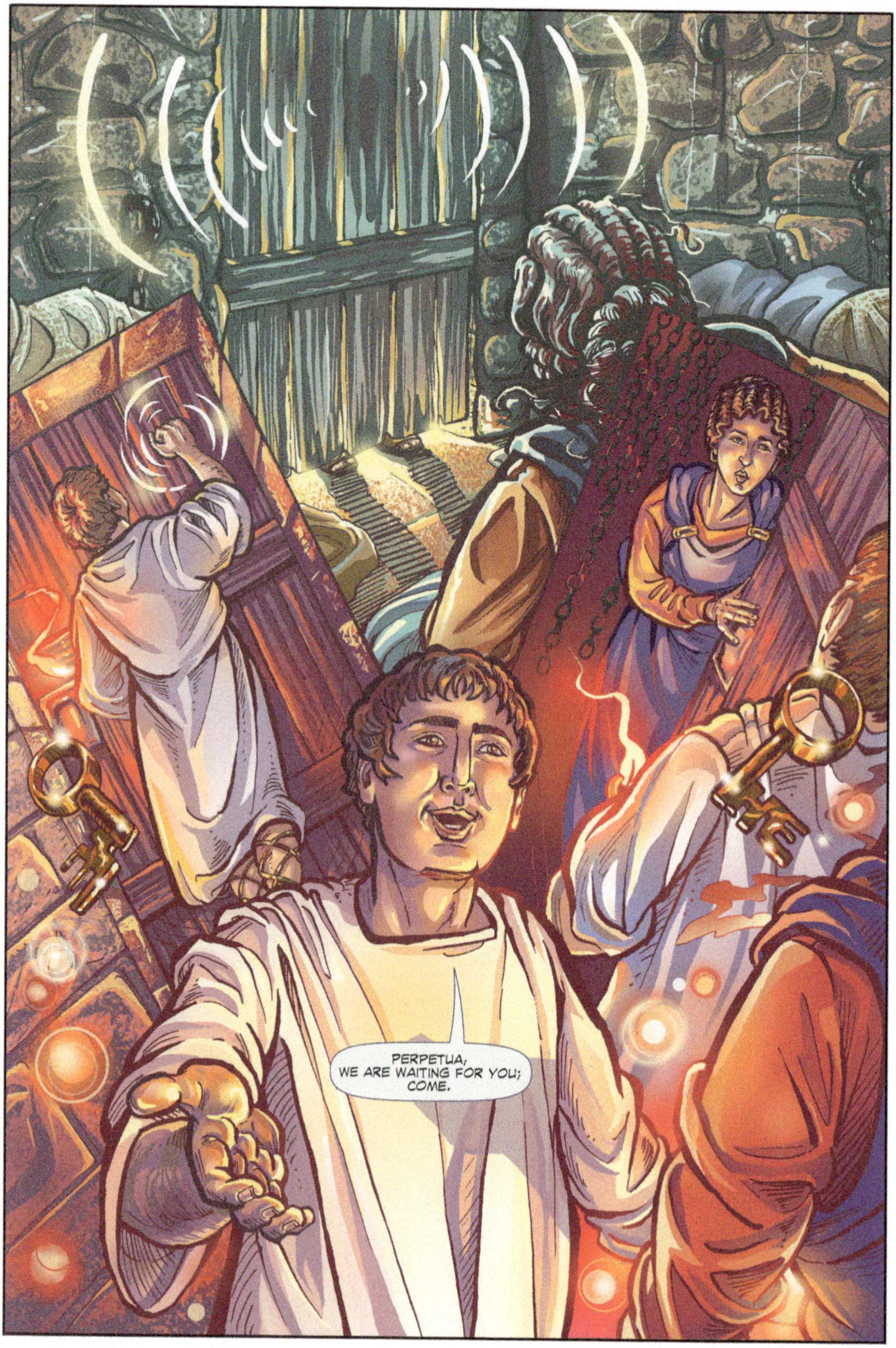
PERPETUA, WE ARE WAITING FOR YOU; COME.

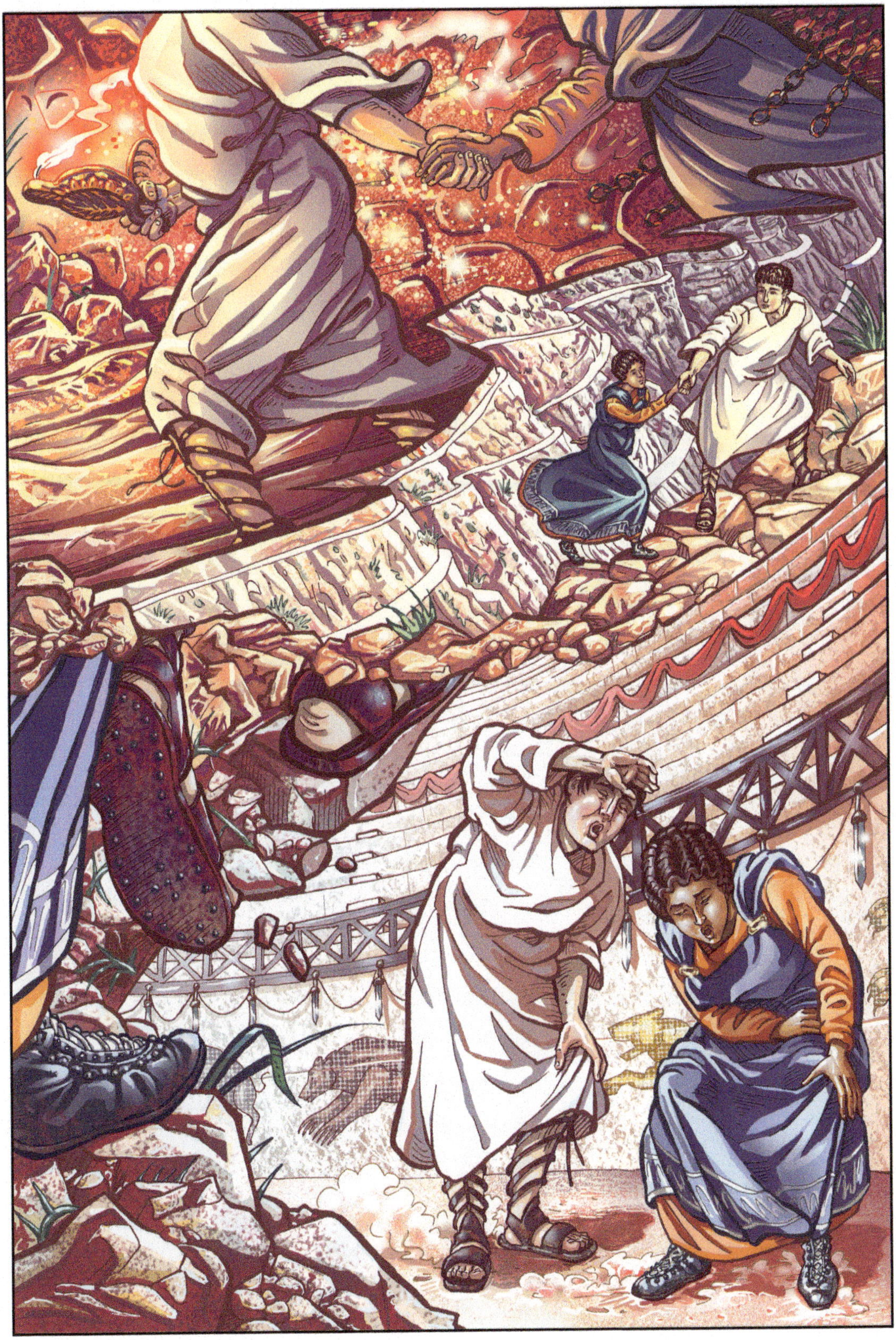

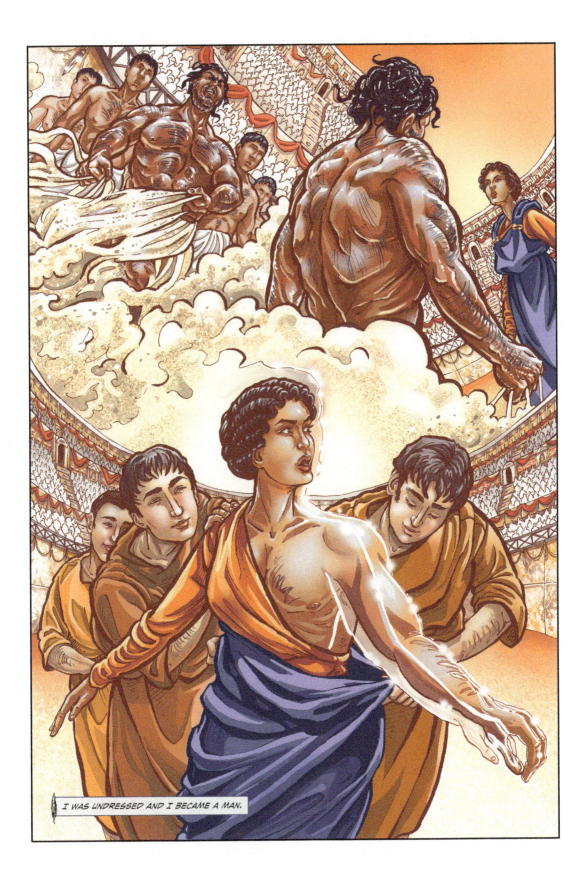

I WAS UNDRESSED AND I BECAME A MAN.

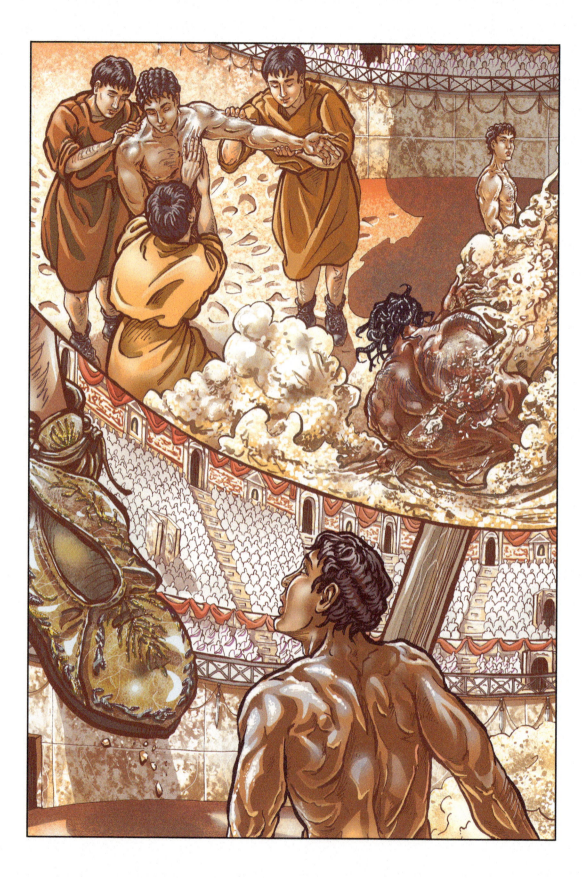

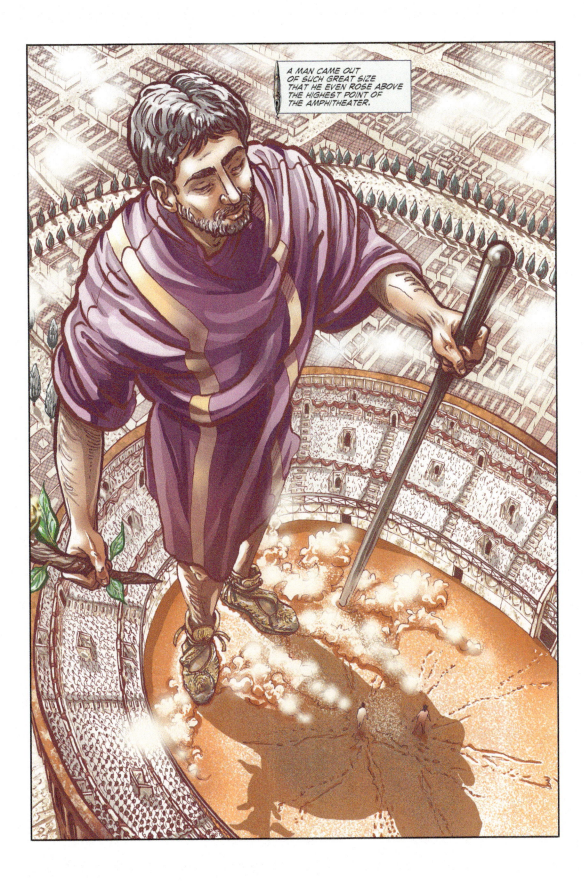

A MAN CAME OUT OF SUCH GREAT SIZE THAT HE EVEN ROSE ABOVE THE HIGHEST POINT OF THE AMPHITHEATER.

39

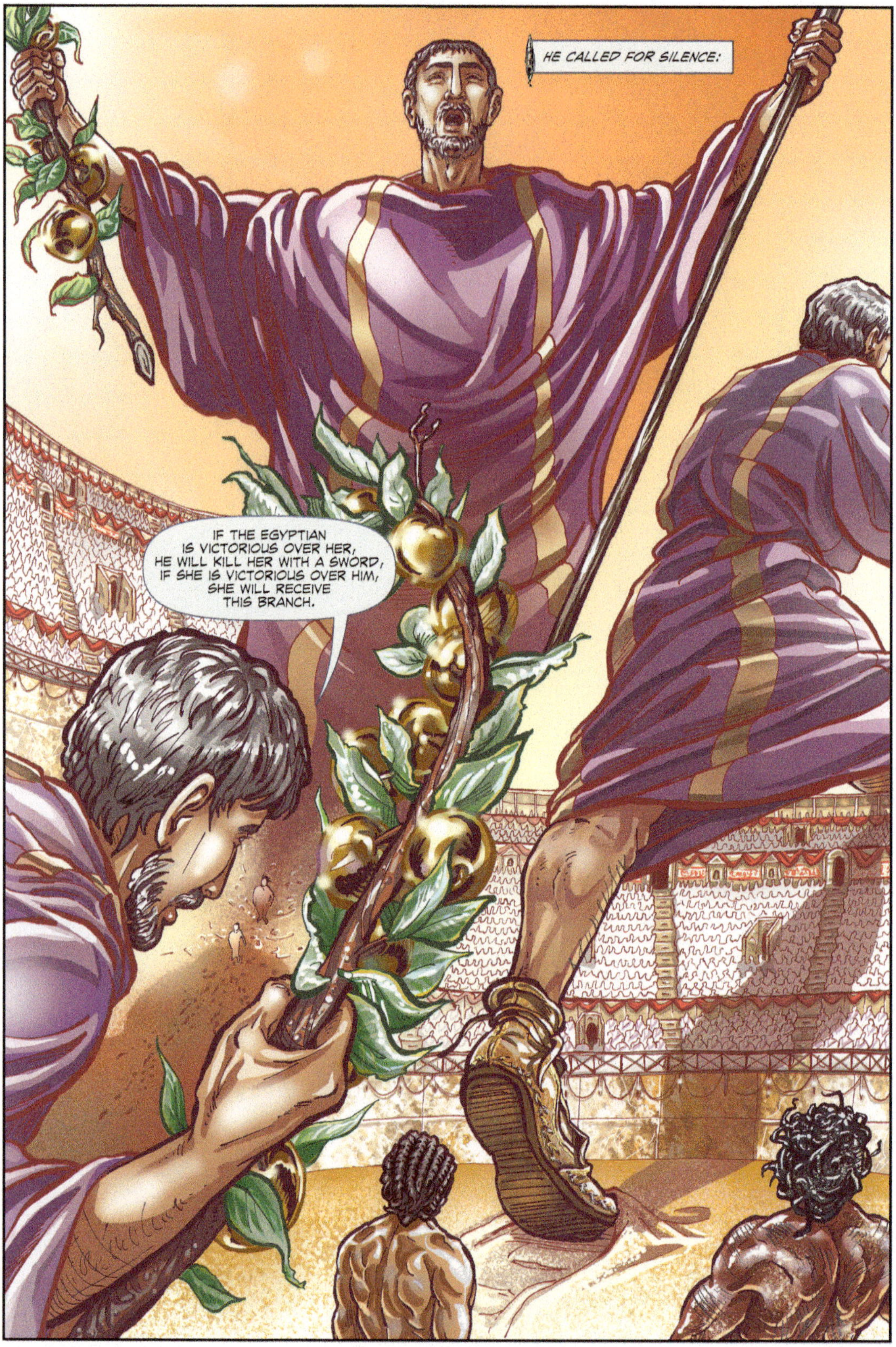
HE CALLED FOR SILENCE:
IF THE EGYPTIAN IS VICTORIOUS OVER HER, HE WILL KILL HER WITH A SWORD; IF SHE IS VICTORIOUS OVER HIM, SHE WILL RECEIVE THIS BRANCH.

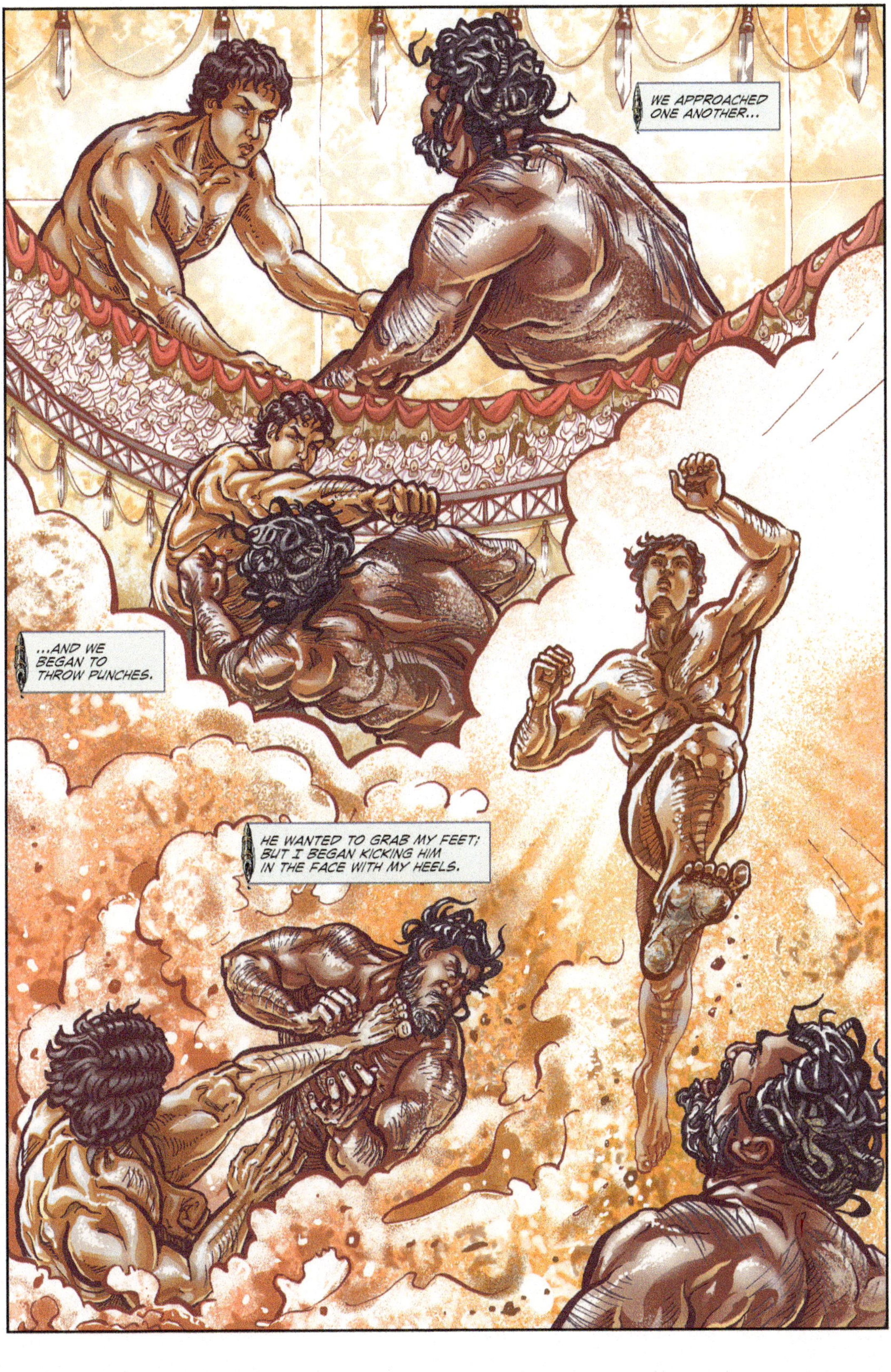
WE APPROACHED ONE ANOTHER...
...AND WE BEGAN TO THROW PUNCHES.
HE WANTED TO GRAB MY FEET; BUT I BEGAN KICKING HIM IN THE FACE WITH MY HEELS.

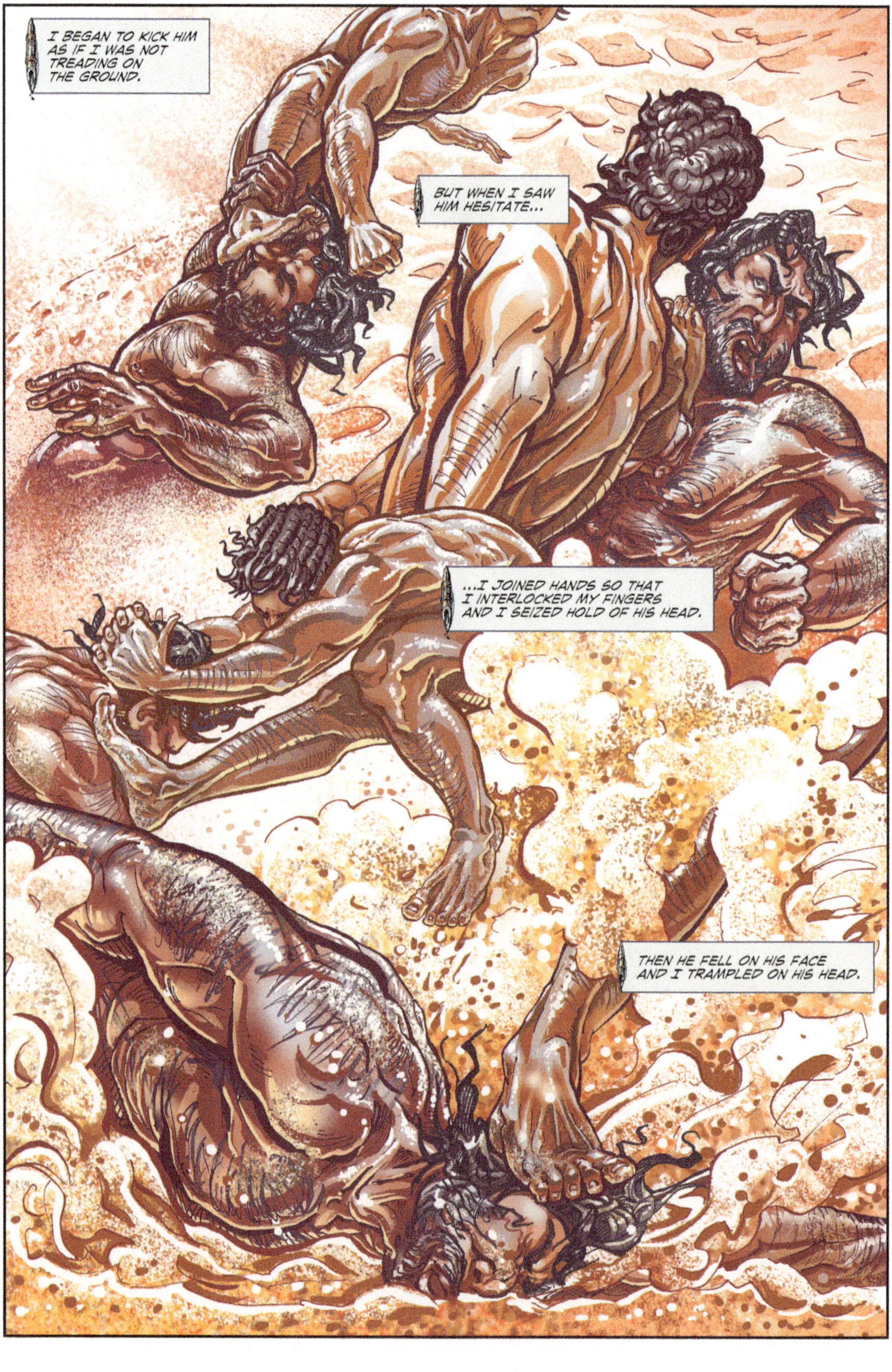
I BEGAN TO KICK HIM AS IF I WAS NOT TREADING ON THE GROUND.
BUT WHEN I SAW HIM HESITATE...
...I JOINED HANDS SO THAT I INTERLOCKED MY FINGERS AND I SEIZED HOLD OF HIS HEAD.
THEN HE FELL ON HIS FACE AND I TRAMPLED ON HIS HEAD.

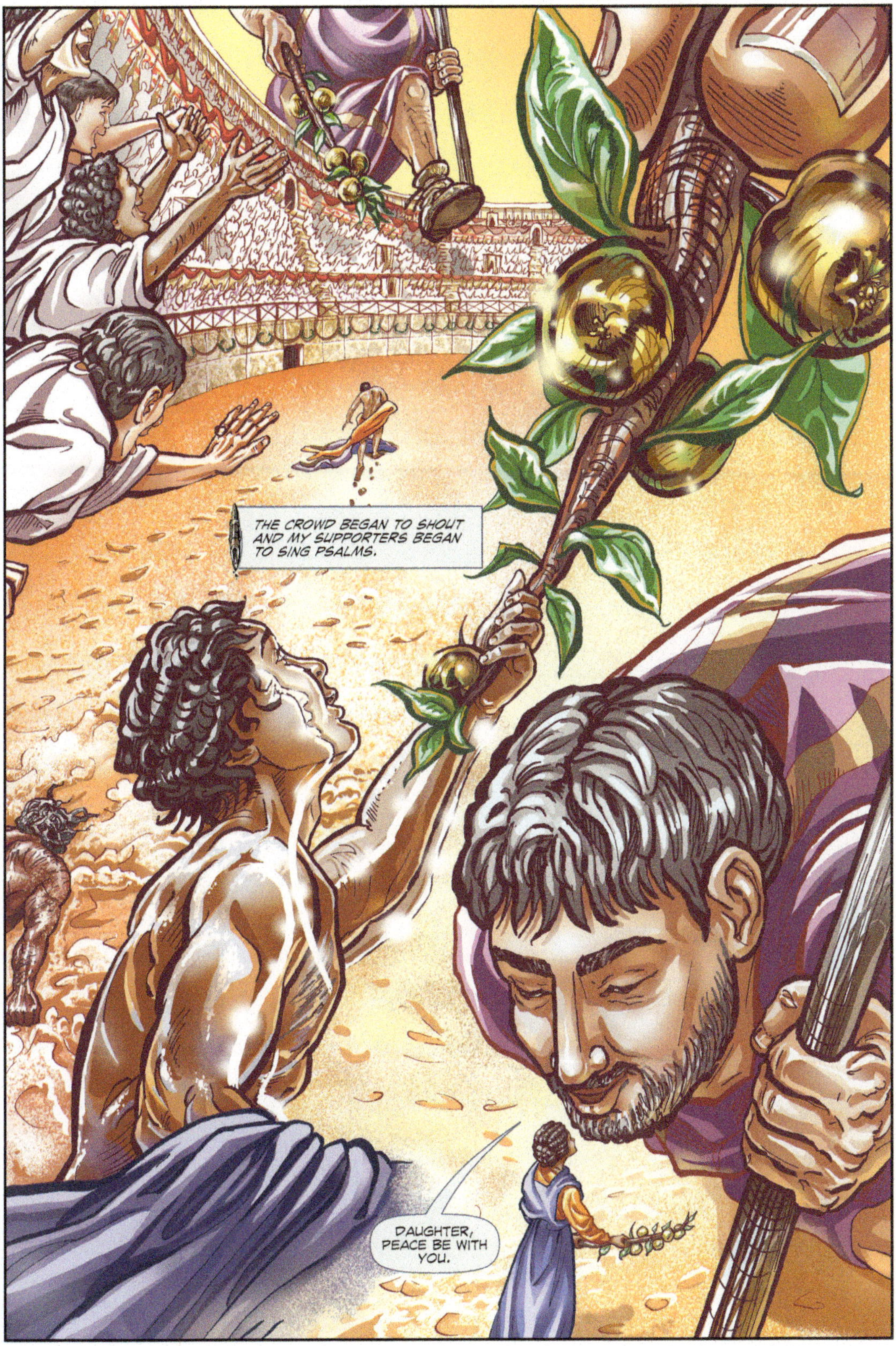
THE CROWD BEGAN TO SHOUT AND MY SUPPORTERS BEGAN TO SING PSALMS.
DAUGHTER, PEACE BE WITH YOU.

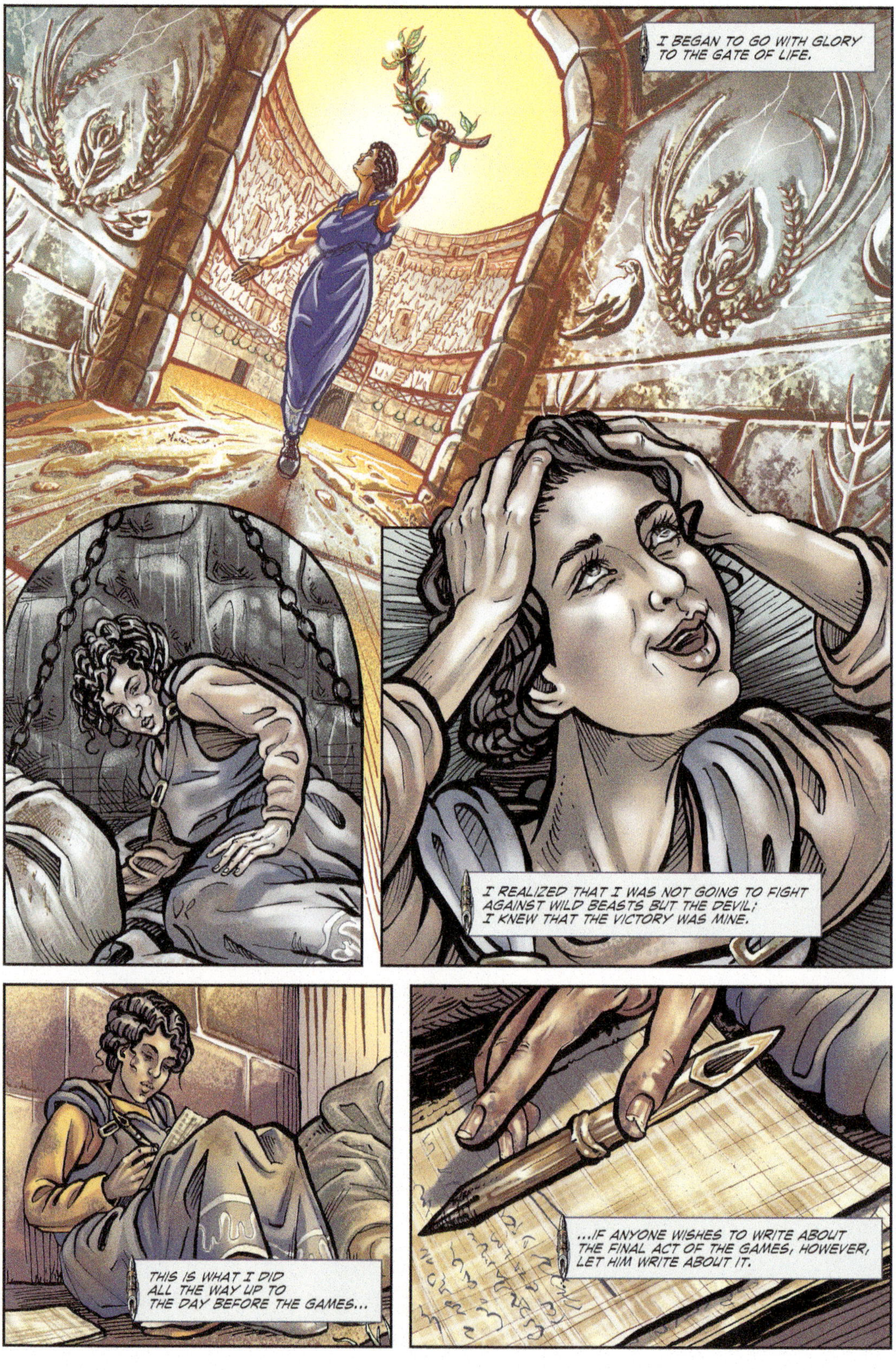
I BEGAN TO GO WITH GLORY TO THE GATE OF LIFE.
I REALIZED THAT I WAS NOT GOING TO FIGHT AGAINST WILD BEASTS BUT THE DEVIL; I KNEW THAT THE VICTORY WAS MINE.
THIS IS WHAT I DID ALL THE WAY UP TO THE DAY BEFORE THE GAMES...
...IF ANYONE WISHES TO WRITE ABOUT THE FINAL ACT OF THE GAMES, HOWEVER, LET HIM WRITE ABOUT IT.

CHAPTER 3
IN VIRIDIARIO, "IN THE GARDEN"

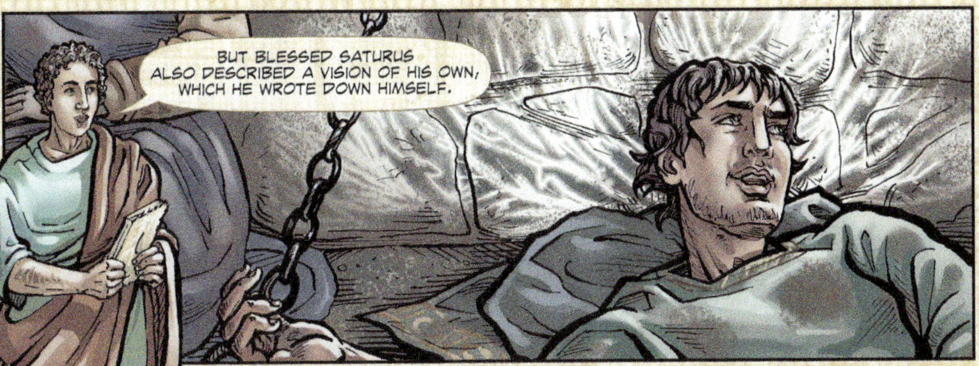
BUT BLESSED SATURUS ALSO DESCRIBED A VISION OF HIS OWN, WHICH HE WROTE DOWN HIMSELF.

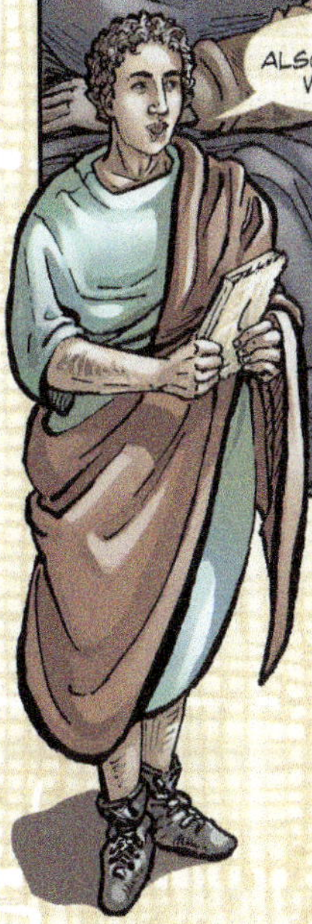

We had experienced martyrdom, he said, and we withdrew from the flesh and we began to be carried off towards the east by four angels, whose hands did not touch us. But we were going, not lying on our backs facing upwards, but as if we were climbing a gently sloping hill. And when we were first set free from this world, we saw an immense light, and I said to Perpetua—for she was by my side—"This is what God has promised to us: we have received His promise." And while we were being carried by the four angels, a great promenade appeared before us. It was a sort of pleasure-garden containing rose trees and flowers of every kind. The trees were as tall as cypress trees and their leaves were falling without stopping. But there in the garden were four other angels, brighter than the others, who, when they saw us, gave us honor, and they said to the other angels: "Here they are! Here they are!" with admiration. And the four angels who were carrying us were very frightened and they put us down. And we went on foot across the park. There we found Iocundus and Saturninus and Artaxius, who were burned alive in the same persecution as us, and Quintus, a martyr who himself had departed from life while in prison. And we asked them where the others were. The angels said to us, "First come, enter and greet the Lord."

And we came near a place whose walls appeared to be built from light, and before the entrance of that place, four angels were standing, and they dressed those who entered in white robes. We came in and we heard a chorus say in unison, "Holy, holy, holy," and they did not stop. And we saw someone sitting in that same place who looked as if he were an old man: he had snow-white hair but his face appeared youthful. We did not see his feet. On his right and on his left there were four elders, and many other elders were standing behind them. We came in and we stood before the throne in admiration, and the four angels raised us up and we kissed him. And with his hand he touched us lightly on our faces. And the other elders said to us, "Let us stand." And we stood, and gave the kiss of peace. And the elders said to us, "Go and play." And I said to Perpetua, "You have what you want!" And she said to me, "I give thanks to God that just as I was happy in the flesh, now I am even happier here."

We went out, and we saw before the gates the bishop Optatus to the right and on the left the learned elder Aspasius, and they were sad and set apart. And they prostrated themselves at our feet and said to us: "Make peace between us, since you have departed and left us behind in this way." We said to them: "Surely you, our bishop and priest, are not the sort to throw yourselves at our feet?" We were moved and we embraced them. Perpetua began to speak to them in Greek, and we led them aside in the pleasure-garden under a rose tree. And while we were talking with them, the angels said to them: "Allow them to rest, and if you have any disagreements between yourselves, forgive one another." And the angels rebuked them and said to Optatus: "Restore order among your people, since they have come to you as if returning from the races and arguing about the teams." Thus it seemed to us as if they wished to close the gates. And we began to recognize many brothers there, also martyrs. We were all nurtured and left satisfied by an indescribable scent.

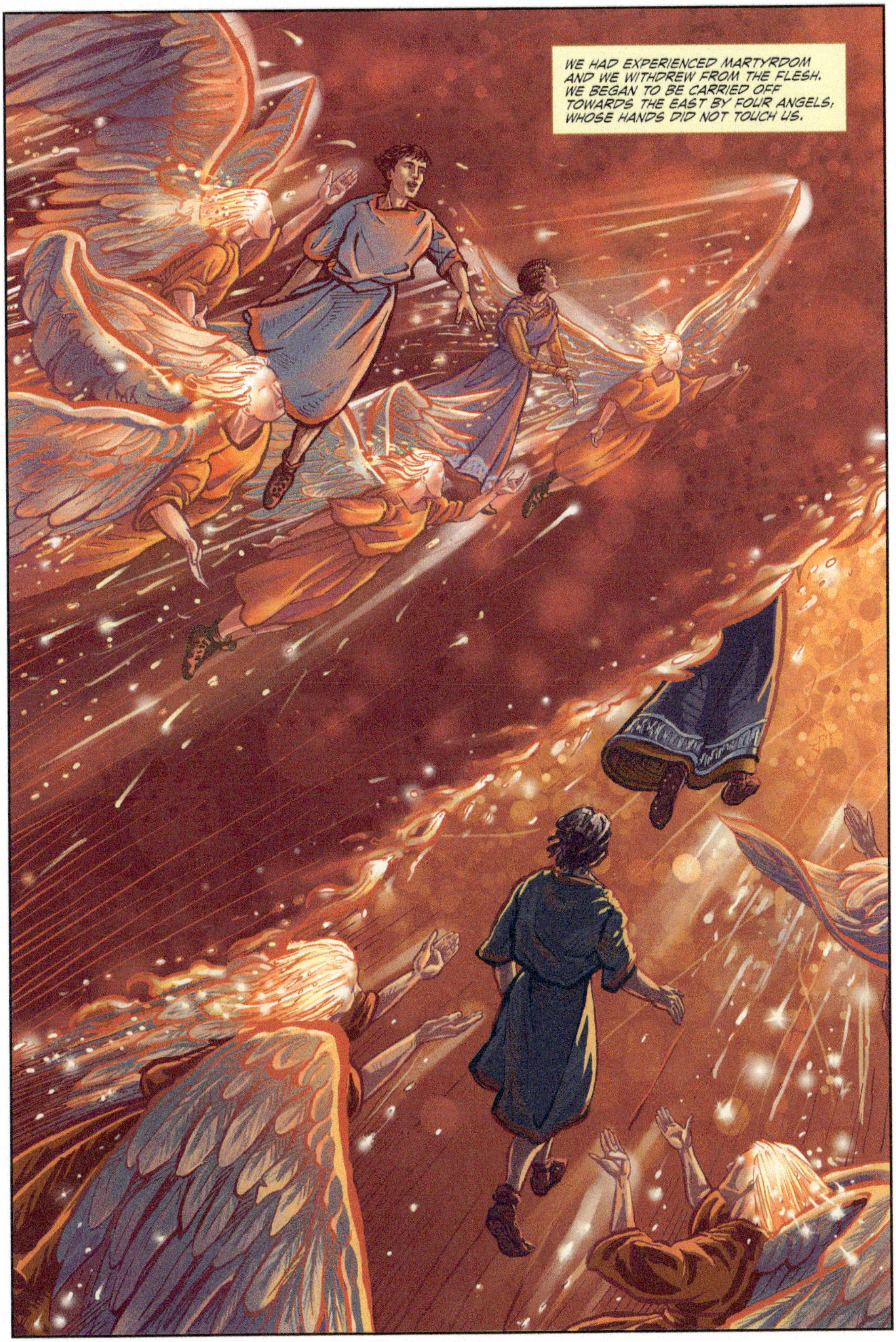
WE HAD EXPERIENCED MARTYRDOM AND WE WITHDREW FROM THE FLESH. WE BEGAN TO BE CARRIED OFF TOWARDS THE EAST BY FOUR ANGELS, WHOSE HANDS DID NOT TOUCH US.

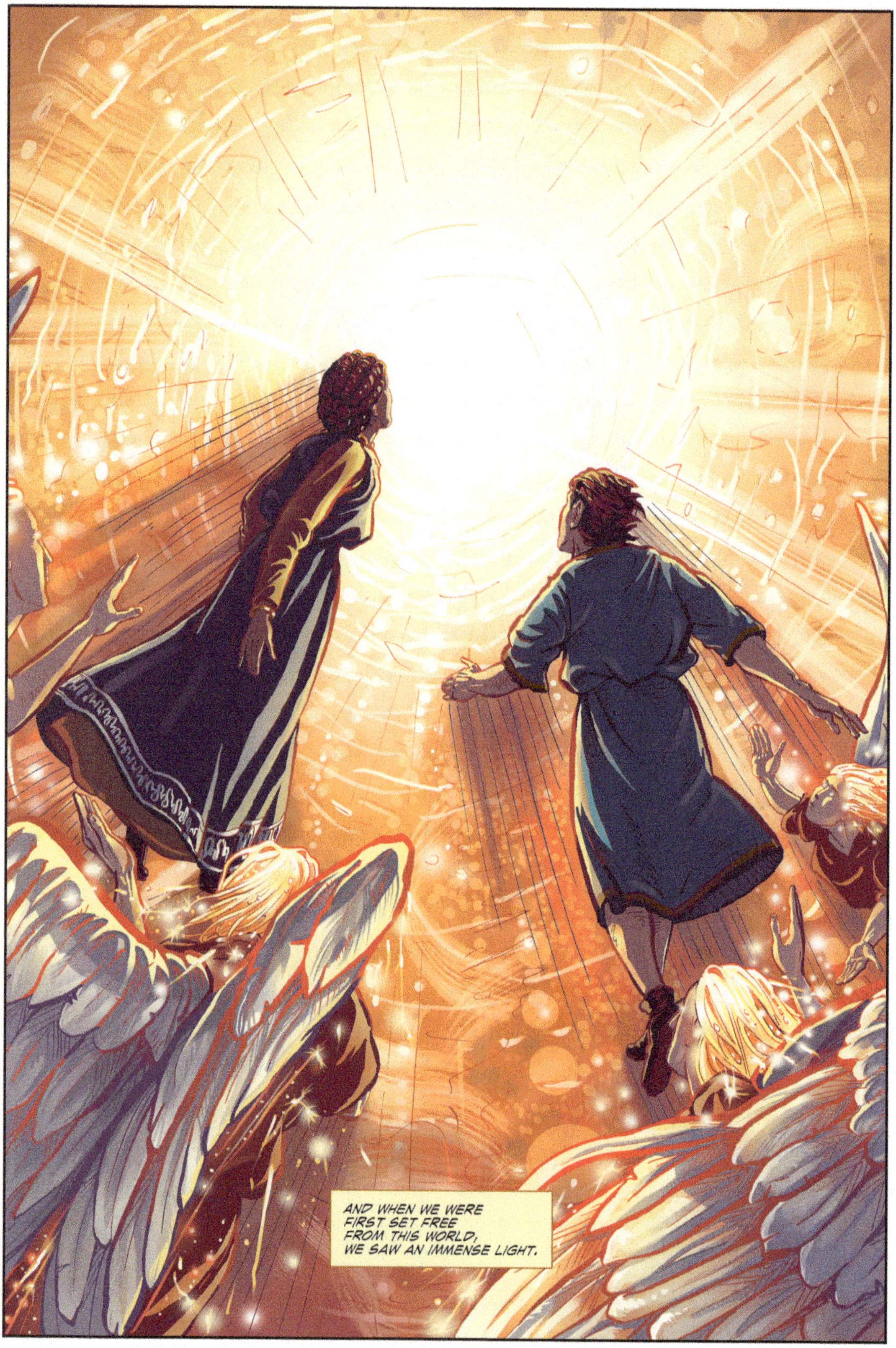
AND WHEN WE WERE FIRST SET FREE FROM THIS WORLD, WE SAW AN IMMENSE LIGHT.

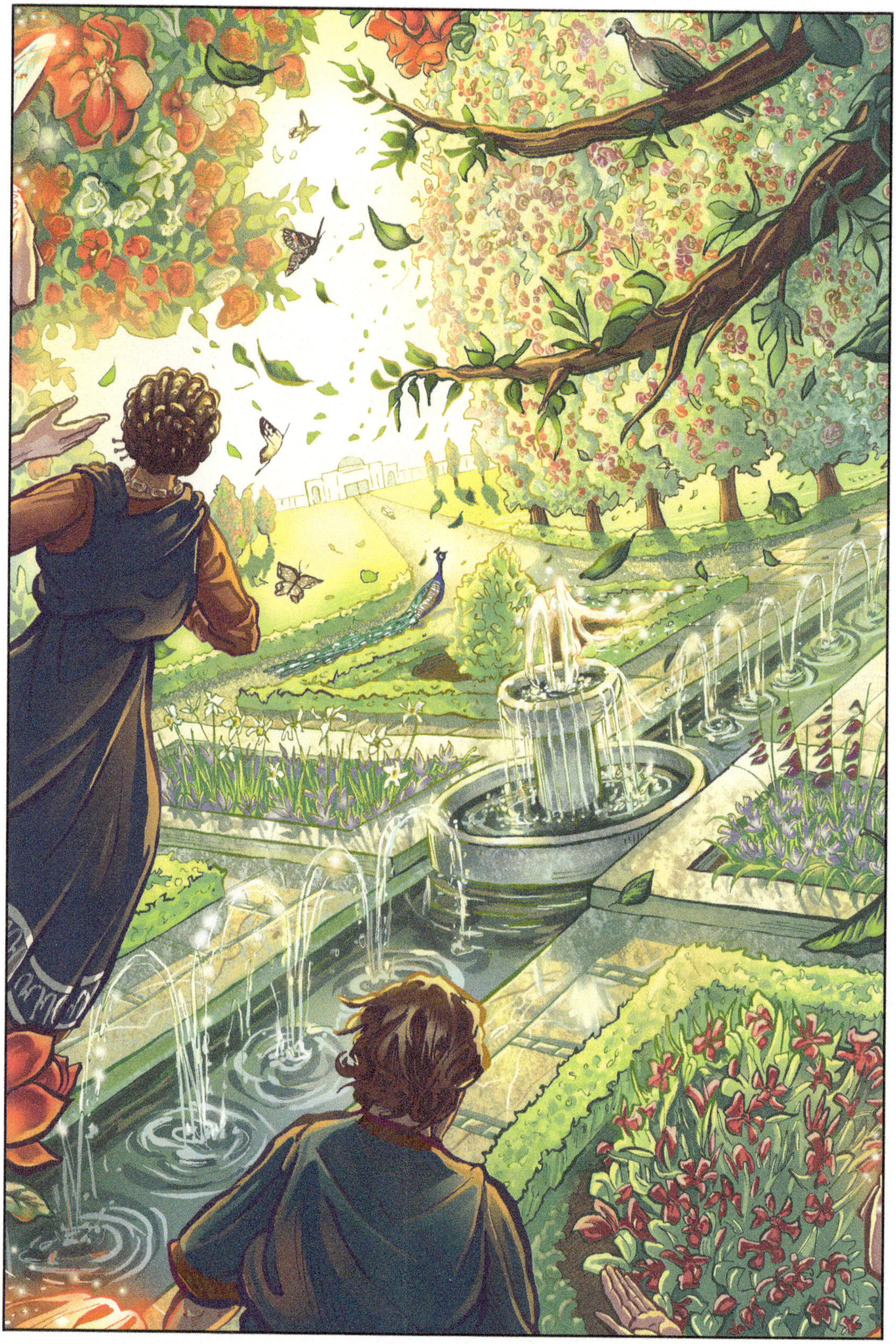

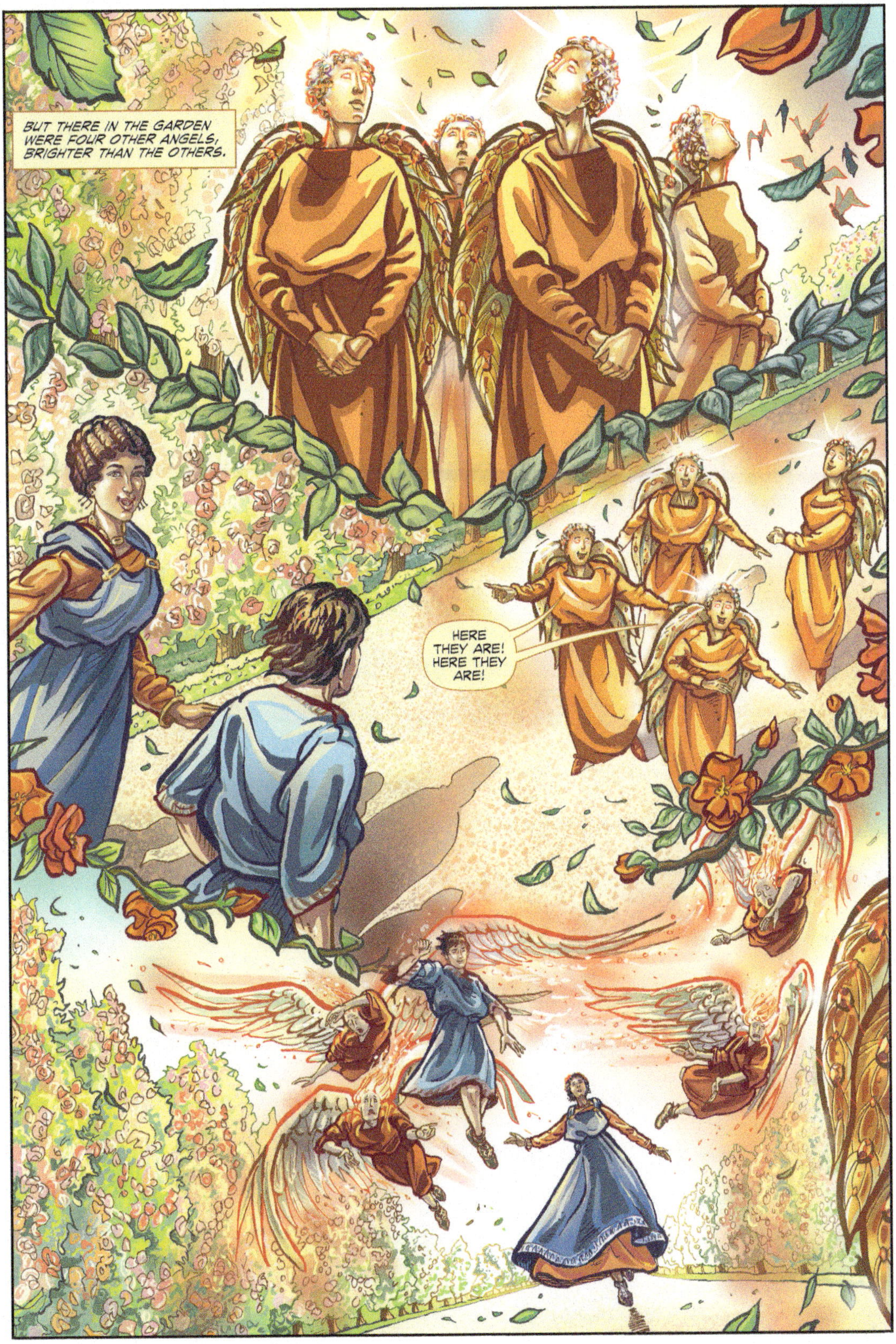
BUT THERE IN THE GARDEN WERE FOUR OTHER ANGELS, BRIGHTER THAN THE OTHERS.
HERE THEY ARE! HERE THEY ARE!

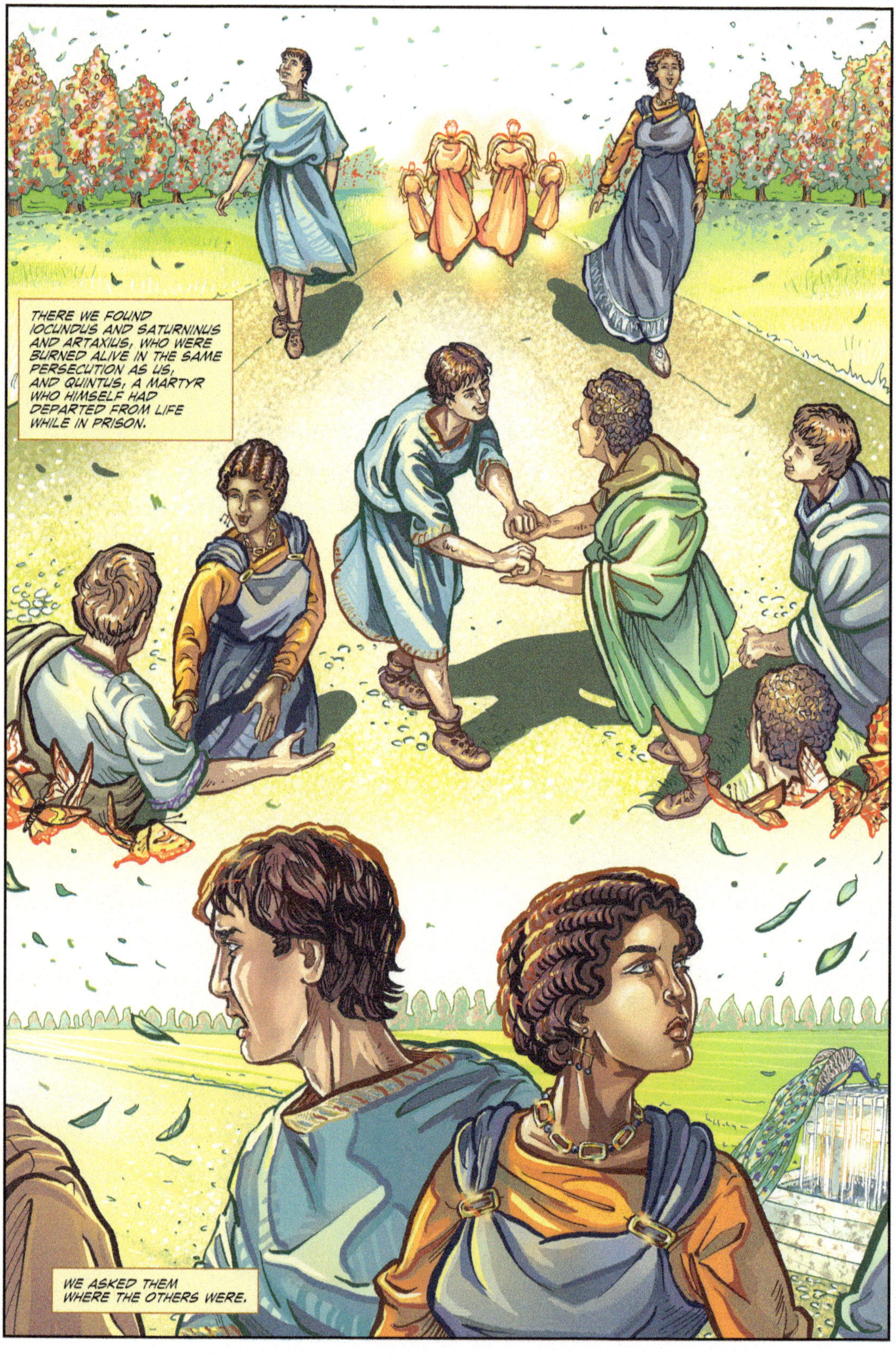
THERE WE FOUND IOCUNDUS AND SATURNINUS AND ARTAXIUS, WHO WERE BURNED ALIVE IN THE SAME PERSECUTION AS US, AND QUINTUS, A MARTYR WHO HIMSELF HAD DEPARTED FROM LIFE WHILE IN PRISON.
WE ASKED THEM WHERE THE OTHERS WERE.

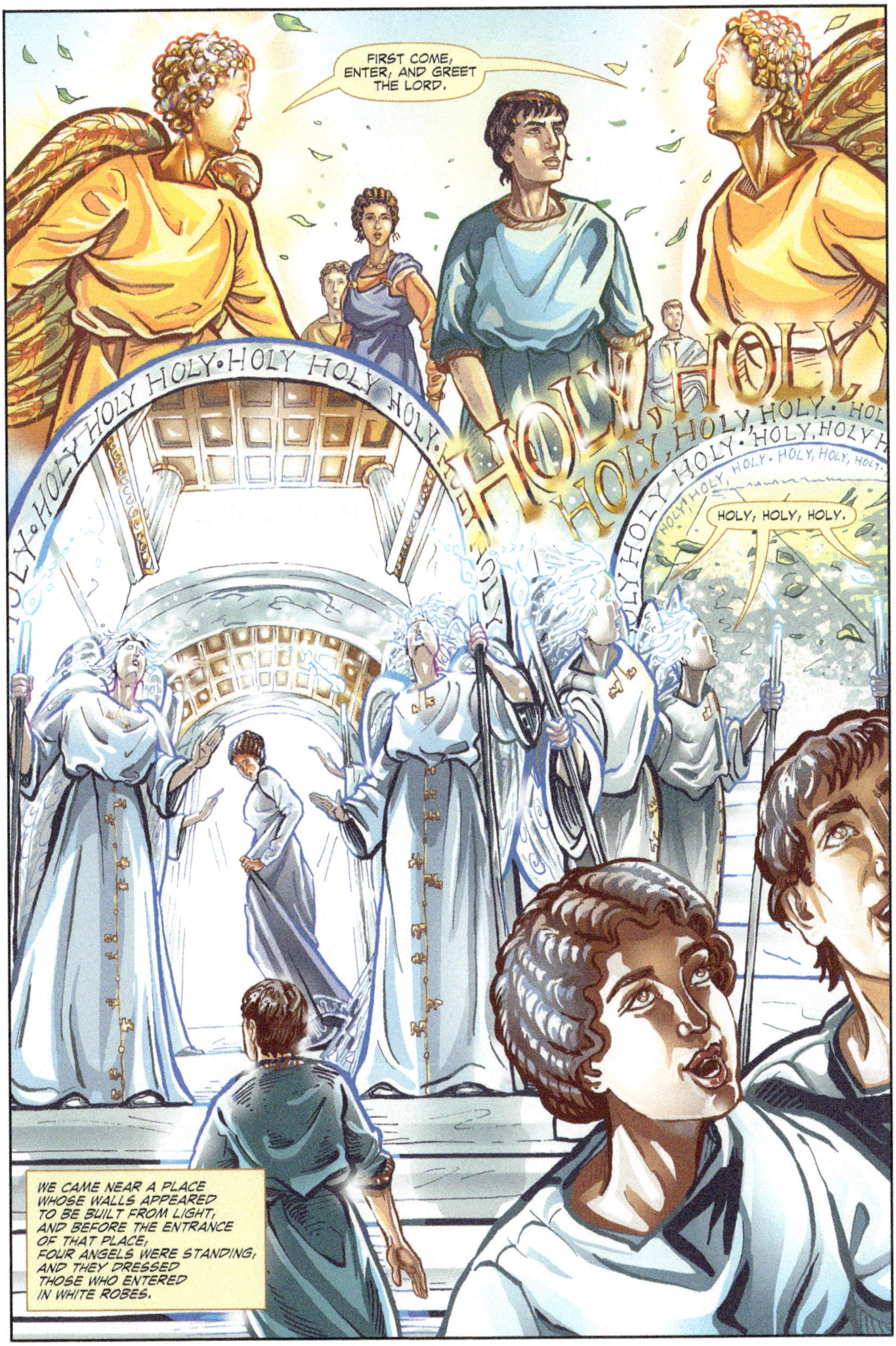
FIRST COME, ENTER, AND GREET THE LORD.
HOLY, HOLY, HOLY.
HOLY, HOLY, HOLY.
WE CAME NEAR A PLACE WHOSE WALLS APPEARED TO BE BUILT FROM LIGHT, AND BEFORE THE ENTRANCE OF THAT PLACE, FOUR ANGELS WERE STANDING, AND THEY DRESSED THOSE WHO ENTERED IN WHITE ROBES.

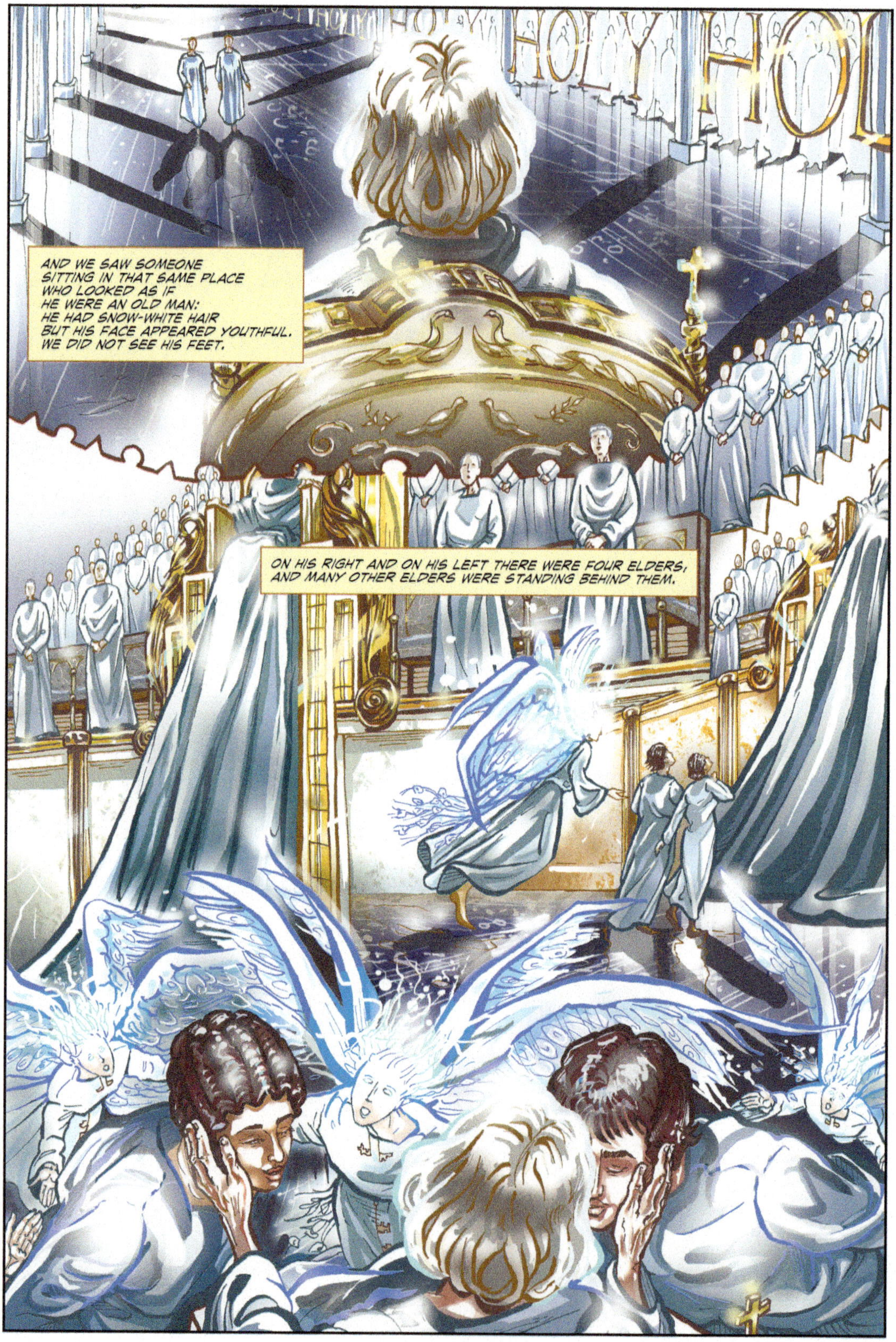
HOLY HOLY HOL
AND WE SAW SOMEONE SITTING IN THAT SAME PLACE WHO LOOKED AS IF HE WERE AN OLD MAN: HE HAD SNOW-WHITE HAIR BUT HIS FACE APPEARED YOUTHFUL. WE DID NOT SEE HIS FEET.
ON HIS RIGHT AND ON HIS LEFT THERE WERE FOUR ELDERS, AND MANY OTHER ELDERS WERE STANDING BEHIND THEM.

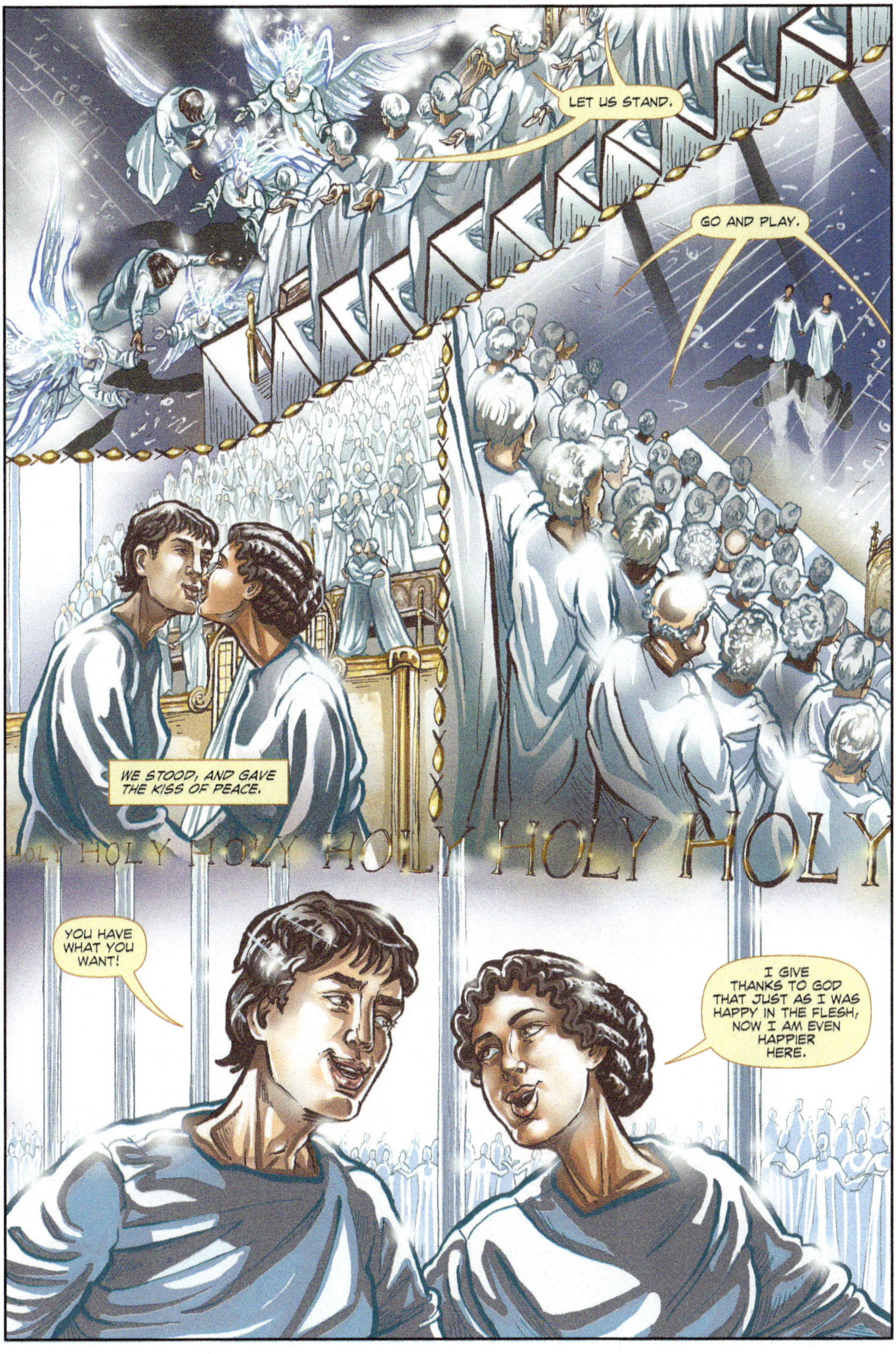
LET US STAND.
GO AND PLAY.
WE STOOD, AND GAVE THE KISS OF PEACE.
HOLY HOLY HOLY HOLY HOLY HOLY
YOU HAVE WHAT YOU WANT!
I GIVE THANKS TO GOD THAT JUST AS I WAS HAPPY IN THE FLESH, NOW I AM EVEN HAPPIER HERE.

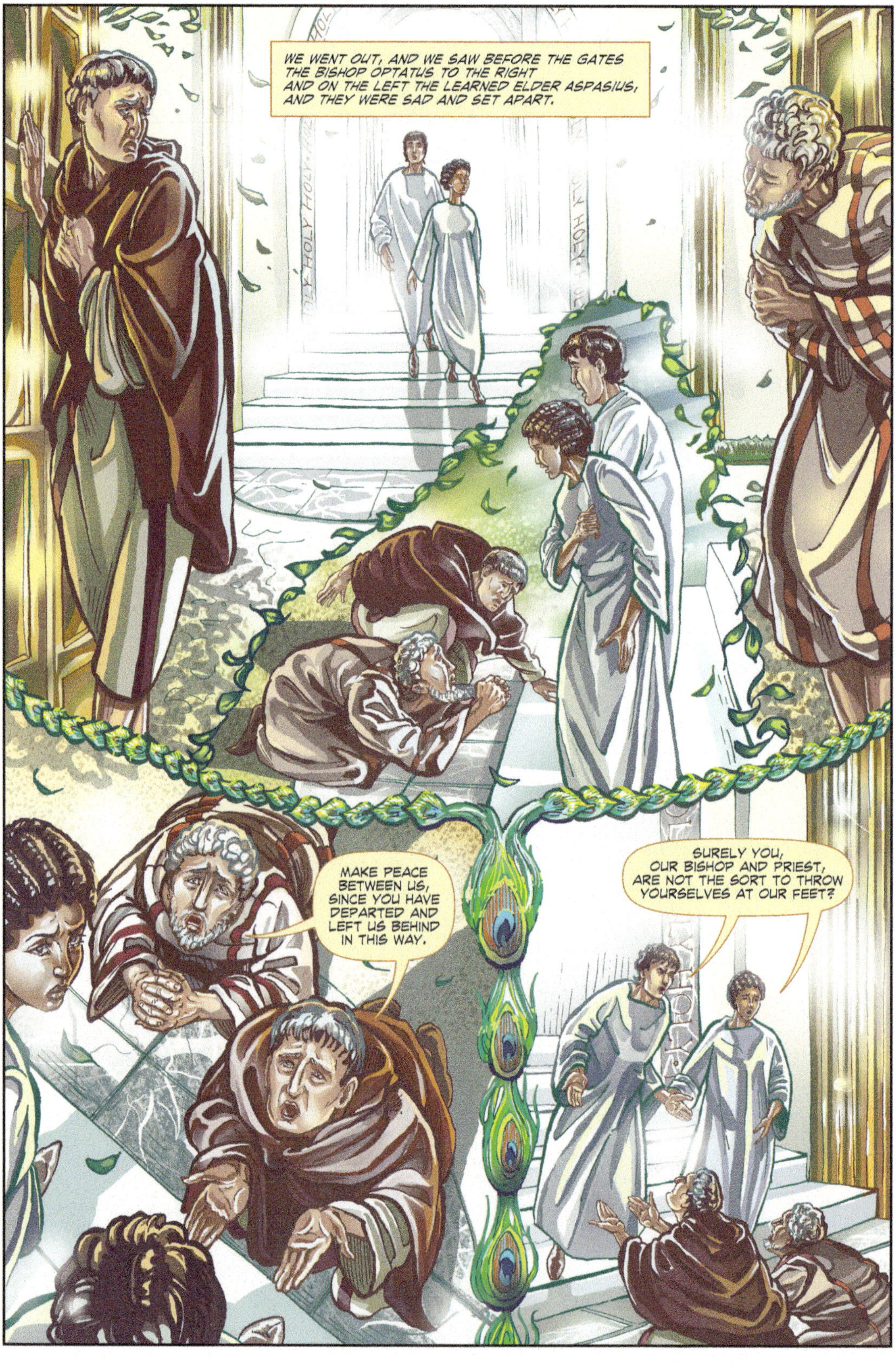
WE WENT OUT, AND WE SAW BEFORE THE GATES THE BISHOP OPTATUS TO THE RIGHT AND ON THE LEFT THE LEARNED ELDER ASPASIUS, AND THEY WERE SAD AND SET APART.
MAKE PEACE BETWEEN US, SINCE YOU HAVE DEPARTED AND LEFT US BEHIND IN THIS WAY.
SURELY YOU, OUR BISHOP AND PRIEST, ARE NOT THE SORT TO THROW YOURSELVES AT OUR FEET?

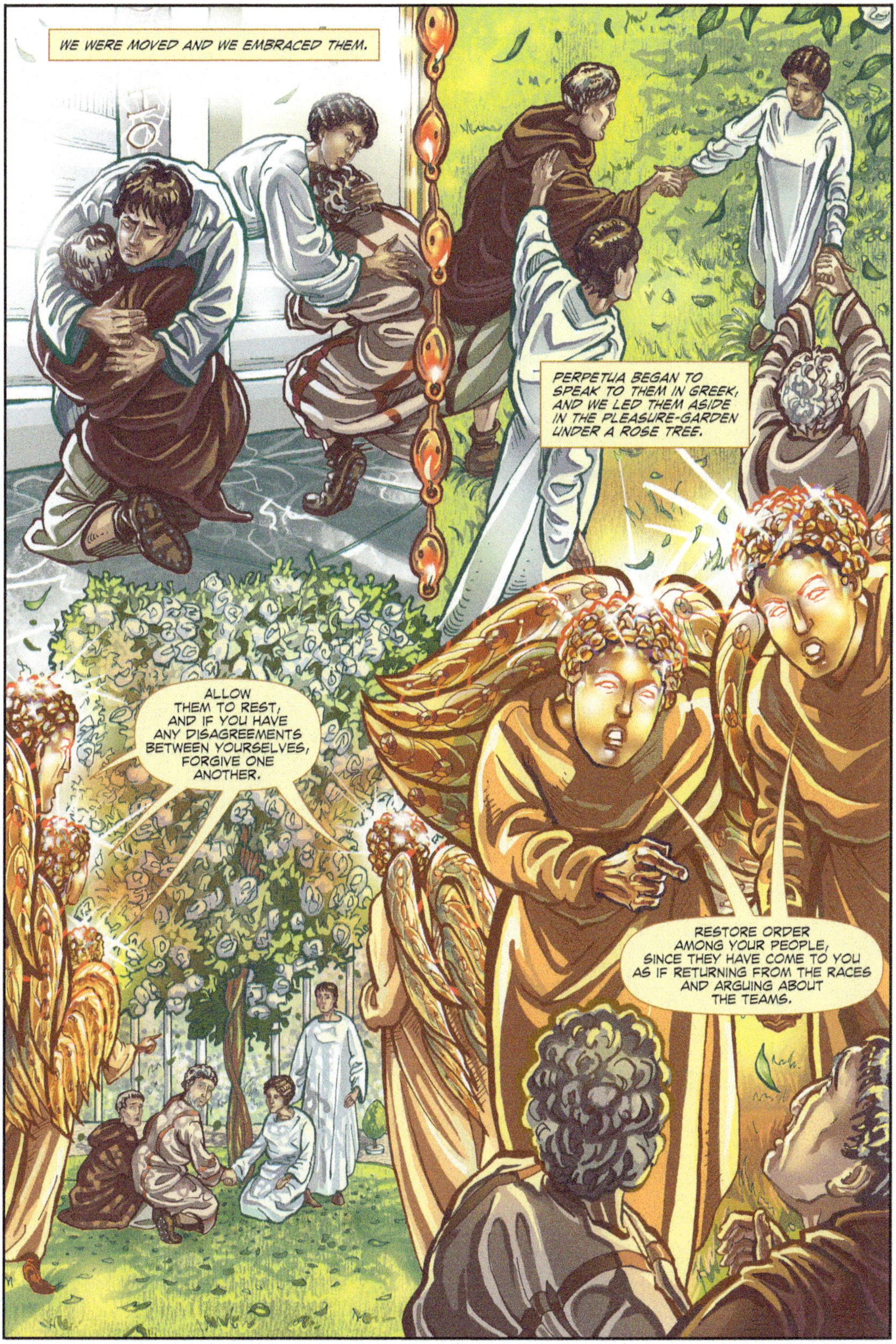
WE WERE MOVED AND WE EMBRACED THEM.
PERPETUA BEGAN TO SPEAK TO THEM IN GREEK, AND WE LED THEM ASIDE IN THE PLEASURE-GARDEN UNDER A ROSE TREE.
ALLOW THEM TO REST, AND IF YOU HAVE ANY DISAGREEMENTS BETWEEN YOURSELVES, FORGIVE ONE ANOTHER.
RESTORE ORDER AMONG YOUR PEOPLE, SINCE THEY HAVE COME TO YOU AS IF RETURNING FROM THE RACES AND ARGUING ABOUT THE TEAMS.

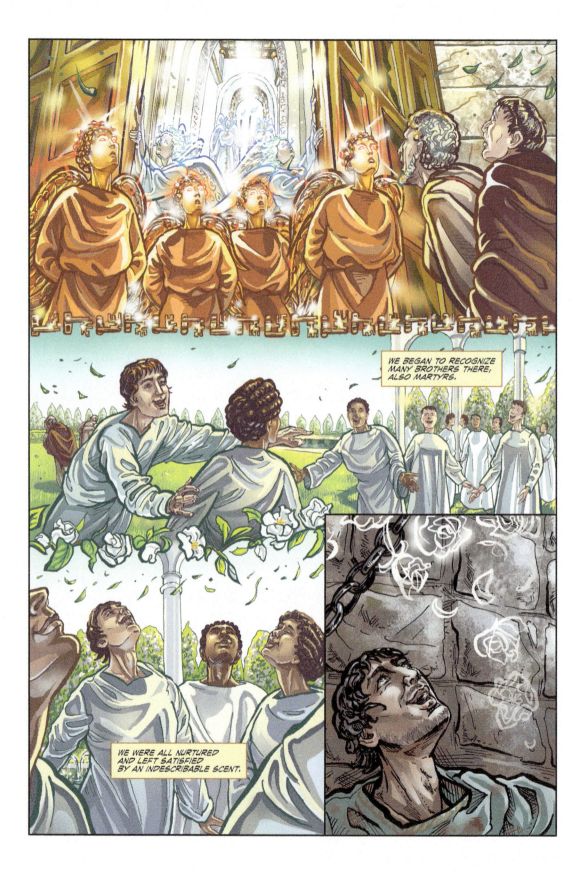

WE BEGAN TO RECOGNIZE MANY BROTHERS THERE; ALSO MARTYRS.

WE WERE ALL NURTURED AND LEFT SATISFIED BY AN INDESCRIBABLE SCENT.

CHAPTER 4
DAMNATIO AD BESTIAS, "CONDEMNED TO THE BEASTS"

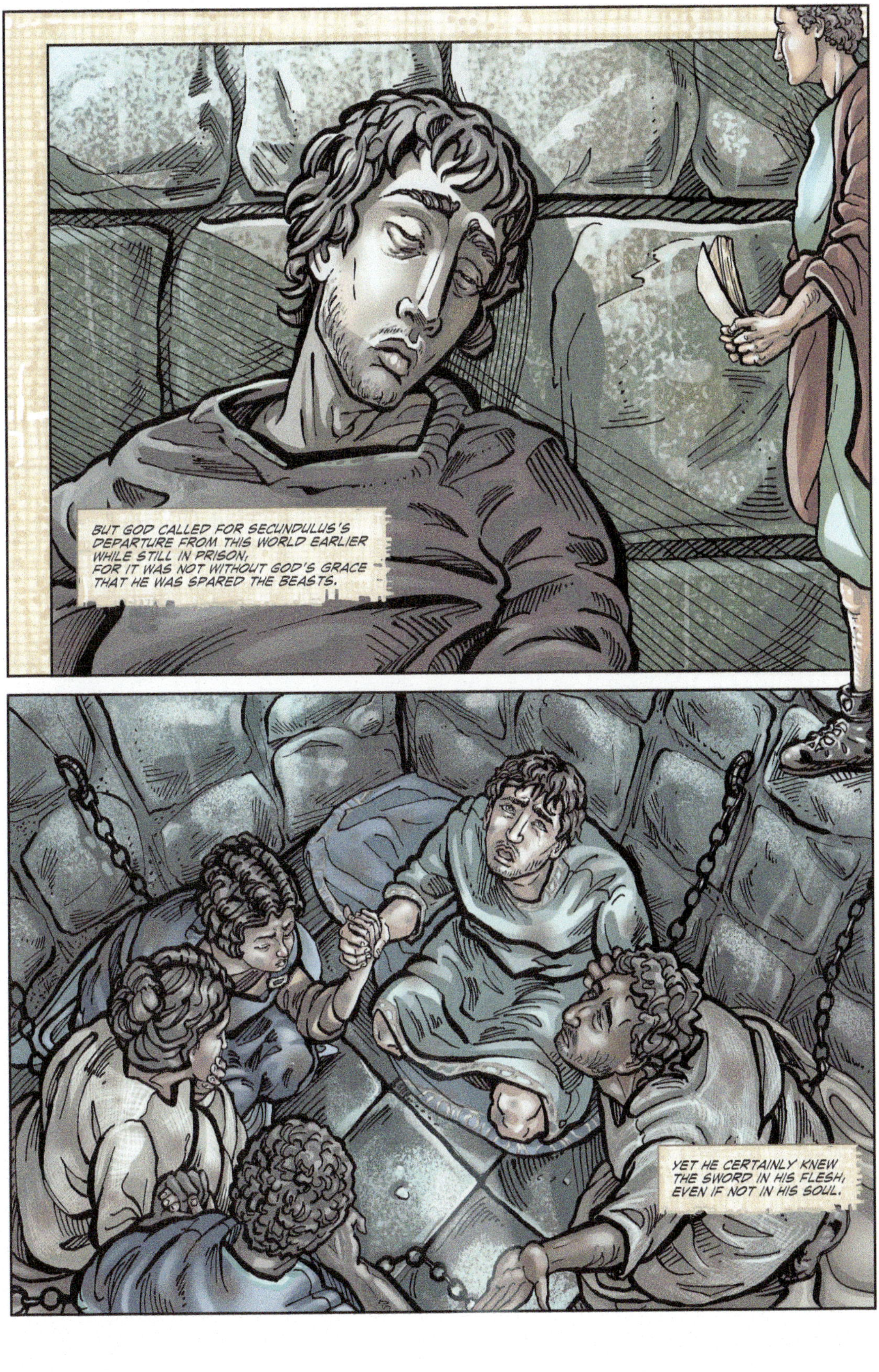
BUT GOD CALLED FOR SECUNDULUS'S DEPARTURE FROM THIS WORLD EARLIER WHILE STILL IN PRISON, FOR IT WAS NOT WITHOUT GOD'S GRACE THAT HE WAS SPARED THE BEASTS.
YET HE CERTAINLY KNEW THE SWORD IN HIS FLESH, EVEN IF NOT IN HIS SOUL.

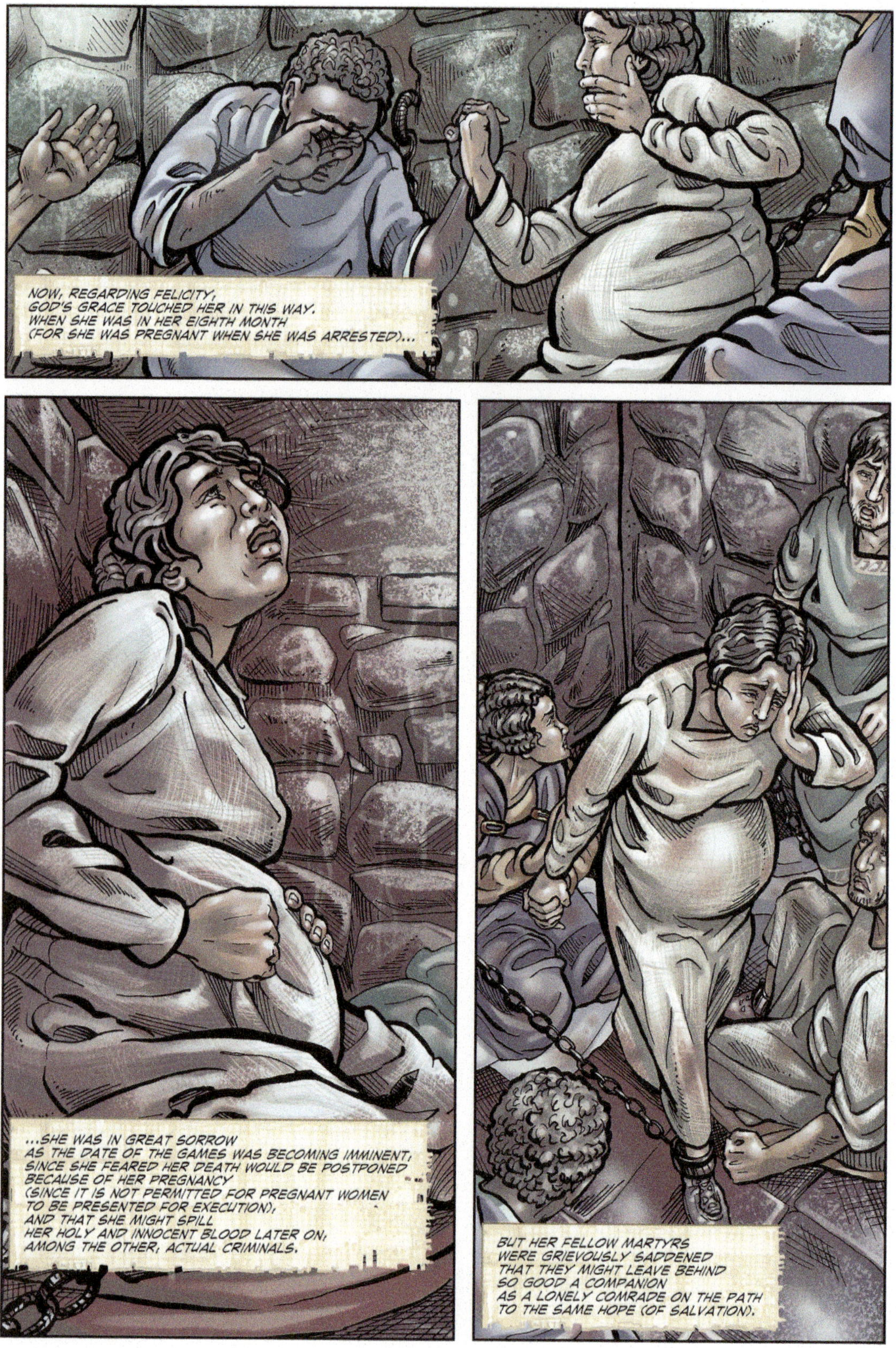
NOW, REGARDING FELICITY,
GOD'S GRACE TOUCHED HER IN THIS WAY.
WHEN SHE WAS IN HER EIGHTH MONTH
(FOR SHE WAS PREGNANT WHEN SHE WAS ARRESTED)...
...SHE WAS IN GREAT SORROW
AS THE DATE OF THE GAMES WAS BECOMING IMMINENT,
SINCE SHE FEARED HER DEATH WOULD BE POSTPONED
BECAUSE OF HER PREGNANCY
(SINCE IT IS NOT PERMITTED FOR PREGNANT WOMEN
TO BE PRESENTED FOR EXECUTION),
AND THAT SHE MIGHT SPILL
HER HOLY AND INNOCENT BLOOD LATER ON,
AMONG THE OTHER, ACTUAL CRIMINALS.
BUT HER FELLOW MARTYRS
WERE GRIEVOUSLY SADDENED
THAT THEY MIGHT LEAVE BEHIND
SO GOOD A COMPANION
AS A LONELY COMRADE ON THE PATH
TO THE SAME HOPE (OF SALVATION).

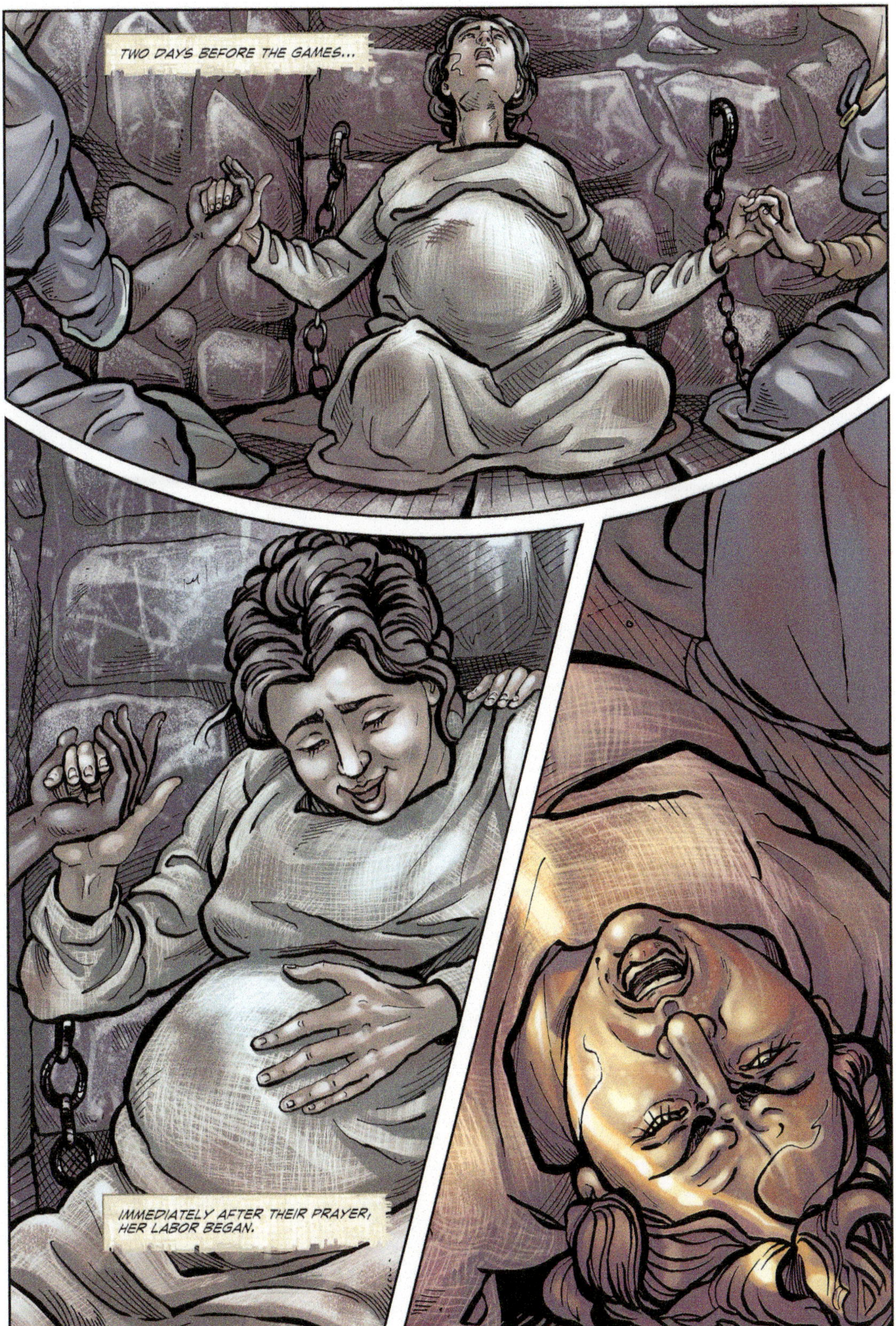
TWO DAYS BEFORE THE GAMES...
IMMEDIATELY AFTER THEIR PRAYER, HER LABOR BEGAN.

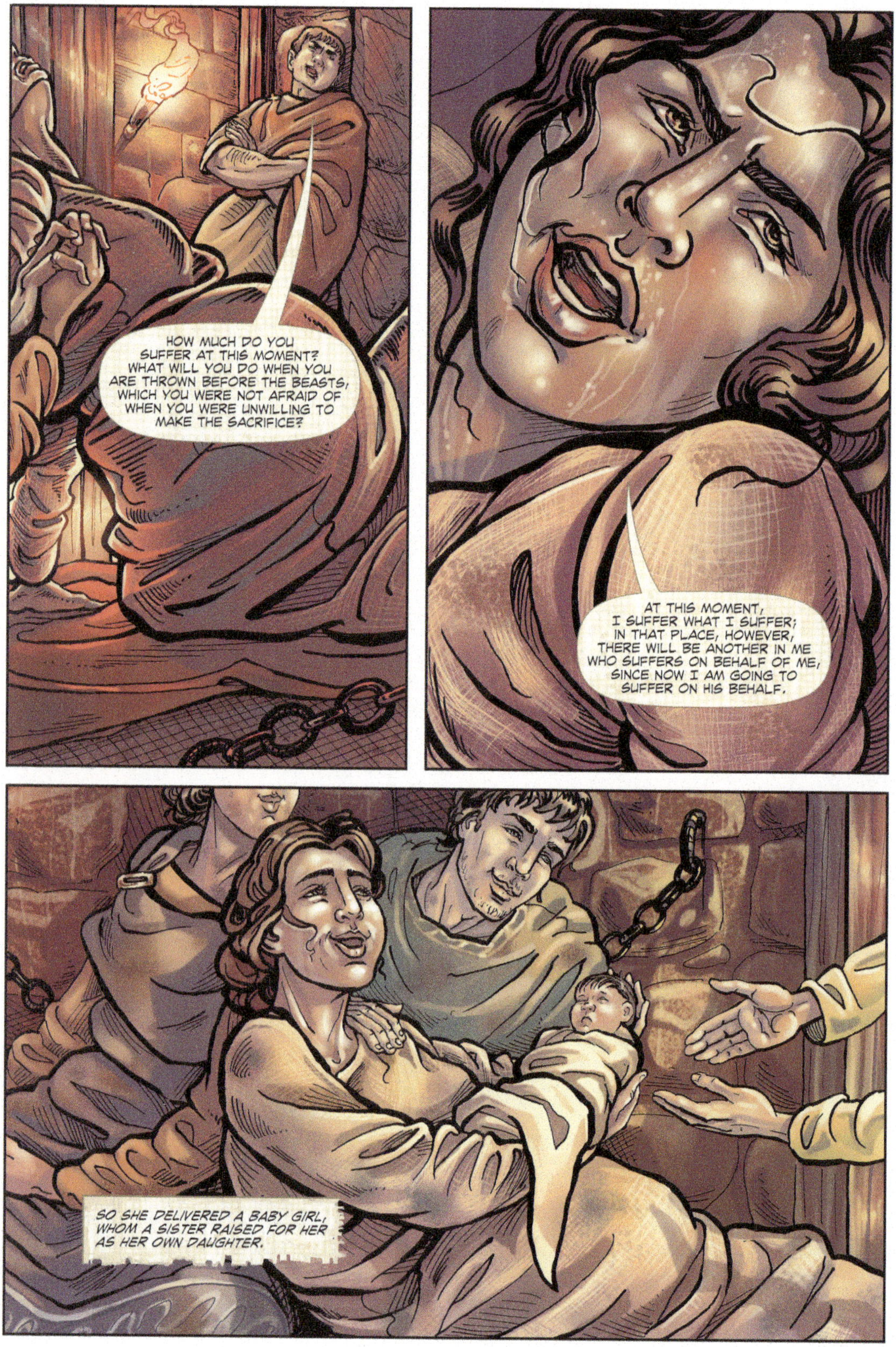
HOW MUCH DO YOU SUFFER AT THIS MOMENT? WHAT WILL YOU DO WHEN YOU ARE THROWN BEFORE THE BEASTS, WHICH YOU WERE NOT AFRAID OF WHEN YOU WERE UNWILLING TO MAKE THE SACRIFICE?
AT THIS MOMENT, I SUFFER WHAT I SUFFER; IN THAT PLACE, HOWEVER, THERE WILL BE ANOTHER IN ME WHO SUFFERS ON BEHALF OF ME, SINCE NOW I AM GOING TO SUFFER ON HIS BEHALF.
SO SHE DELIVERED A BABY GIRL, WHOM A SISTER RAISED FOR HER AS HER OWN DAUGHTER.

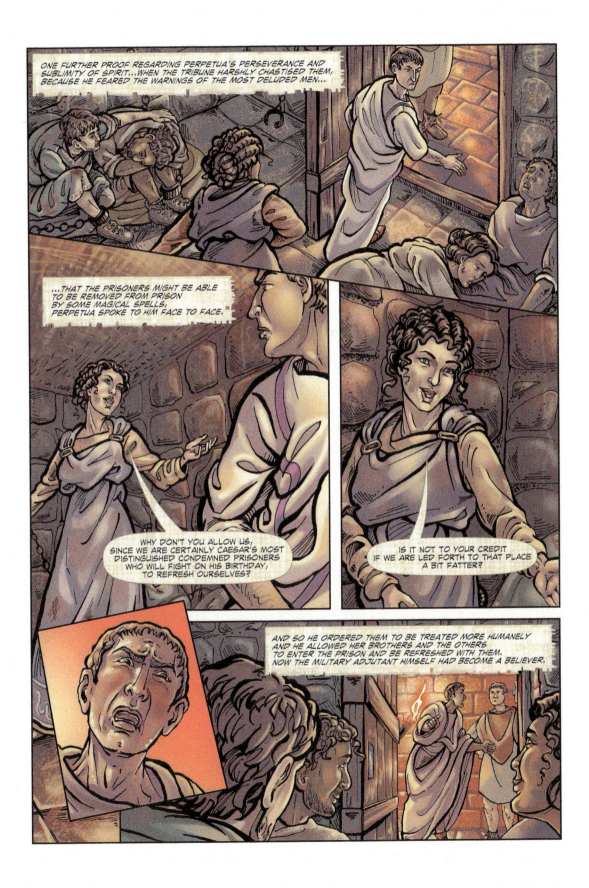

ONE FURTHER PROOF REGARDING PERPETUA'S PERSEVERANCE AND SUBLIMITY OF SPIRIT...WHEN THE TRIBUNE HARSHLY CHASTISED THEM, BECAUSE HE FEARED THE WARNINGS OF THE MOST DELUDED MEN...

...THAT THE PRISONERS MIGHT BE ABLE TO BE REMOVED FROM PRISON BY SOME MAGICAL SPELLS, PERPETUA SPOKE TO HIM FACE TO FACE."

WHY DON'T YOU ALLOW US, SINCE WE ARE CERTAINLY CAESAR'S MOST DISTINGUISHED CONDEMNED PRISONERS WHO WILL FIGHT ON HIS BIRTHDAY, TO REFRESH OURSELVES?

IS IT NOT TO YOUR CREDIT IF WE ARE LED FORTH TO THAT PLACE A BIT FATTER?

AND SO HE ORDERED THEM TO BE TREATED MORE HUMANELY AND HE ALLOWED HER BROTHERS AND THE OTHERS TO ENTER THE PRISON AND BE REFRESHED WITH THEM. NOW THE MILITARY ADJUTANT HIMSELF HAD BECOME A BELIEVER.

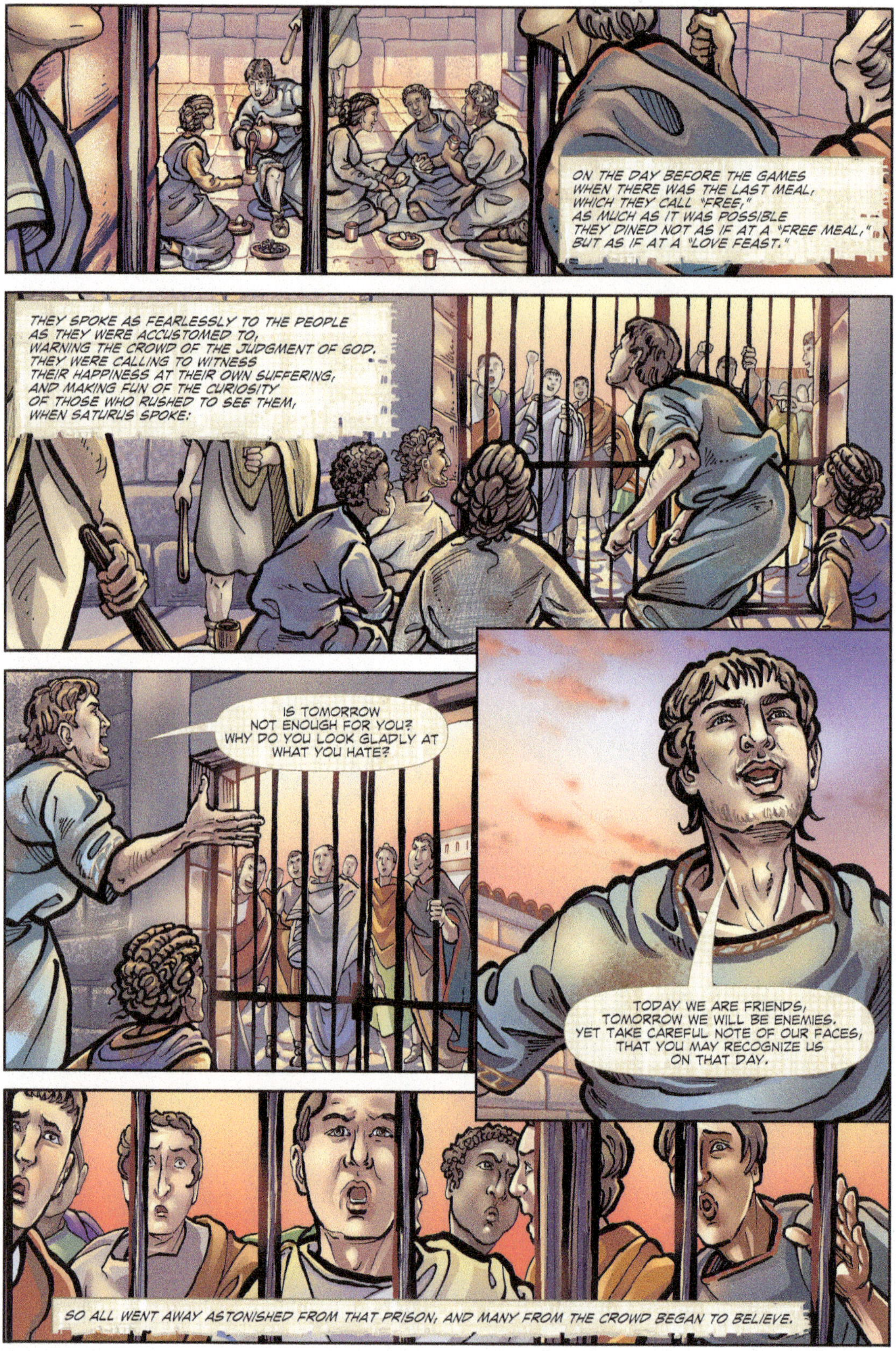
ON THE DAY BEFORE THE GAMES WHEN THERE WAS THE LAST MEAL, WHICH THEY CALL "FREE," AS MUCH AS IT WAS POSSIBLE THEY DINED NOT AS IF AT A "FREE MEAL," BUT AS IF AT A "LOVE FEAST."
THEY SPOKE AS FEARLESSLY TO THE PEOPLE AS THEY WERE ACCUSTOMED TO, WARNING THE CROWD OF THE JUDGMENT OF GOD. THEY WERE CALLING TO WITNESS THEIR HAPPINESS AT THEIR OWN SUFFERING, AND MAKING FUN OF THE CURIOSITY OF THOSE WHO RUSHED TO SEE THEM, WHEN SATURUS SPOKE:
IS TOMORROW NOT ENOUGH FOR YOU? WHY DO YOU LOOK GLADLY AT WHAT YOU HATE?
TODAY WE ARE FRIENDS, TOMORROW WE WILL BE ENEMIES. YET TAKE CAREFUL NOTE OF OUR FACES, THAT YOU MAY RECOGNIZE US ON THAT DAY.
SO ALL WENT AWAY ASTONISHED FROM THAT PRISON, AND MANY FROM THE CROWD BEGAN TO BELIEVE.

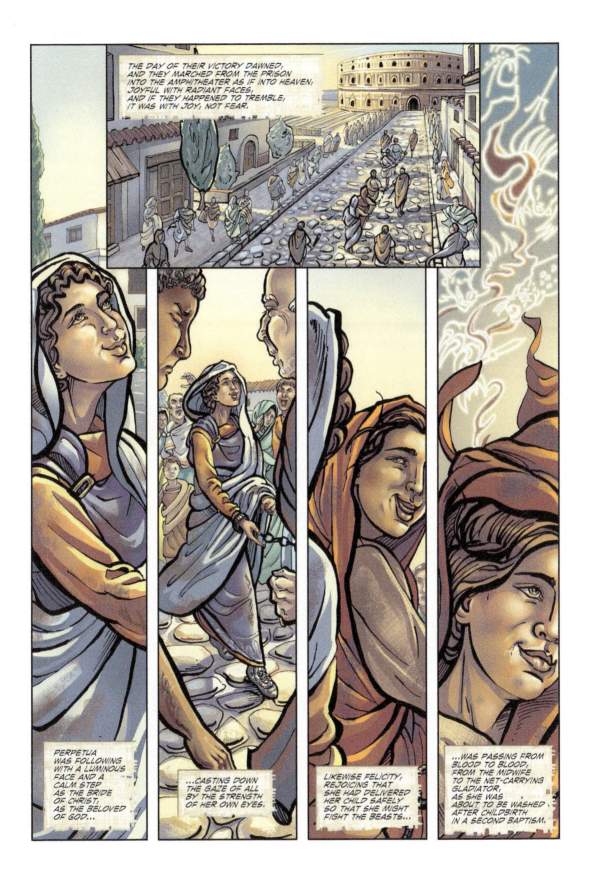

THE DAY OF THEIR VICTORY DAWNED,
AND THEY MARCHED FROM THE PRISON
INTO THE AMPHITHEATER AS IF INTO HEAVEN,
JOYFUL WITH RADIANT FACES,
AND IF THEY HAPPENED TO TREMBLE,
IT WAS WITH JOY, NOT FEAR.

PERPETUA
WAS FOLLOWING
WITH A LUMINOUS
FACE AND A
CALM STEP
AS THE BRIDE
OF CHRIST,
AS THE BELOVED
OF GOD...

...CASTING DOWN
THE GAZE OF ALL
BY THE STRENGTH
OF HER OWN EYES.

LIKEWISE FELICITY,
REJOICING THAT
SHE HAD DELIVERED
HER CHILD SAFELY
SO THAT SHE MIGHT
FIGHT THE BEASTS...

...WAS PASSING FROM
BLOOD TO BLOOD,
FROM THE MIDWIFE
TO THE NET-CARRYING
GLADIATOR,
AS SHE WAS
ABOUT TO BE WASHED
AFTER CHILDBIRTH
IN A SECOND BAPTISM.

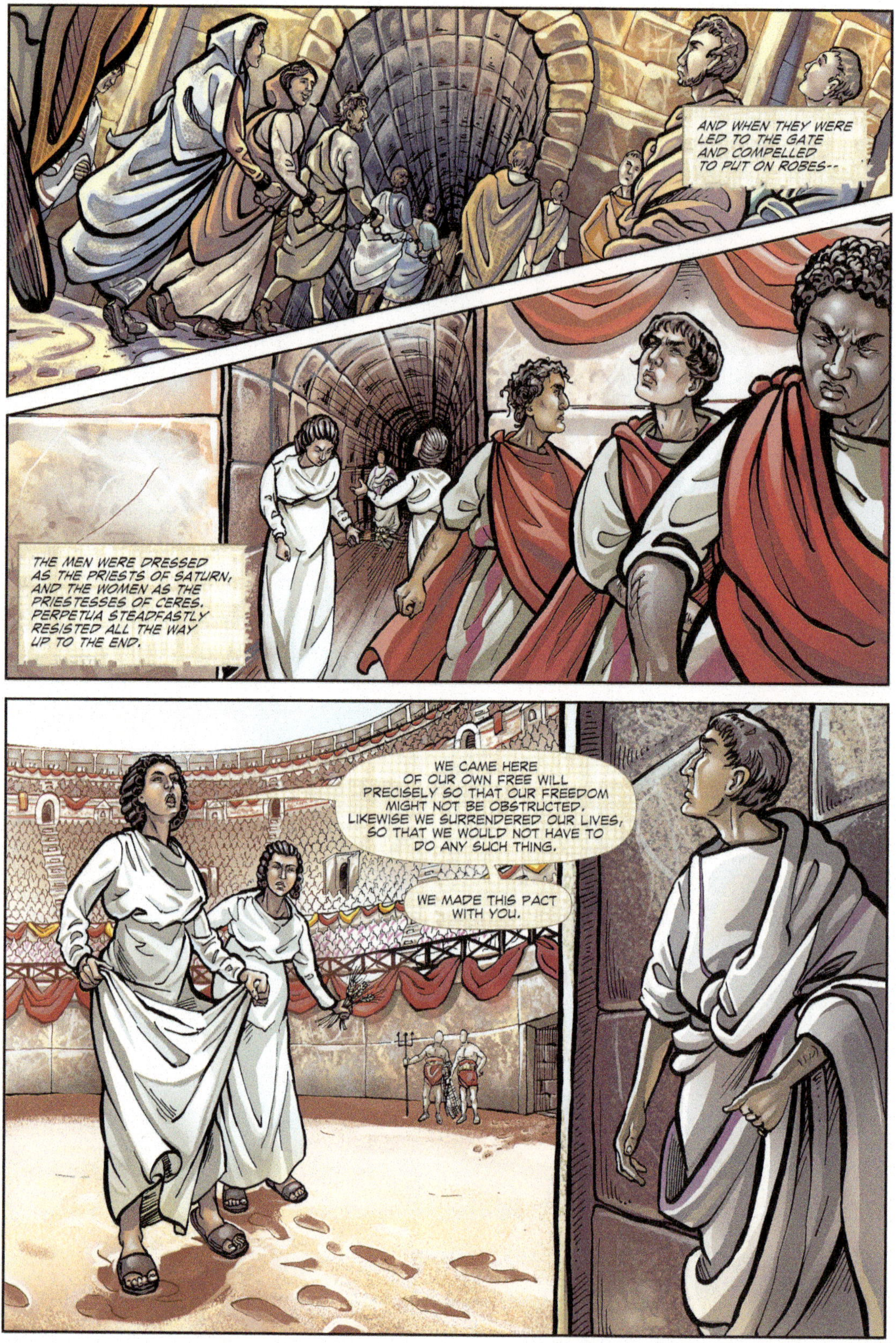
AND WHEN THEY WERE LED TO THE GATE AND COMPELLED TO PUT ON ROBES--
THE MEN WERE DRESSED AS THE PRIESTS OF SATURN, AND THE WOMEN AS THE PRIESTESSES OF CERES. PERPETUA STEADFASTLY RESISTED ALL THE WAY UP TO THE END.
WE CAME HERE OF OUR OWN FREE WILL PRECISELY SO THAT OUR FREEDOM MIGHT NOT BE OBSTRUCTED. LIKEWISE WE SURRENDERED OUR LIVES, SO THAT WE WOULD NOT HAVE TO DO ANY SUCH THING.
WE MADE THIS PACT WITH YOU.

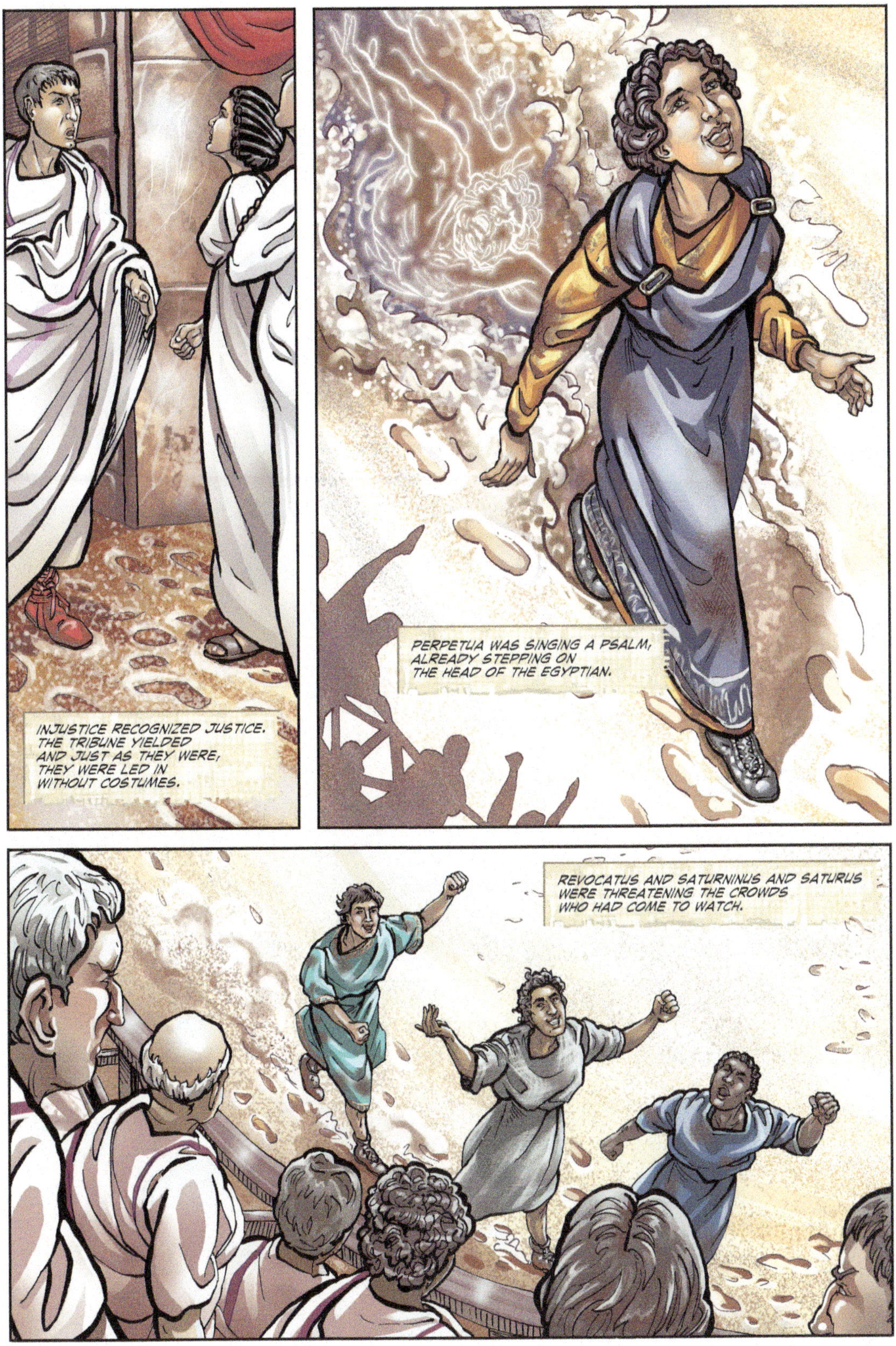
INJUSTICE RECOGNIZED JUSTICE. THE TRIBUNE YIELDED AND JUST AS THEY WERE, THEY WERE LED IN WITHOUT COSTUMES.
PERPETUA WAS SINGING A PSALM, ALREADY STEPPING ON THE HEAD OF THE EGYPTIAN.
REVOCATUS AND SATURNINUS AND SATURUS WERE THREATENING THE CROWDS WHO HAD COME TO WATCH.

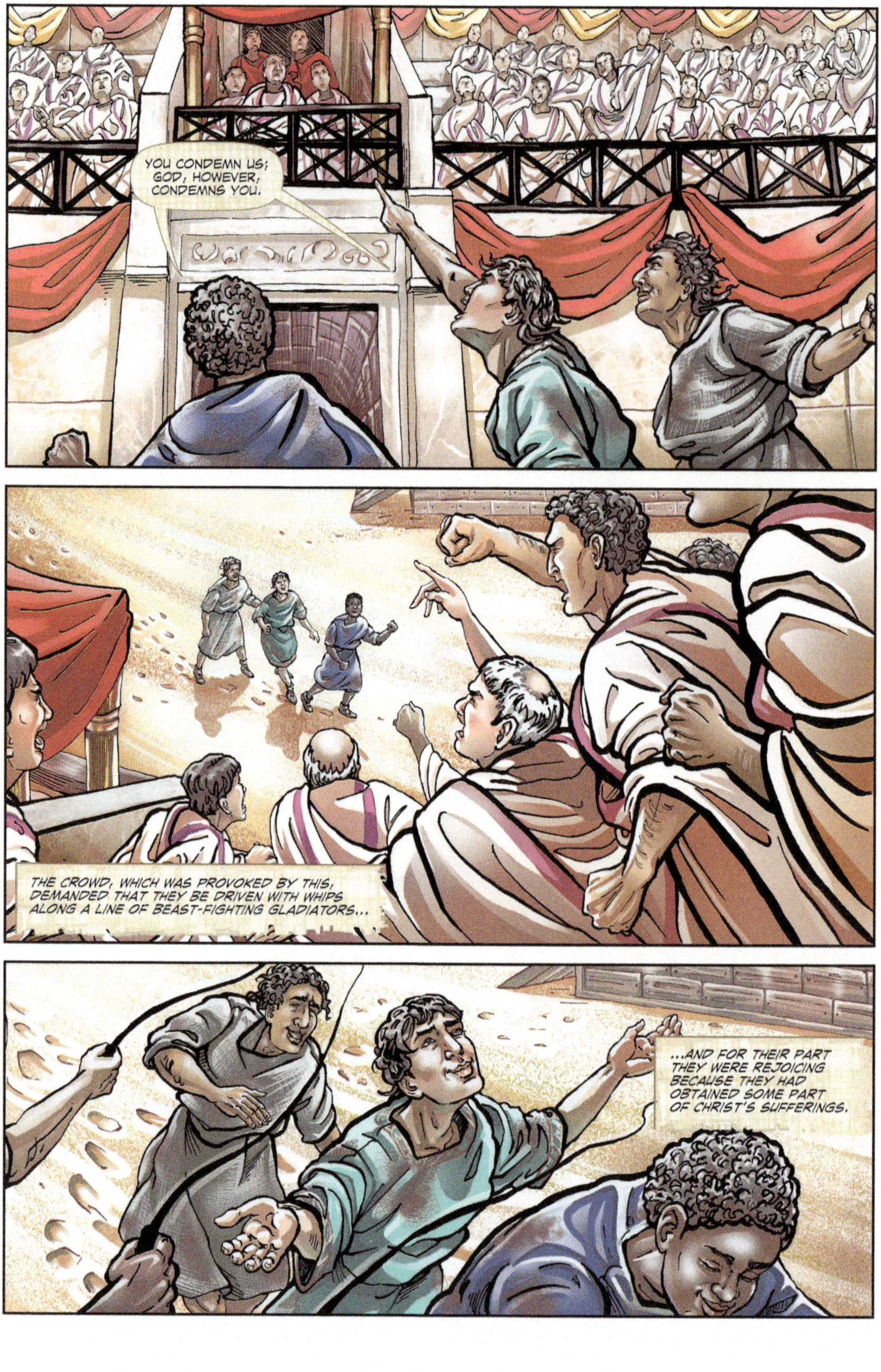
YOU CONDEMN US; GOD, HOWEVER, CONDEMNS YOU.
THE CROWD, WHICH WAS PROVOKED BY THIS, DEMANDED THAT THEY BE DRIVEN WITH WHIPS ALONG A LINE OF BEAST-FIGHTING GLADIATORS...
...AND FOR THEIR PART THEY WERE REJOICING BECAUSE THEY HAD OBTAINED SOME PART OF CHRIST'S SUFFERINGS.

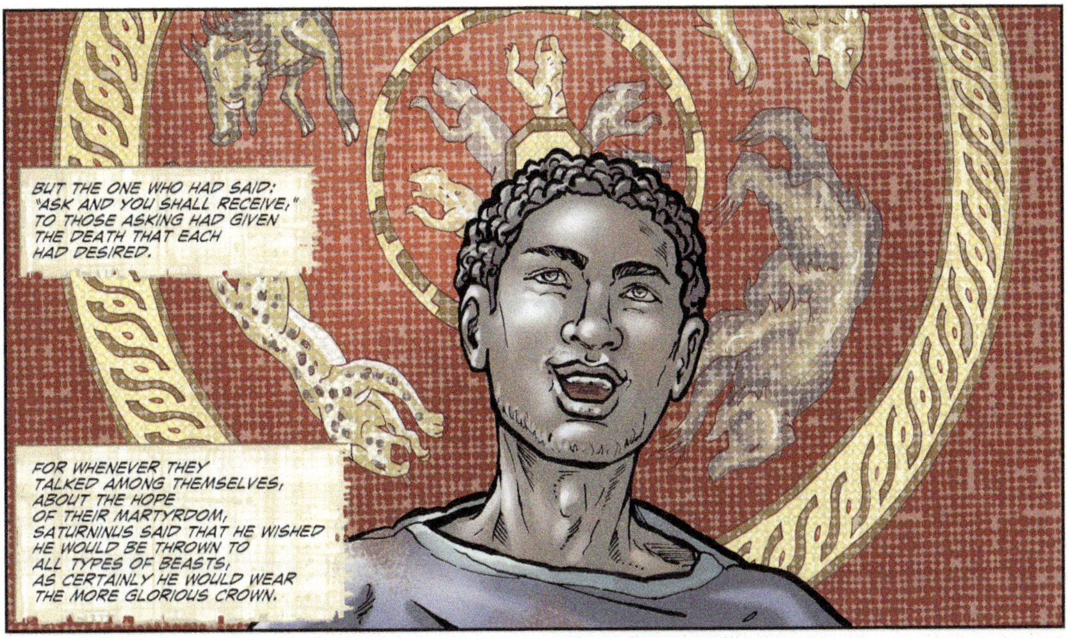
BUT THE ONE WHO HAD SAID: "ASK AND YOU SHALL RECEIVE," TO THOSE ASKING HAD GIVEN THE DEATH THAT EACH HAD DESIRED.
FOR WHENEVER THEY TALKED AMONG THEMSELVES, ABOUT THE HOPE OF THEIR MARTYRDOM, SATURNINUS SAID THAT HE WISHED HE WOULD BE THROWN TO ALL TYPES OF BEASTS, AS CERTAINLY HE WOULD WEAR THE MORE GLORIOUS CROWN.

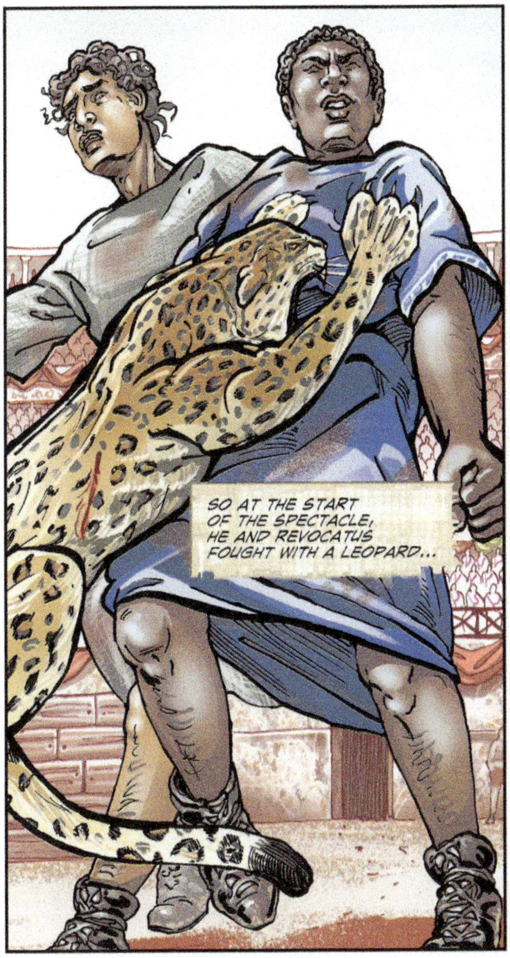
SO AT THE START OF THE SPECTACLE, HE AND REVOCATUS FOUGHT WITH A LEOPARD...

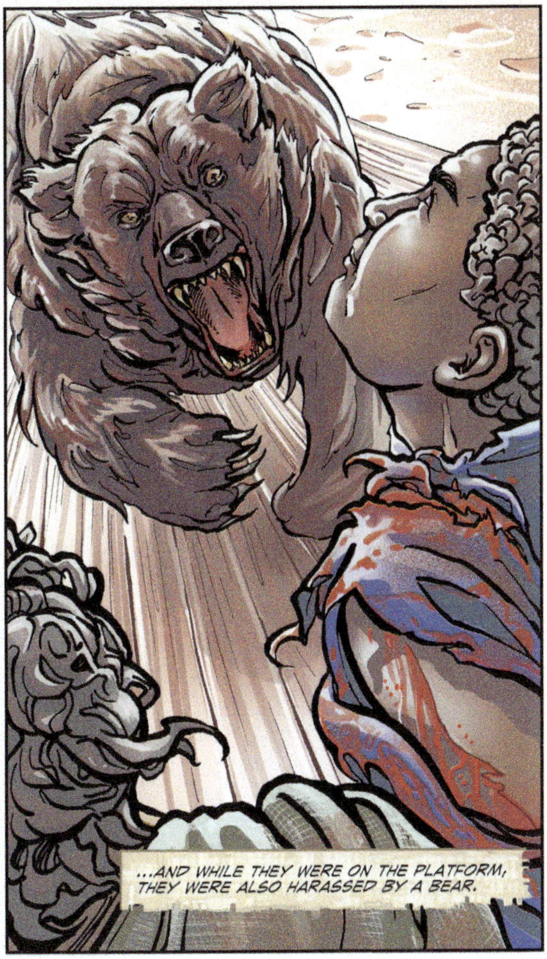
...AND WHILE THEY WERE ON THE PLATFORM, THEY WERE ALSO HARASSED BY A BEAR.

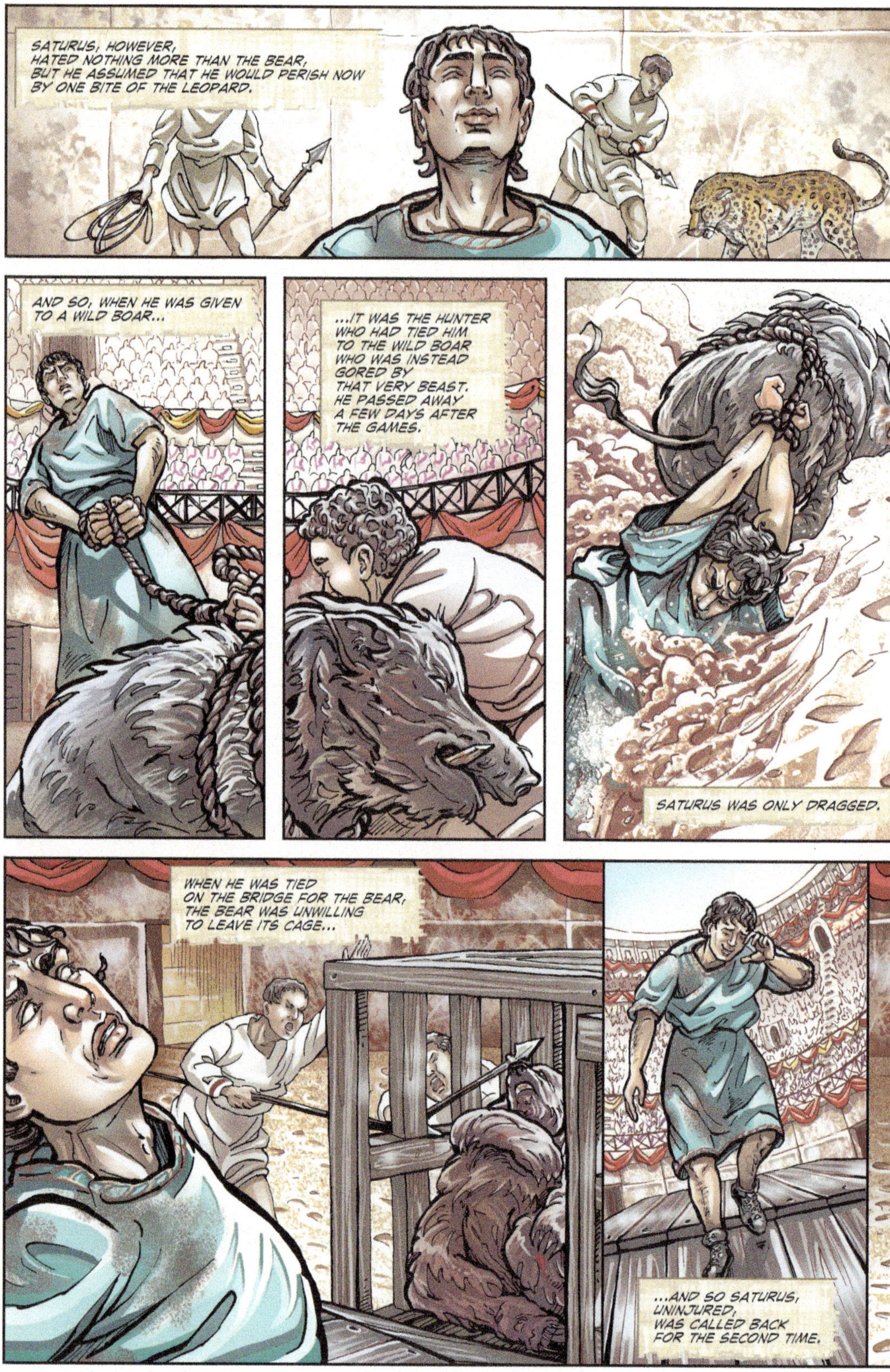
SATURUS, HOWEVER, HATED NOTHING MORE THAN THE BEAR, BUT HE ASSUMED THAT HE WOULD PERISH NOW BY ONE BITE OF THE LEOPARD.
AND SO, WHEN HE WAS GIVEN TO A WILD BOAR...
...IT WAS THE HUNTER WHO HAD TIED HIM TO THE WILD BOAR WHO WAS INSTEAD GORED BY THAT VERY BEAST. HE PASSED AWAY A FEW DAYS AFTER THE GAMES.
SATURUS WAS ONLY DRAGGED.
WHEN HE WAS TIED ON THE BRIDGE FOR THE BEAR, THE BEAR WAS UNWILLING TO LEAVE ITS CAGE...
...AND SO SATURUS, UNINJURED, WAS CALLED BACK FOR THE SECOND TIME.

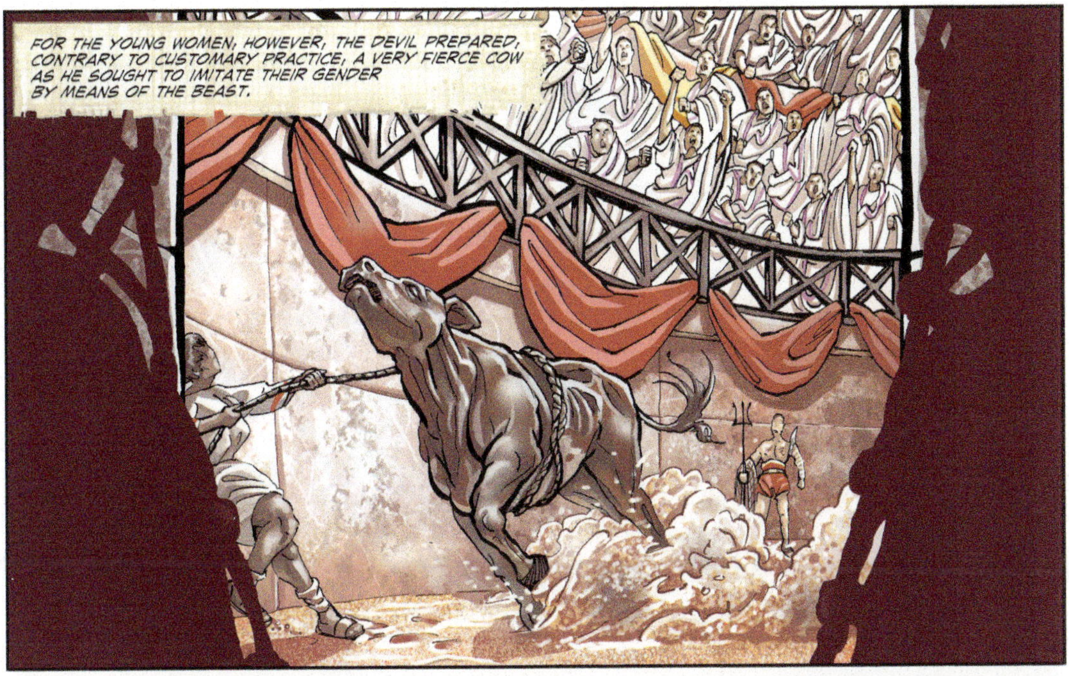
FOR THE YOUNG WOMEN, HOWEVER, THE DEVIL PREPARED, CONTRARY TO CUSTOMARY PRACTICE, A VERY FIERCE COW AS HE SOUGHT TO IMITATE THEIR GENDER BY MEANS OF THE BEAST.

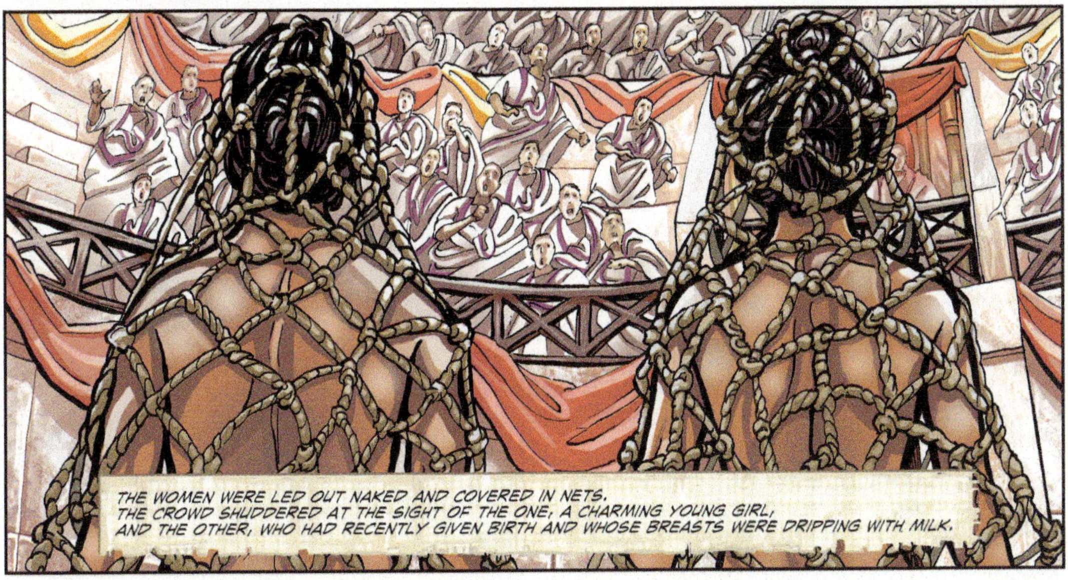
THE WOMEN WERE LED OUT NAKED AND COVERED IN NETS. THE CROWD SHUDDERED AT THE SIGHT OF THE ONE, A CHARMING YOUNG GIRL, AND THE OTHER, WHO HAD RECENTLY GIVEN BIRTH AND WHOSE BREASTS WERE DRIPPING WITH MILK.

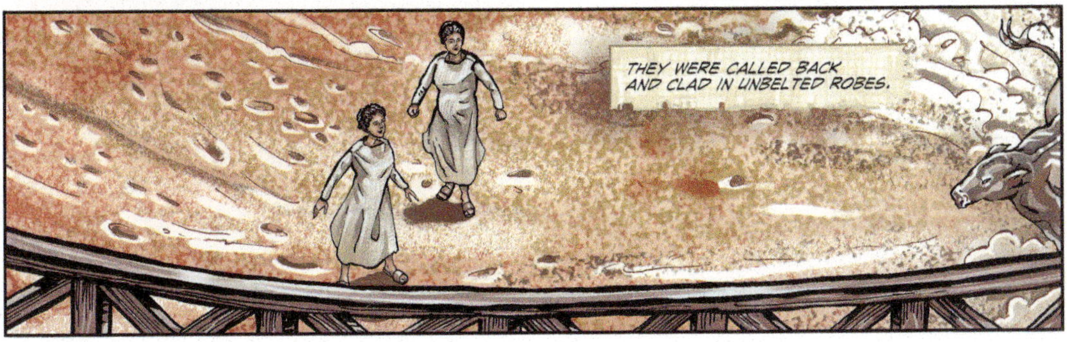
THEY WERE CALLED BACK AND CLAD IN UNBELTED ROBES.

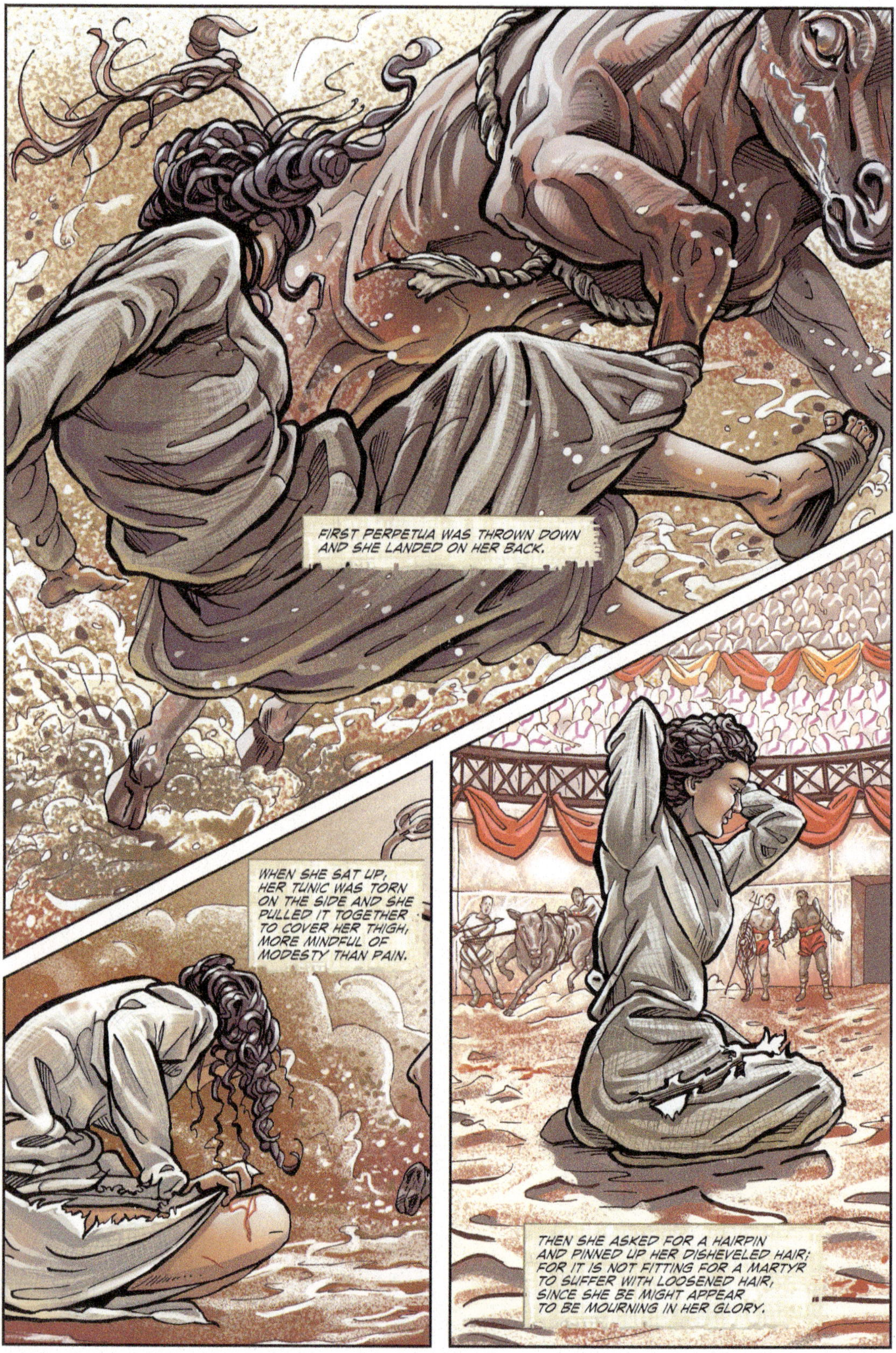
FIRST PERPETUA WAS THROWN DOWN AND SHE LANDED ON HER BACK.
WHEN SHE SAT UP, HER TUNIC WAS TORN ON THE SIDE AND SHE PULLED IT TOGETHER TO COVER HER THIGH; MORE MINDFUL OF MODESTY THAN PAIN.
THEN SHE ASKED FOR A HAIRPIN AND PINNED UP HER DISHEVELED HAIR; FOR IT IS NOT FITTING FOR A MARTYR TO SUFFER WITH LOOSENED HAIR, SINCE SHE BE MIGHT APPEAR TO BE MOURNING IN HER GLORY.

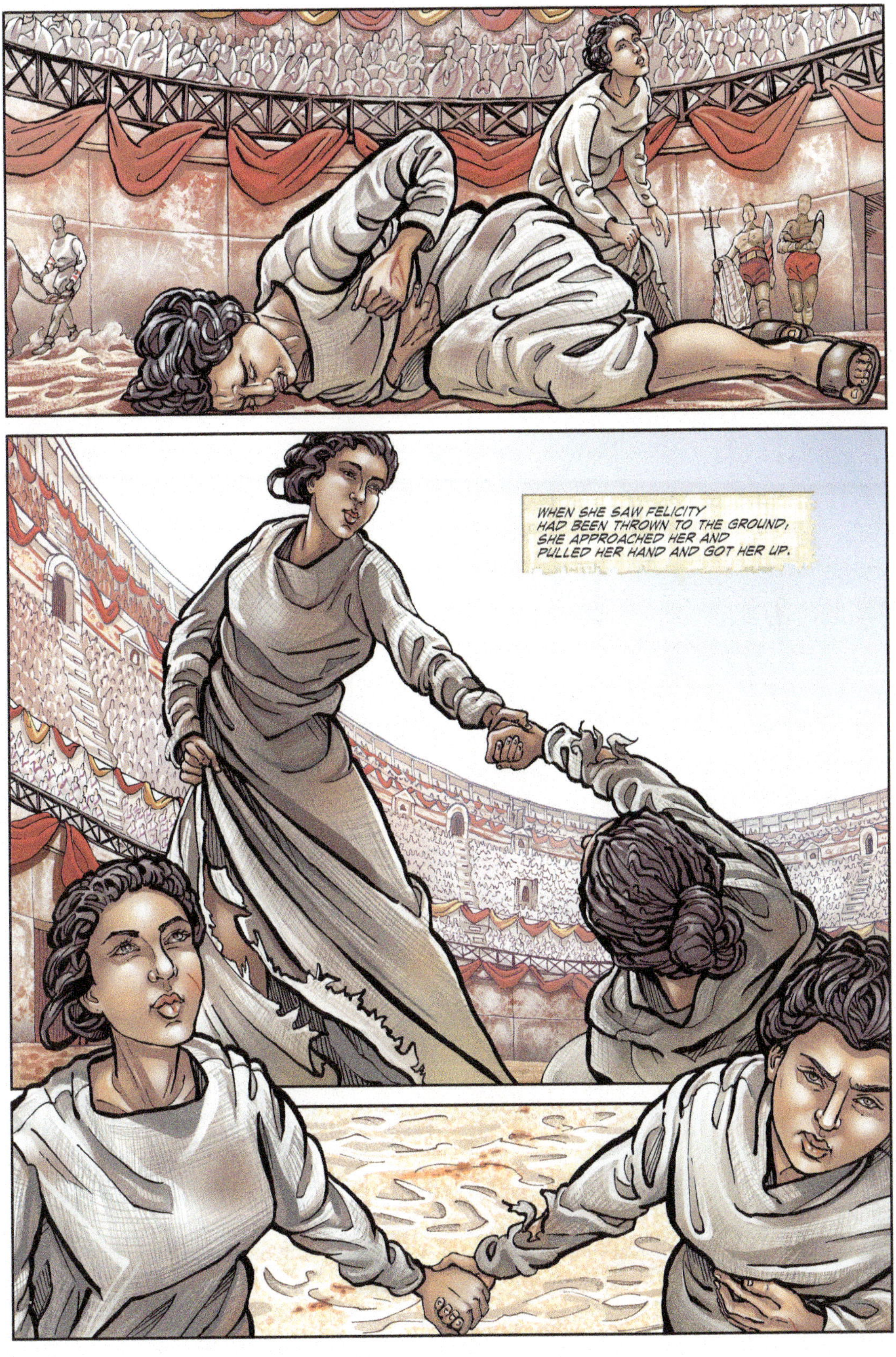
WHEN SHE SAW FELICITY HAD BEEN THROWN TO THE GROUND, SHE APPROACHED HER AND PULLED HER HAND AND GOT HER UP.

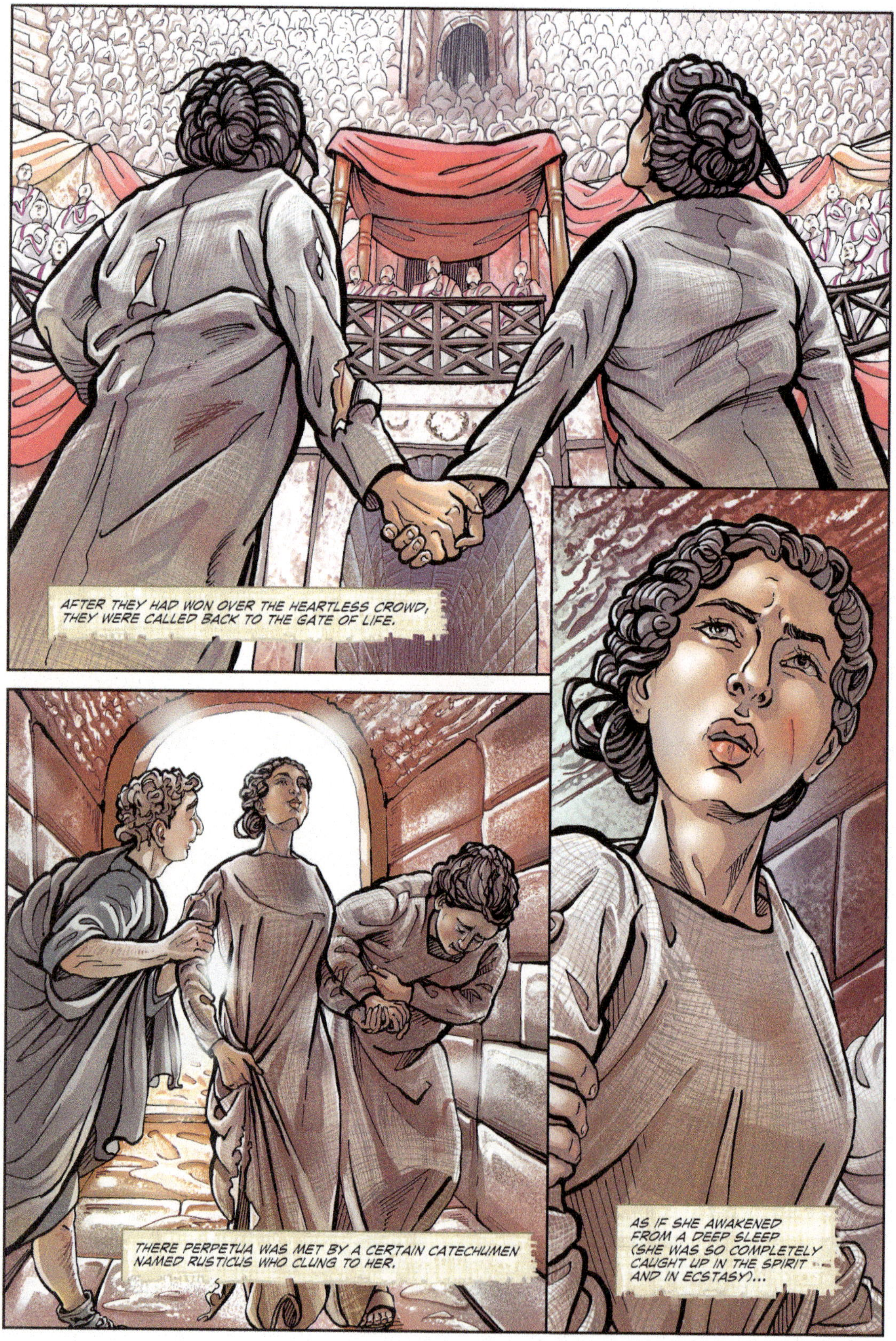
AFTER THEY HAD WON OVER THE HEARTLESS CROWD, THEY WERE CALLED BACK TO THE GATE OF LIFE.
THERE PERPETUA WAS MET BY A CERTAIN CATECHUMEN NAMED RUSTICUS WHO CLUNG TO HER.
AS IF SHE AWAKENED FROM A DEEP SLEEP (SHE WAS SO COMPLETELY CAUGHT UP IN THE SPIRIT AND IN ECSTASY)...

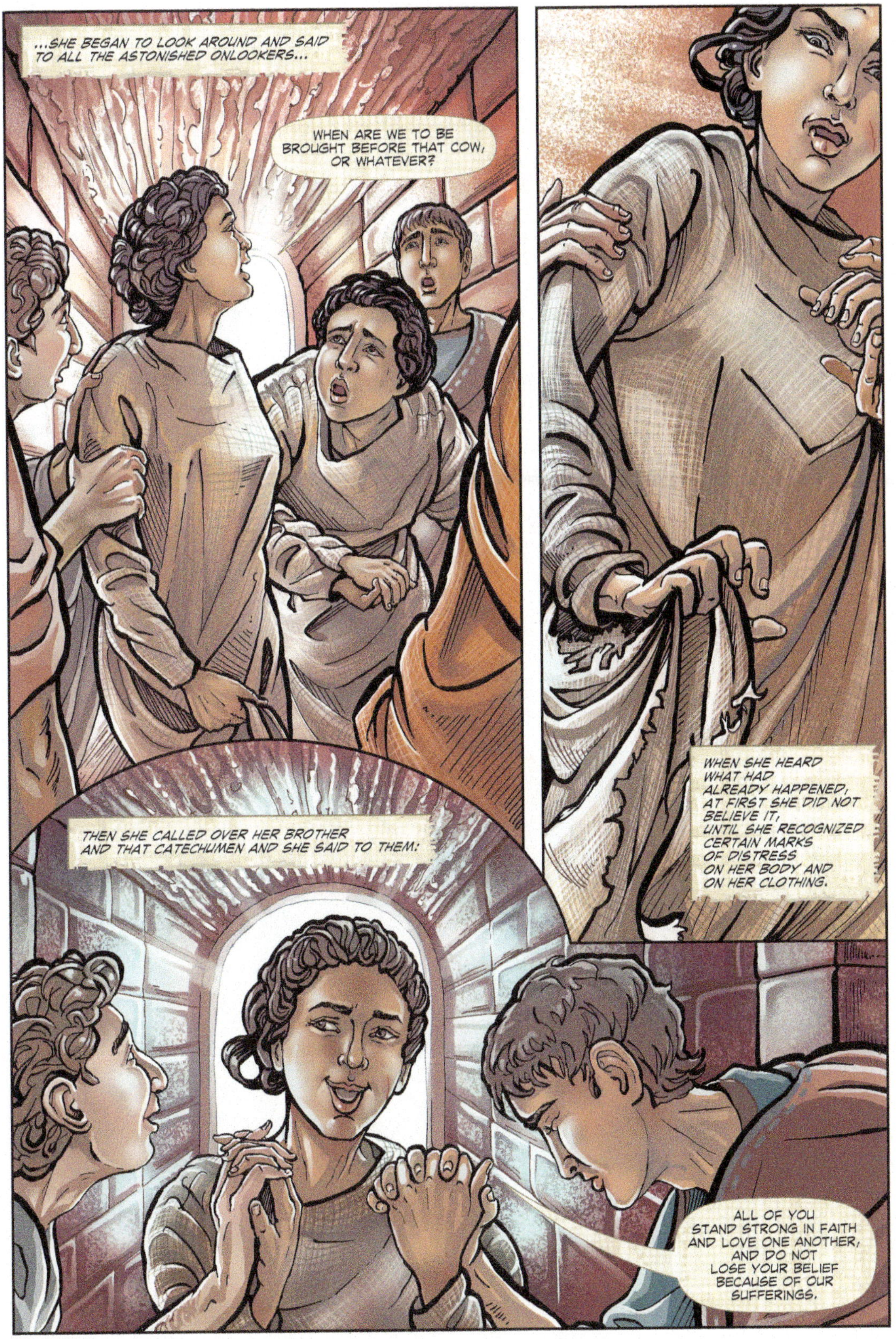
...SHE BEGAN TO LOOK AROUND AND SAID TO ALL THE ASTONISHED ONLOOKERS...
WHEN ARE WE TO BE BROUGHT BEFORE THAT COW, OR WHATEVER?
WHEN SHE HEARD WHAT HAD ALREADY HAPPENED, AT FIRST SHE DID NOT BELIEVE IT, UNTIL SHE RECOGNIZED CERTAIN MARKS OF DISTRESS ON HER BODY AND ON HER CLOTHING.
THEN SHE CALLED OVER HER BROTHER AND THAT CATECHUMEN AND SHE SAID TO THEM:
ALL OF YOU STAND STRONG IN FAITH AND LOVE ONE ANOTHER, AND DO NOT LOSE YOUR BELIEF BECAUSE OF OUR SUFFERINGS.

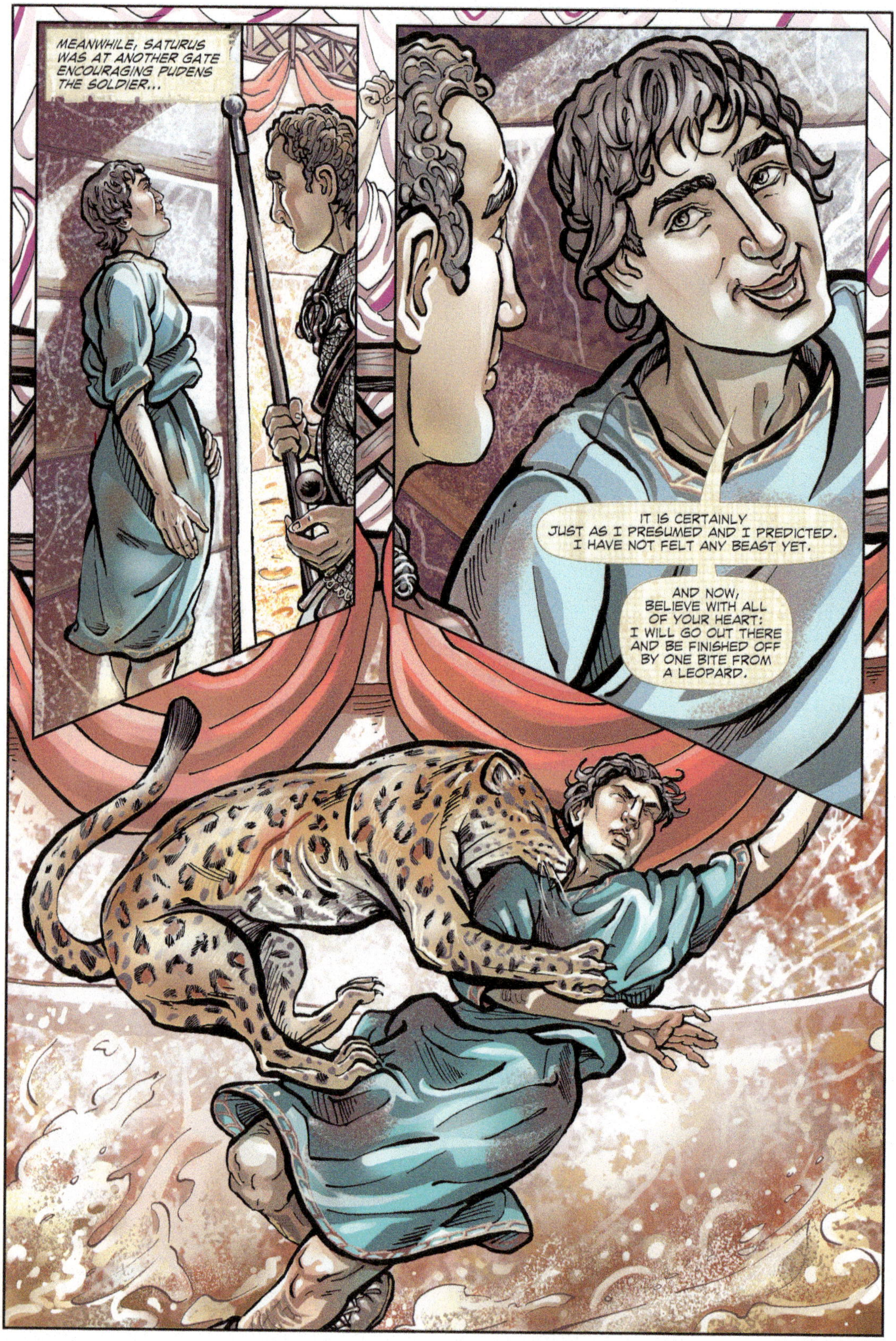
MEANWHILE, SATURUS WAS AT ANOTHER GATE ENCOURAGING PUDENS THE SOLDIER...
IT IS CERTAINLY JUST AS I PRESUMED AND I PREDICTED. I HAVE NOT FELT ANY BEAST YET.
AND NOW, BELIEVE WITH ALL OF YOUR HEART: I WILL GO OUT THERE AND BE FINISHED OFF BY ONE BITE FROM A LEOPARD.

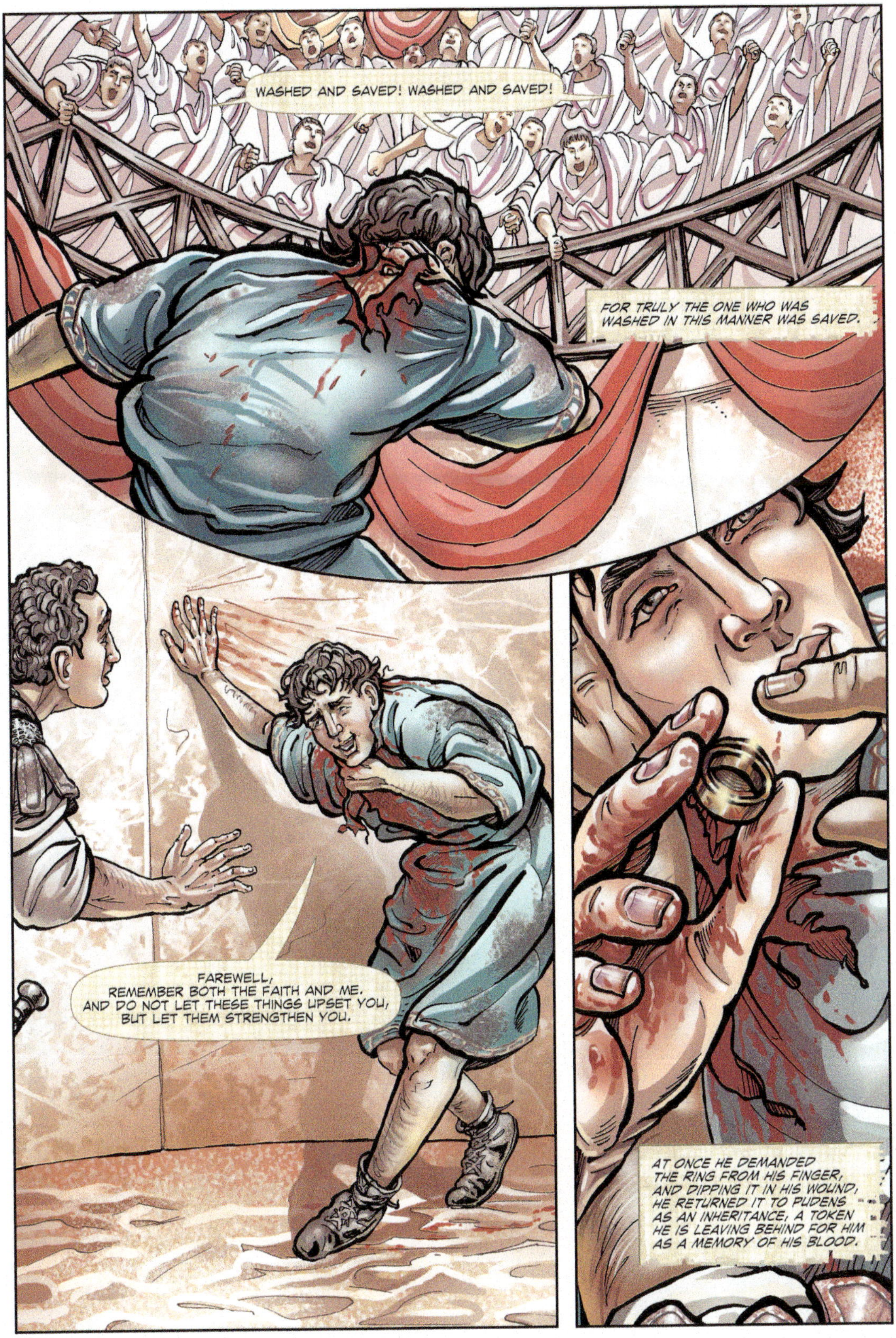
WASHED AND SAVED! WASHED AND SAVED!
FOR TRULY THE ONE WHO WAS WASHED IN THIS MANNER WAS SAVED.
FAREWELL, REMEMBER BOTH THE FAITH AND ME. AND DO NOT LET THESE THINGS UPSET YOU, BUT LET THEM STRENGTHEN YOU.
AT ONCE HE DEMANDED THE RING FROM HIS FINGER, AND DIPPING IT IN HIS WOUND, HE RETURNED IT TO PUDENS AS AN INHERITANCE, A TOKEN HE IS LEAVING BEHIND FOR HIM AS A MEMORY OF HIS BLOOD.

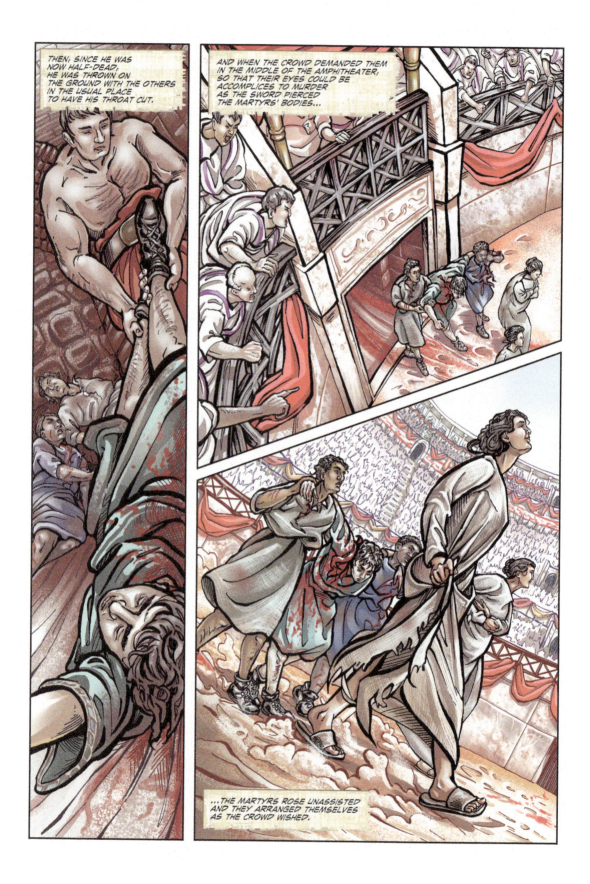

THEN, SINCE HE WAS NOW HALF-DEAD, HE WAS THROWN ON THE GROUND WITH THE OTHERS IN THE USUAL PLACE TO HAVE HIS THROAT CUT.

AND WHEN THE CROWD DEMANDED THEM IN THE MIDDLE OF THE AMPHITHEATER, SO THAT THEIR EYES COULD BE ACCOMPLICES TO MURDER AS THE SWORD PIERCED THE MARTYRS' BODIES...

...THE MARTYRS ROSE UNASSISTED AND THEY ARRANGED THEMSELVES AS THE CROWD WISHED.

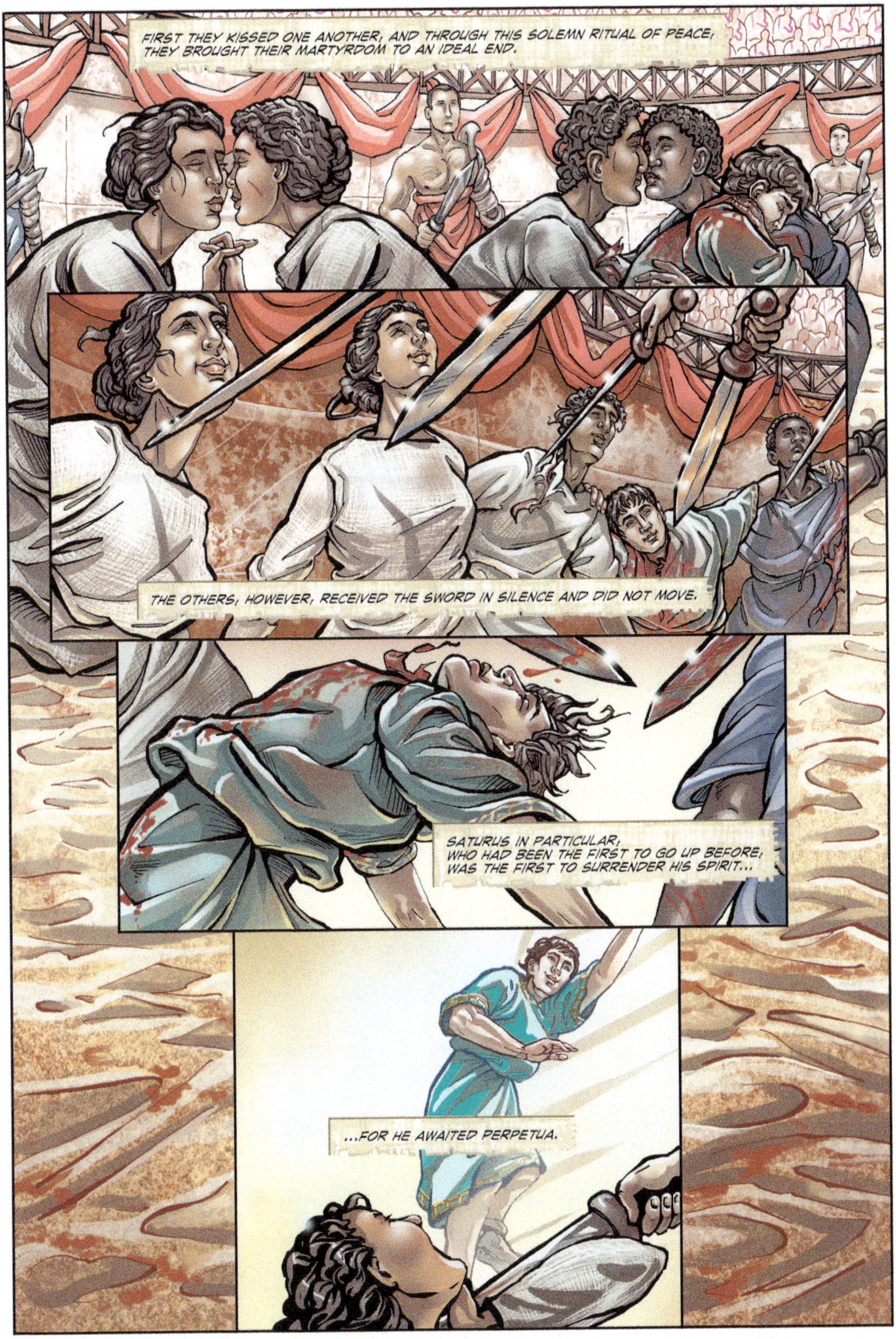
FIRST THEY KISSED ONE ANOTHER, AND THROUGH THIS SOLEMN RITUAL OF PEACE, THEY BROUGHT THEIR MARTYRDOM TO AN IDEAL END.
THE OTHERS, HOWEVER, RECEIVED THE SWORD IN SILENCE AND DID NOT MOVE.
SATURUS IN PARTICULAR, WHO HAD BEEN THE FIRST TO GO UP BEFORE, WAS THE FIRST TO SURRENDER HIS SPIRIT...
...FOR HE AWAITED PERPETUA.

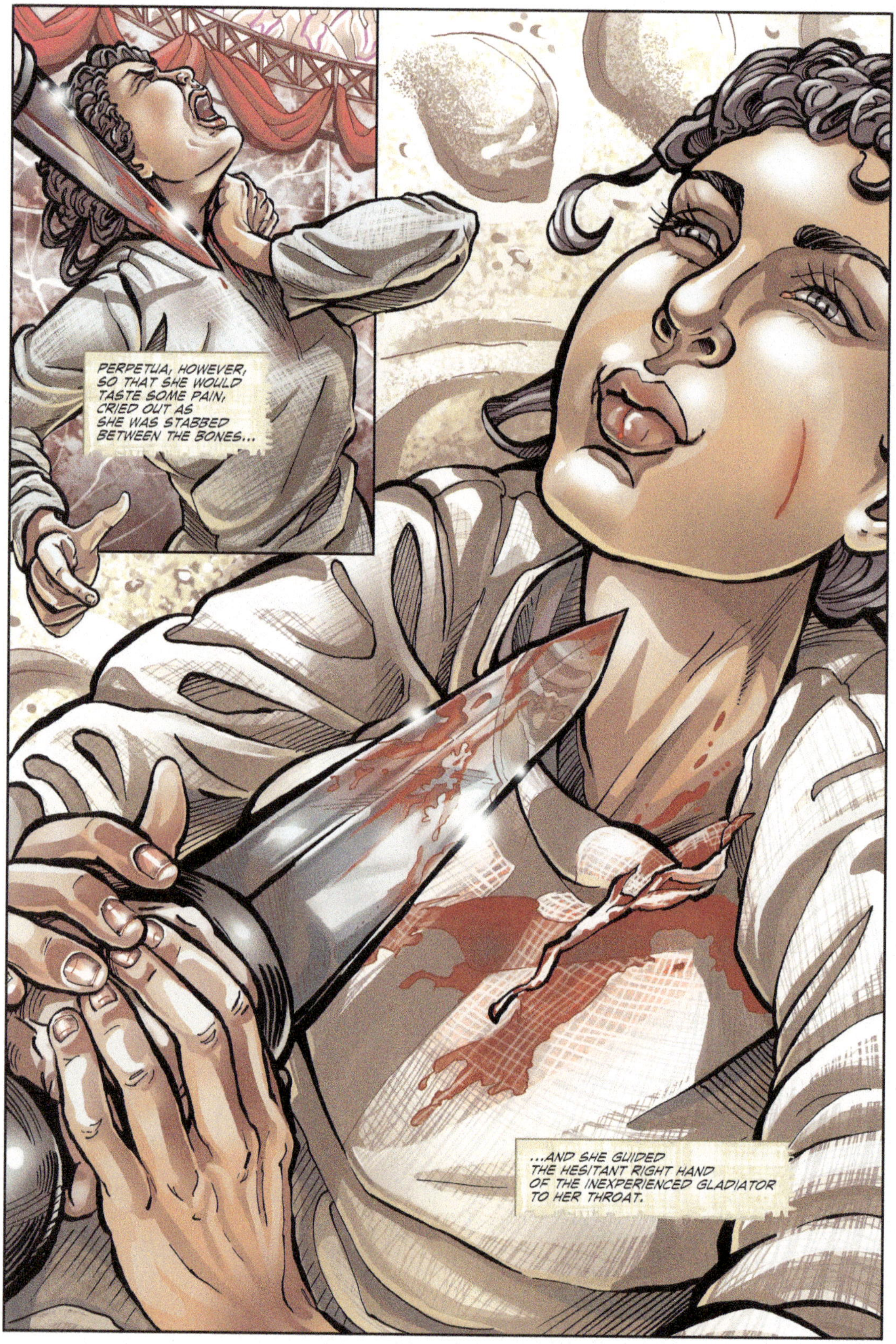
PERPETUA, HOWEVER, SO THAT SHE WOULD TASTE SOME PAIN, CRIED OUT AS SHE WAS STABBED BETWEEN THE BONES...
...AND SHE GUIDED THE HESITANT RIGHT HAND OF THE INEXPERIENCED GLADIATOR TO HER THROAT.

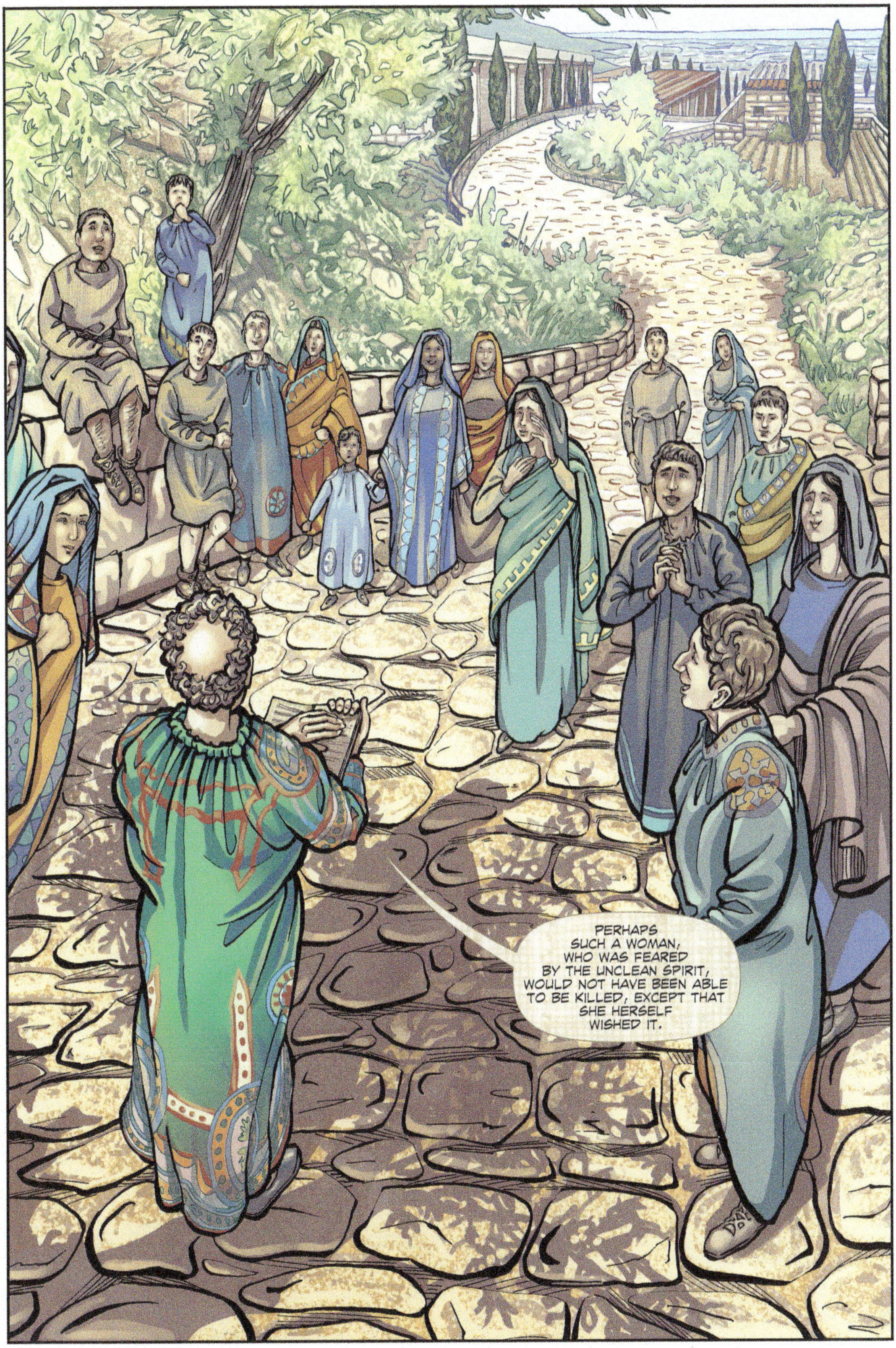
PERHAPS SUCH A WOMAN, WHO WAS FEARED BY THE UNCLEAN SPIRIT, WOULD NOT HAVE BEEN ABLE TO BE KILLED, EXCEPT THAT SHE HERSELF WISHED IT.

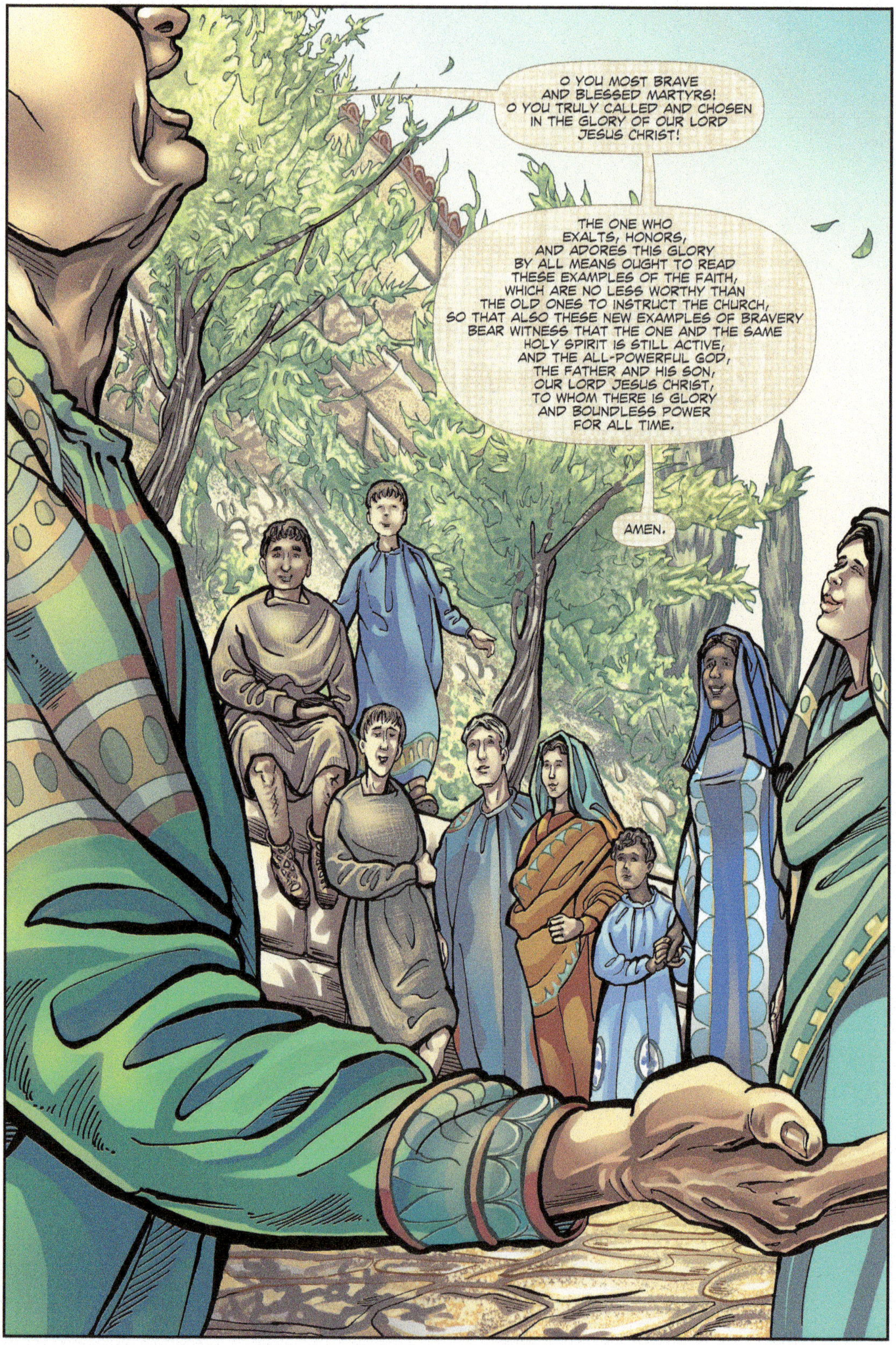
O YOU MOST BRAVE AND BLESSED MARTYRS! O YOU TRULY CALLED AND CHOSEN IN THE GLORY OF OUR LORD JESUS CHRIST!
THE ONE WHO EXALTS, HONORS, AND ADORES THIS GLORY BY ALL MEANS OUGHT TO READ THESE EXAMPLES OF THE FAITH, WHICH ARE NO LESS WORTHY THAN THE OLD ONES TO INSTRUCT THE CHURCH, SO THAT ALSO THESE NEW EXAMPLES OF BRAVERY BEAR WITNESS THAT THE ONE AND THE SAME HOLY SPIRIT IS STILL ACTIVE, AND THE ALL-POWERFUL GOD, THE FATHER AND HIS SON, OUR LORD JESUS CHRIST, TO WHOM THERE IS GLORY AND BOUNDLESS POWER FOR ALL TIME.
AMEN.

PART II
HISTORICAL AND SOCIAL CONTEXT

THE ROMAN EMPIRE

The term *Roman Empire* can refer to "a territory, a form of government, and a period of history" (see "Timeline of Events in History").[1] This commentary will cover all three aspects of the empire since each one is relevant to Perpetua's story. The Roman historian Livy states that Rome began as a monarchy founded via strife by the legendary first king Romulus (Livy, *Ab Urbe Condita* 1.7). The first people who resided in Rome, therefore, were called the Romans. The city of Rome expanded over time from its humble and legendary origins to a cosmopolitan metropolis. By the third century CE, the Roman Empire had spread throughout the entire Mediterranean world (see Map 1).

But what does the term *Roman* or the description of a people as *the Romans* mean to someone living in Carthage in 203 CE? Indeed, *Roman* does not just indicate a person living within Rome's city limits. While I use the term *the Romans* throughout this work when discussing key aspects of Perpetua's story, it is necessary to understand that it does not merely define a group who lived within a certain geographical territory at a certain period of time in history. Think instead about the Romans as the community of imperial Rome, or as a group of persons who shared some common aspects of a culture and values.

Under the reign of the Roman monarchy, from the fifth to the third century BCE the Romans began to expand their territory until they ruled the Italian peninsula. As Rome became a world power in the Mediterranean, they challenged the ruling powers of Greece and Carthage for control of the seas and trade, and Roman forces leveled the city of Carthage. By the first century BCE, Rome had expanded its territory as far as Gaul (modern-day France) through the conquests of Julius Caesar. Subsequently the military invasions of the first Roman emperor, Augustus, expanded the border to the Danube and the Rhine. The emperor Claudius expanded Rome's territory to include Britain in the latter part of the first century CE, and at the start of the second century the emperor Trajan had added Dacia (modern-day Romania). By 203 CE, Rome had established itself as a world power.

---

1 Rives (2007, 1).

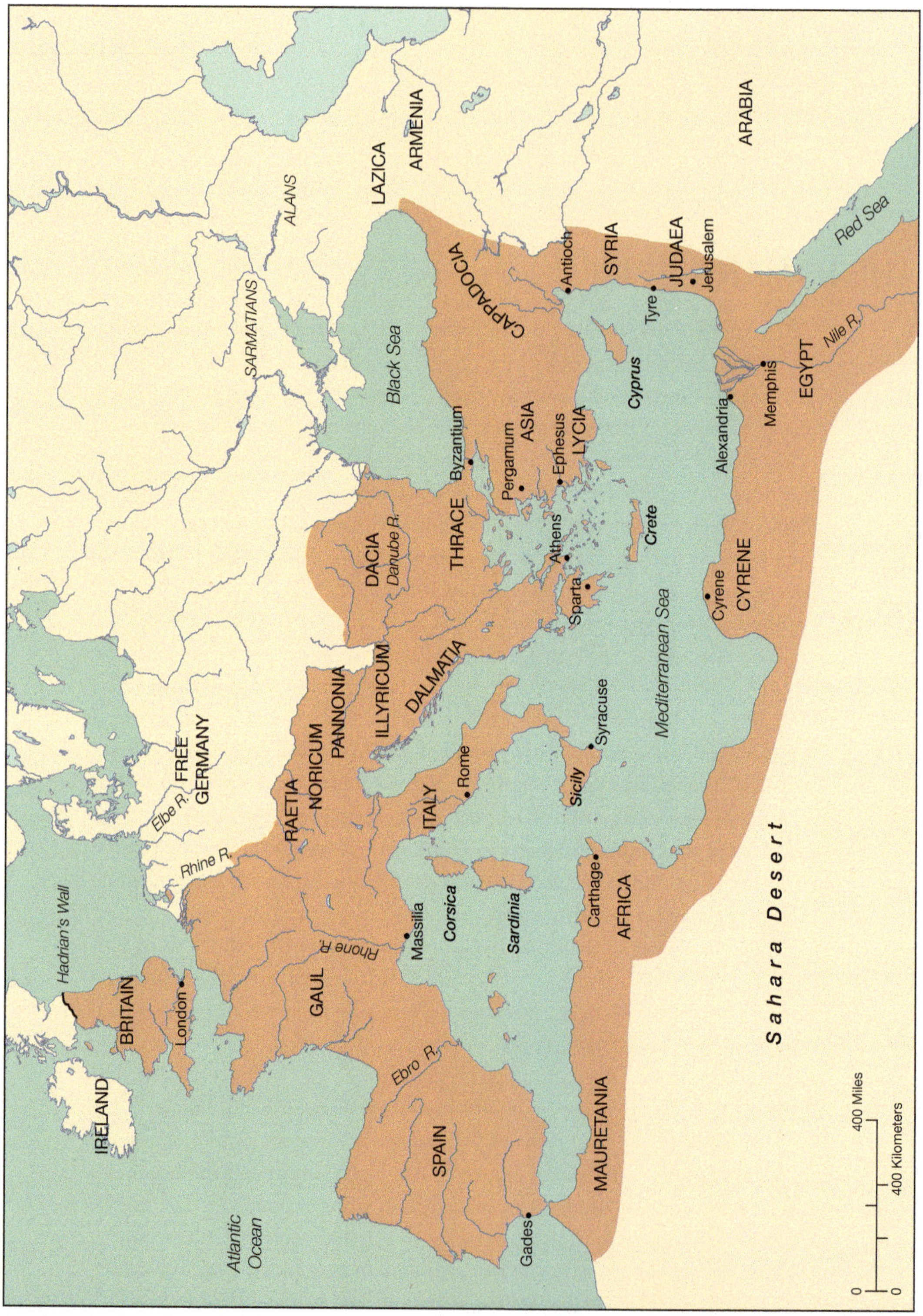

ARABIA
ARMENIA
LAZICA
ALANS
SARMATIANS
Red Sea
Nile R.
EGYPT
Memphis
Alexandria
JUDAEA
Jerusalem
SYRIA
Tyre
Antioch
CAPPADOCIA
Cyprus
Black Sea
Byzantium
ASIA
Pergamum
Ephesus
LYCIA
THRACE
Athens
Crete
Sparta
DACIA
Danube R.
ILLYRICUM
DALMATIA
Cyrene
CYRENE
Mediterranean Sea
Syracuse
Sicily
PANNONIA
NORICUM
RAETIA
FREE GERMANY
Elbe R.
Rhine R.
ITALY
Rome
Carthage
AFRICA
Sahara Desert
Hadrian's Wall
Massilia
Corsica
Sardinia
Rhone R.
GAUL
BRITAIN
London
IRELAND
Ebro R.
SPAIN
MAURETANIA
Gades
Atlantic Ocean
0
400 Miles
0
400 Kilometers

The Roman Empire in the Third Century CE

What did it mean to be living in a part of the Romans' imperial territory during the Roman Empire? Locals in the Roman territories, known as provinces, could have the opportunity to gain citizenship if they were not slaves.[2] Roman officials would set in place policies such as taxation. They placed Roman governors and their retinues in the provinces, along with other appointed officials. They also situated military legions in the provinces as needed, to enforce Roman rule and to protect provinces from outside threats. The Romans set up an infrastructure that included empowering locals to enforce Roman policies. While they permitted locals in provinces to retain many of their customs and traditions, the introduction of Roman city design and engineering meant that following Roman occupation, cities such as Carthage would gain enhancements such as Roman baths and arenas as part of their urban development.

As a governing body, the Roman Empire lasted from 31 BCE, when the first emperor, Augustus, began his rule, until Constantinople fell in 1453 CE to the Ottoman Turks. This commentary will focus on the historical period of the early third century and events that took place in the province of Roman Africa, but the next section, "Roman Africa," will offer more historical background regarding Carthage and Roman occupation since that enhances our understanding of Perpetua's story. The majority of Perpetua's story takes place in the city of Carthage, although we do not know exactly where she lived, or even if her family's home was located in Carthage.

CARTHAGE BEFORE ROME

The city of Carthage is located in modern-day Tunisia across from Sicily and its name means "New City" in Phoenician. It was one of the largest cities in antiquity and contained a diverse population because of its influence over maritime trade. Situated as a coastal metropolis that one would encounter when sailing between Sicily and Tunisia's coast,[3] the natural topography facilitated cultural diversity and enabled Carthage to control the sea in that part of the world (see Map 2).

The indigenous people of the area were called Berbers, named from the Greek word *barbaros*, which means "foreign."[4] In the twelfth century BCE, the Phoenicians, who were seafaring merchants, began to trade with the Berbers. This agricultural trade led to the Phoenicians becoming interested in acquiring other goods from around the Mediterranean; eventually

---

2   See Rives (2007, 1–4) for an overview of Rome's history and the rise of the Roman Empire.

3   Bullard (2001, 188).

4   Bullard (2001, 183–84).

ITALY
Athens
Caesarea
Carthage
Syracuse
MAURETANIA
NUMIDIA
Mediterranean Sea
Sabratha
Leptis Magna
Cyrene
CYRENAICA
TRIPOLITANIA
A f r i c a
0 300 Miles
0 300 Kilometers
N

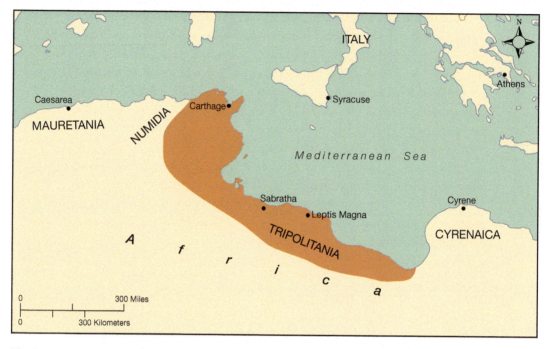

The Roman Province of Proconsular Africa

the Phoenicians would colonize the area, late in the second millennium BCE. When the native Berbers and the Phoenician settlers mixed their languages and cultures together, the resulting language and culture was known as Punic. The Phoenicians came from Tyre (in modern-day Lebanon) to Carthage. For this reason, Tyre is sometimes referred to as Carthage's "parent city."

Primary sources for Carthage's history include the Greek and Roman historians, along with inscriptional evidence from buildings and monuments. Carthage's founding is sometimes recorded as taking place in the ninth century C BCE, before the city of Rome's founding (Justin, *Epitome of Pompeius Trogus* 18.6.9). Greek historians state that the Phoenician Queen Dido (or Queen Elissa, as she is sometimes called) founded Carthage. The traditional story of Carthage's founding, which historians regard as a legend, is as follows: Dido was a Phoenician who fled from Tyre after the death of her husband and ended up settling in Carthage. When Dido arrived at Carthage, she made a deal with the local residents to buy all of the land that the hide of a bull could cover. She then cut up the hide into thin strips, tied the strips together, and gained a large piece of territory upon which she and her people could settle.[5]

5 Desmond (1994, 24–26) offers a summary of the historical sources for Dido. Dido's story is also found in the Roman author Vergil's epic work the *Aeneid*, which Perpetua may have read (see "Roman Education").

Carthage became more powerful due to its wealth and resources, and the historian Herodian tells us that Carthage was second only to Rome as a world power (vii.6.1). As a result, Rome became the city's rival. In addition to its successful maritime commerce, Carthage exported a number of locally made products, including wine, silk, pottery, perfumes, mirrors, and furniture. Agriculture and horse breeding were also profitable enterprises. The city's topography meant that it was well protected from attacks: low hills and an ample supply of fish from the lake of Tunis meant that the residents had a place to retreat and a food supply should the enemy attack. One low hill, known as the Byrsa, contained a citadel that the population could retreat into when in danger. By 300 BCE, Carthage was the unrivaled master of the western Mediterranean seas, with its navy and merchant fleet unparalleled.

Carthage clashed with the Greeks for control over Sicily, and this eventually led to a conflict with Rome over Roman interest in Sicily. The First Punic War was fought between the Romans and the Carthaginians from 264–241 BCE over control of Sicily. The Romans lacked a major naval fleet and realized that they would have no chance of winning a war with Carthage without one, so they built ships. Their military strength lay in their army, so their ships included a device known as a *corvus*, or a gangplank that allowed their soldiers to board the enemy Carthaginian ships. By 241 BCE, the Romans had gained control of the seas off of Sicily and the Carthaginians surrendered Sicily to them.

When Carthage's military leader Hannibal invaded Italy during the Second Punic War (218–201 BCE), the Roman army suffered defeat at first. The Carthaginians had by this time assembled an army of mercenary soldiers, including men from North Africa, Gaul, and Spain. Hannibal's legendary march through the Alps included 40,000 mercenary soldiers and dozens of elephants. In 216 BCE, at the Battle of Cannae in southern Italy, Hannibal secured southern Italy for Carthage. The Roman dominance over Italy was threatened, but the Romans rallied quickly and at the battle of Zama in 202 BCE, under the leadership of Publius Cornelius Scipio Africanus, also known as Scipio Africanus the Elder, they regained control over the territory.

After the battle of Zama, Carthage yielded all territories outside of Africa to Rome and could no longer wage war without Rome's permission. Thus, Carthage became a Roman client-state. The historian Plutarch tells us that Cato gave a rousing speech in 150 BCE to encourage his fellow Romans to resume fighting against the Carthaginians. Cato repeatedly used the phrase "Carthago delenda est," or "Carthage must be destroyed," to emphasize that the Romans ought to emerge from battle as the sole supreme power in the Mediterranean (Plutarch, *Life of Cato the Elder* 27.1).

The Third Punic War occurred when Scipio Aemilianus launched the final attack on Carthage in 149 BCE and took control of the city's forum, after which he was able to invade the rest of the city. When the Romans began burning neighborhoods and attacking the fortress on top of the Byrsa hill, the Carthaginian general Hasdrubal surrendered. In 146 BCE, Roman soldiers under Scipio Aemilianus's leadership burned the city to the ground. The city was abandoned and much of Carthage's population was enslaved.

ROMAN AFRICA

After Rome defeated Carthage in the Third Punic War, the Romans succeeded in establishing a province in Africa in 146 BCE. (see Map 2).[6] By 38 BCE, the capital of the Roman province in Africa was Carthage, which is the city where the events of the *Passio* take place.[7] Despite Roman occupation, Carthage's inhabitants continued to speak Punic, although residents could also be exposed to Latin and Greek, as well as Berber. The province was governed by a proconsul and would remain under Roman control until the fifth century CE, when Germanic invasions allowed the Vandals to establish their own kingdom.

The historian Appian describes how Julius Caesar was instrumental in the success of the Romans' overseas colonization. In particular, Carthage was a city that Julius Caesar repopulated and that Emperor Augustus rebuilt about one hundred years after it was abandoned (Appian, *Punic Wars* 136). The Romans wanted to take advantage of the port location since they exported wheat from Africa and Carthage was one of the supplying cities. Olive oil was added as an export soon afterward. The system of agricultural estates owned by wealthy persons with slaves tending the crops sustained the export system.[8] When Augustus rebuilt the city, the Carthaginians received the Romans' grid system of roads and the residents gained a new city center on the Byrsa hill.

By 35 BCE, Carthage had become the Roman provincial governor's center of operations and the administrative base for the province. Rome passed laws that enabled colonists to emigrate to Carthage, and the city was governed through a combination of Roman oversight and local administration. The Romans still allowed the Carthaginians to worship

---

6   There is some dispute among scholars over using the term "Africa Proconsularis" to describe the province formed in 146 BCE. For a discussion of the modern historical debate on the formation of *Africa Proconsularis*, see D. Fishwick (1993, 53–62).

7   Miles (2003, 133).

8   Salisbury (1997, 35–44).

their traditional gods, although they introduced Roman traditions and religious practices (see "Religion in the Roman Empire"). The colonists could elect magistrates to serve as local officials and hold elections for priests and other religious officials. Political and religious officials held many duties within the city, including holding games in celebration of Roman gods, overseeing the grain supply, and maintaining public works, such as the upkeep of roads.[9] As the colony continued to grow and develop in the first and second centuries CE, it became a center of trade. Roman merchants purchased commodities such as building materials, wheat, wool, and ivory from the North African frontier for use in Rome and Carthage, and wealthy Romans settled in the estates formerly owned by Berber ruling families.[10]

Carthage in the early third century CE contained a diverse population that would have included Judeans, Christians, Greeks, Romans, Africans (Libyans), and Phoenicians. It was a successful and prosperous Roman colony, and in Perpetua's time the buildings in the city would have included an amphitheater, the lavish Antonine baths, aqueducts, a forum, and a theater. These hallmarks of Roman architecture were on display to show residents and visitors that the symbols of Roman power could be seen everywhere, and were endowed with decorative stone, mosaic floors, and statues. The Romans not only quarried the local stone from north of Thuburbo Maius but also imported Carrara marble from Italy and building materials from Greece and Asia Minor.

Agricultural estate owners often lived in town and left the running of country estates to an overseer. Many of the homes would have had sea views. The preferred style of the residents' houses consisted of a court-yard, which could contain a fountain, surrounded by rooms with elaborate mosaic floors. Mosaics that depicted gardens and mythological scenes, along with the popular hunting scene motif, could have been crafted at the mosaic workshop that began in the city in the second century CE.[11] At the center of urban activity was the Byrsa hill, on which the Romans constructed a forum, with plazas, colonnaded walkways, a library, a judicial basilica, and temples. The Romans had flattened out the Byrsa hill to construct the forum on top of the Punic ruins, and redistributed the earth removed from the top to the sides of the hill to create a wider base upon which to begin their construction. In Perpetua's time, the forum would have been the intellectual center of the city, with its densely packed

---

9   Rives (1995, 28–34).

10   Bullard (2001, 196–97).

11   The Bardo Museum in Tunis contains mosaics from the houses of Roman Africa.

residential area leading up to the top of the hill. In the *Passio*, when the large crowd gathers to see Perpetua's trial as she is brought before the procurator Hilarianus in the forum (6.1), it is possible that the majority of the crowd came from this part of the city.

The date that Christianity was first introduced in Roman Africa is uncertain, although an account of martyrdom in 180 CE meant that evidence of Christianity in the area existed before Perpetua's martyrdom (see "Roman Religion and Early Christianity").[12] The fact that there were many ports in Africa and a diverse, thriving trade and commerce that involved many populations means that exactly where knowledge of the early Christian teachings came from is also unknown. Early Christian documents were written in both Greek and Latin, and thus we cannot say with certainty that Christian texts came from Rome first. But Romanization contributed to the spread of the early church. The main archaeological evidence for the spread of Christianity can be dated to after the third century CE, and once Christianity was established, inscriptions, churches, martyrs' tombs, and mosaics tell the story of its expansion throughout Roman Africa.

THE EMPEROR SEPTIMIUS SEVERUS

Lucius Septimius Severus (11 April 145–4 February 211 CE) was the Roman Empire's first African-born emperor. He ruled as emperor from 193 to 211 CE. His succession to the title of emperor was not accomplished without difficulty. The year in which he became emperor was known as the Year of the Five Emperors. Severus had to conquer his rivals before securing a spot as emperor (Dio Cassius, *Roman History* LXXIV). After the death of the emperor Pertinax, Septimius Severus was declared emperor by his military troops while in the provinces, in Carnuntum (in modern-day Austria). When he returned to Rome, however, he found Didius Julianus had bought the emperorship via auction. After Julianus was killed, Septimius Severus had to fight Pescennius Niger, who had claimed the throne, and then had to defeat one more rival following Niger's death, Clodius Albinus. Severus claimed the emperor Marcus Aurelius as his adoptive father in 195 CE, so that he could justify his rule.[13] At the battle of Lugdunum (in modern-day Lyon), Clodius Albinus was killed, thus securing Severus's position as the fifth emperor in that year.

---

12   See Binder (2010, 188–89). See also Rives (1995, 223–25) and Rankin (1995, 10–11).

13   Cooley (2007, 385–86) discusses how Severus establishes continuity between his reign and those of earlier emperors.

The accounts of the historians contain varying details about his life, but a brief biographical sketch will add to the context for events in the *Passio*.[14] He was born to Publius Septimius Geta and Fulvia Pia in Leptis Magna (sometimes spelled Lepcis Magna) in Tripolitania (in present-day Libya) and was of Italian and Punic descent. As a young man growing up in an African province, he would have had instruction in Latin and Greek, and he would have spoken Punic as well (*Sev.* 1.1). His family was wealthy and of the equestrian rank. He was approximately eighteen years old when he first went to Rome, and he entered public service around 162 CE. With the help of Emperor Marcus Aurelius, who gave him senatorial rank, he entered the *cursus honorum*, which was a sequence of offices that allowed Roman men to advance their careers in politics. After a brief first marriage to Paccia Marciana, he married a Syrian named Julia Domna. She gave him two sons, Lucius Septimius Bassianus (known as Caracalla) and Publius Septimius Geta.

Severus claimed to be an heir to the Antonine family, declaring himself the emperor Nerva's great-great-great-grandson through his constructed family lineage.[15] By establishing a sense of continuity between himself and prior emperors, Severus attempted to reinforce the idea that during his reign, the Roman Empire would remain in an enduring period of stability. Yet Severus's own reign did not last.

Severus died in 211 at Eboracum (modern-day York) after falling ill while on a military campaign in Britain. He was sixty-six years old. When he was succeeded by his son Caracalla, the Severan Dynasty began. Caracalla, who had ruled with his father jointly until his death, then ruled jointly with his brother Geta afterward. Severus's last words to his sons, as quoted in Anthony Birley's biography *Septimius Severus: The African Emperor*, were, "Do not disagree between yourselves, give money to the soldiers and despise everyone else."[16]

Visitors to the Roman Forum can still see the Arch of Septimius Severus standing in the northwest corner near the Temple of Saturn. The monument was erected to commemorate the Severan victories in Parthia (modern-day Iran) in 203 CE, the same year that the *Passio* describes Perpetua's death on Geta's birthday. Geta's image and inscriptions on his behalf were originally on the arch, but after his assassination in 211, all indications of Geta's part in the Parthian conquests were removed. By 217 Geta's brother, Caracalla, had also been assassinated.

---

14   The main historical sources for the life of Septimius Severus include Dio Cassius, Herodian, and the *Historia Augusta*, which contains the *Life of Septimius Severus*.

15   Cooley (2007, 386). Marcus Aurelius was related to Nerva through adoption.

16   Birley (1999, 187); quotes Dio Cassius 76.15.2.

Figure 2.1 Clockwise from top left: Portrait of Julia Domna, Septimius Severus, Caracalla, and Geta (later erased) from Egypt, c. 200 CE.

TERTULLIAN

Tertullian was a Christian author who lived in Carthage during the third century CE. He is sometimes referred to, by historians writing after his death, as a founding theologian or founding church father because he was a prolific writer at the time early Christian theology was emerging.[17] His writings examine the development of the Christian church in the West, which is sometimes referred to as Latin Christianity. Questions of faith, salvation, and identity as a Christian are all topics that he covers in his extant works (written in Latin, although he also wrote in Greek).

We do not know much about his life, but from his work we know that he was raised in Carthage in a wealthy family and married. His texts also

---

17   See, for example, Daniel-Hughes (2011, 1), who refers to Tertullian as the "'first theologian of the west'" based on the title of Osborn's 1997 study and also refers to him as a "church father."

indicate that he was well educated, most likely in rhetoric as well as law. A Christian convert, he was not afraid to critique the lives of his fellow Christians. In his *Apology* he stated "Christians are made, not born" (xviii). He criticized Christians who avoided being punished by Roman officials through bribes and did not like the unwillingness of some Christians to be martyred. He censured a church more interested in politics than religion. But he also defended Christians when he dispelled rumors of infant sacrifice. His later writings show the influence of the Montanist movement (see "Montanism"), but there is no reason to think that he was excluded from the larger Christian community in Carthage due to his Montanist beliefs.[18] Tertullian died around 220 CE.

Tertullian mentions the martyrdom of Perpetua and Felicity (*De Anima* 55.4) and approves of women's prophecy (*De Anima* 9.4), yet he denies women the right to teach, or to baptize or perform any other functions that a priest could (*De Virginibus Velandis* 9.1). While some scholars have even suggested he might be the anonymous editor-narrator who introduces the text and provides a conclusion to it, there is no existing proof for this. Although Tertullian writes about a Christian community and advises Christians on matters such as dress and conduct in his writings, his work should not be taken as evidence that there existed in Perpetua's day a "stable" or "consistent" group of Christians that thought of themselves as existing in "a separate Christian world," set apart from non-Christians.[19] Or that, for example, all Christian women gave up adornment based on the advice he offered in his sermons.

Tertullian's writings are just one of the sources that offer us a way to determine what life was like in Carthage in the third century. We have already talked about the fact that there is no definite way to know how Christianity came to Roman Africa, nor is there much written about Carthage extant from the time period (see "Roman Africa"). But Tertullian contributes to the development of the church, and his doctrine on women allows a modern audience to understand the ways in which women's roles were recognized, defined, and even limited by the early Christian church.

ROMAN RELIGION AND EARLY CHRISTIANITY

Religious practices in antiquity were as diverse and complex as they are in modern times. The sheer variety of deities and traditions that existed in antiquity means that writing "a history of Roman religion" or even

---

18   See Rankin (1995, 27–40).

19   See Rebillard (2012, 33): "Christianness was only one of the many affiliations that mattered in everyday life."

"religion in the Roman Empire during the early third century" would be a task outside the scope of this work. Discussing Roman religious practices is not a simple undertaking: ancient Roman authors and modern scholars alike recognize that the discourse needs to acknowledge that the concepts of what is appropriate or inappropriate conduct in terms of the worship of the gods shifts over time, and the key to understanding begins with recognition of this fluidity.[20] It would also be incorrect to assume that when the imperial Roman community's religious practices were introduced into the provinces, an imperial Roman religious identity was forged that unified all who were under the rule of the Roman Empire. But we can start by talking about what modern assumptions we might have about religion and how they differ from the ways in which the ancients thought about religious phenomena: comprehending their festivals, the games, the sacrifices they made to deities, and other traditional behaviors can help us understand more about life in Perpetua's time.

When we talk about religion, what exactly are we talking about? One modern way to define religion, as James Rives has noted, would be to distinguish a set of beliefs in or interactions with the divine that is set apart from other aspects of daily life.[21] But the Romans did not separate religion from other aspects of their daily lives. For example, public officials performed religious duties along with their other responsibilities. By the time of the empire, the emperor functioned as both the leading religious figure in society and the political leader.

The community viewed the relationship with the gods as one in which an individual who was sanctioned to act on behalf of the community performed the appropriate rituals, and therefore this individual could guarantee the safety and well-being of the people. Thus, the concept of *religion* as is often used today to include a separation of church and state did not exist at this time; instead, the Romans used the term *religio* for their recognition of the cult of the gods as part of their social structure. *Religio* became a term used to define the acceptable way to worship and show honor to the gods. Participation in "public, communal behaviour towards the gods of the state" meant proper devotion to *religio*. Those who failed to do this might be categorized as *superstitio*, or engaging in a form of false worship, which could be anything from "not following the customs of the state" to "excessive devotion towards ritual and the gods" to practicing magic, which is something that the tribune suspects of Perpetua and her

---

20   Beard, North, and Price (1998, 211–18).

21   Rives (2000, 246). See also Rives (2007, 4), where he suggests applying the following definition of religion to imperial Rome's culture: "a desire to please or live in harmony with some superhuman force."

companions in the *Passio* (16.2).[22] *Superstitio* can be broadly defined. But one way to think about it would be to say that anything the Roman officials found to be threatening to the stability and well-being of the state could be categorized as *superstitio*.

The word *religio* was often used by Roman authors when talking about religious traditions.[23] To defy Roman *religio* and to worship as a Christian meant rejecting the *mos maiorum*, or ancestral customs of the Romans, in favor of Christian rites. Because of the relationship in Rome between religion and the state, to defy Roman *religio* also meant rejecting the power of the Roman emperor and the empire itself. Thus, parents took care to teach their children the proper way to venerate the gods, and this instruction took place at home and in public at ceremonial events, not at school (see also "Roman Education"). That is why Perpetua's father appeared so distressed at his daughter's behavior. To him, his daughter's conduct was a reflection of how he had raised her, and in the eyes of the community, to reject his instruction meant that she had brought shame on her family. In Perpetua's day, Christianity was regarded as a form of *superstitio* by those who displayed *religio*.

The relationship between humans and gods in ancient Rome was essential for the well-being of the Roman state. To the community's way of thinking, humans acted in tandem with the gods to benefit Rome. When the community in Rome called upon various gods to protect them in battle against the city, they were invoking that relationship. Roman political leaders also claimed familial ties to divine beings. Julius Caesar and Augustus Caesar, for example, declared themselves to be descendants of the Roman goddess Venus. Julius Caesar was called *Divus Iulius* or "divine Julius" after his death, and most of the Roman emperors were made into deities following their deaths, until the practice became for them to be declared divine while still living (see "Emperor Worship"). Thus, the boundaries or divisions between humans and the gods were not always distinct.

THE ROMAN SENATE

Roman politics and religion were always closely tied. Religious officials took orders from the Roman Senate, but they also advised the Senate on the sacred laws.

---

22   Beard, North, and Price (1998, 216–17).

23   In particular, the Roman author Cicero often used the term *religio* when discussing religious traditions. See, for example, Cicero's *De Natura Deorum* 2.28.72.

The Senate was in charge of the more public aspects of Roman religion, which had less to do with individual beliefs and more to do with communal rituals. During the Roman Republic, the Senate controlled the *sacra publica*, which meant that the Senate could define what kinds of gods could become officially accepted within Roman religion. The *sacra publica* were the public cults of the city, and the local officials in provinces who were put in charge of religion recognized that involvement in cults like these offered a structured way for individuals to participate in civic and religious life.

The Senate was able to add religious practices and new cults as they saw fit, and they could restrict practices they did not think contributed to what Rives calls the "civic model" for religion, where civic authorities attempted to control what was acceptable behavior for individuals when they practiced religious rites.[24] Once a god became part of the *sacra publica*, the Senate was responsible for ensuring the establishment of yearly games in honor of the god or goddess, as well as a date for a sacrifice and the construction of a temple. When the Sibylline books predicted that if the foreign goddess Cybele were brought to Rome, Rome would be victorious over foreign enemies, the community in Rome made arrangements to bring the goddess to the city (Livy, *AUC* 29.10–11, 14). Not all foreign gods were officially accepted into Roman religion. Rather than enforce an outright prohibition on a cult or punish its leaders, sometimes the Senate simply did not encourage a foreign cult.

We know that local cults flourished even after the Romans expanded their territory and that Carthage, for example, had its own *sacra publica*. The city would have had a mixture of Greek, Punic, and Libyan religious traditions before they were introduced to Roman religion. But the Carthaginians would have been allowed to keep those traditions as well as adopt Roman ones. The Romans had a policy of allowing colonies outside Rome to keep their gods as well as introducing the Roman ones to the colonies.

The Roman officials who were in charge of governing the provinces employed social and political controls, such as establishing religious festivals. The festivals helped to foster the concept that the religious traditions citizens in the provinces observed were for the benefit of the Roman Empire. In other words, they helped to maintain the established way of doing things and, by extension, honored the *mos maiorum*.

---

24   Rives (1995, 170–71) argues that the civic model did not give unity to religion throughout the empire, but could inspire a province's identification with Rome. He also points out that transformative and ongoing changes were taking place at the local level in Carthage during the empire, as officials there were put in charge of the *sacra publica*.

RELIGION IN THE ROMAN EMPIRE

So, how did individuals living in the time of the Roman Empire show that they venerated their gods? They did it in ways that were both very public and highly private. Private cults were celebrated by persons, families, and the *gentes* (groups of individuals who shared a claim to a common ancestor). Public cults, on the other hand, could be celebrated by all members of the community of imperial Rome, and celebrations were held at public expense. Here is one example of the difference between public and private veneration of the gods in Rome. Anyone could make a sacrifice to, or pray to, a deity. While a slave might request asylum in a temple of Diana, there was a more public aspect of the goddess Diana that was worshipped as well. The Roman poet Horace composed his *Carmen Saeculare* poem at the request of the emperor Augustus in 17 BCE. The poem was sung at the *Ludi Saeculares*, public games which lasted three days and celebrated Apollo and Diana. It is likely residents would have been encouraged to attend the festival, which included sacrifices and theatrical performances, in the gods' honor.

Jason Davies notes that when the Romans employed these kinds of sacrificial rites to the gods, "they were not just deliberately constructing their identity, they were also negotiating with the future course of events."[25] This meant, for example, public officials would be appointed who would make the appropriate sacrifices to these three gods to ensure the safety of the community and its security in the future. People would gather to watch the spectacle of the rites being performed and to enjoy the entertainment that followed. Some may also have enjoyed the sense of participating in a practice associated with being part of the community of imperial Rome.

So far we have been discussing the importance of ritual to the community and ways of worshipping the gods. But individual persons were free to attend the public rituals or not, as long as they did not attempt to conduct any business on religious festival days. In fact, they would not have thought of worship of their emperor or the public cults as the only form of accepted "religion." Indeed, since the Roman Empire was so widespread, the community was constantly being exposed to new ideas and new traditions. In addition, in the provinces, it was not uncommon to worship gods unique to a particular geographic location, or local versions of Roman gods. So the Romans were not necessarily transferring their gods to the provinces as much as the idea of their gods, which became associated with local gods, such as the Punic goddess Tanit in Carthage, who later

---

25 Davies (2004, 10).

became identified with Juno Lucina, the Roman goddess of childbirth. The community of imperial Romans also added new gods to their traditional lineup. The Egyptian goddess Isis is just one example of a god who was adopted by the community and was worshipped within the city of Rome. Although at first Isis was worshipped within the city limits, it became commonplace by the second century CE to find temples throughout the empire.

EMPEROR WORSHIP

The Roman emperor occupied the central religious position within the empire.[26] For example, the emperor Augustus and members of his family were given divine honors after their deaths; but even before his death, games were celebrated on his behalf, hymns were sung in his honor, and his image was placed in household shrines. Augustus's *numen,* or divine power, was awarded public honors during his lifetime, and the line between man and god was becoming increasingly blurred at this time.[27] Eventually emperors were worshipped as gods while alive, along with the continued practice of worshipping dead emperors as well: "the ritual of sacrifice to both the dead and the living emperors was, in practice, the recognition of a social contract between the ruler and the ruled."[28] Information was mobile about the imperial cult and various religious ceremonies and was easily disseminated to the provinces. By the third century CE, the cult of the emperor would have been given special prominence in Roman Africa, since Septimius Severus and his family maintained strong ties to the region. Making a sacrifice on behalf of Severus and his family's wellbeing and good health would be one way to show loyalty to the Roman Empire and the imperial cult. While the imperial cult helped to maintain the Carthaginian populace's ties to the Roman Empire, disparate religious traditions remained in existence.

THE CULTS OF CERES AND SATURN

Perpetua was asked to dress up as a priestess of Ceres before she entered the arena, but she refused to do so (18.4). Ceres (Greek Demeter) was the Roman goddess associated with grain, and the harvest festival of Cerealia was celebrated in honor of the agricultural goddess. In the fourth century

---

26   Beard, North, and Price (1998, 206).

27   Beard, North, and Price (1998, 208–10).

28   Heffernan (2012, 195).

BCE, the cult of Ceres was imported to Carthage from Syracuse.[29] The *Ludi Cereales*, or public games held in honor of Ceres, would have included rites performed on behalf of the goddess. The male catechumens and Saturus were asked to dress up as priests of Saturn (Saturn can be associated with the pre-Roman Punic god Ba'al).[30] Saturn's cult was very significant within Roman Africa because of the god's association with farming and agriculture in general. When Saturn was imported to Carthage, local traditions were incorporated into his worship. Both Ceres and Saturn were popular gods in Roman Africa, and the cults combined both elements of local and Roman traditions. Ceres, for example, became associated with African grain production.[31] Both cults were part of the *sacra publica* in many cities and offered their followers a way to be a part of both a local and a Roman collective religious identity.

The officials wished to dress up Perpetua and her female companions as priestesses to highlight the fact that they did not participate in one of the state-sanctioned religious activities for women within the culture of imperial Rome.[32] Perpetua objected to the pagan costume, in her own words, because she had been tried and found guilty of having a Christian identity, so she rejected the attire for herself and her fellow prisoners. But it is more than that, given that the priests of Ceres held official Roman offices: she also demonstrated her rejection of the emperor, and by extension the Roman government's authority and ability to regulate her beliefs.

CHRISTIANS IN IMPERIAL ROME

Just as the Romans had religious traditions that were complex and diverse, so did the Christians. The earliest Christians, for example, were members of the Jewish community, and many historians refer to them as Jewish Christians. It is likely that Christianity expanded throughout Roman Africa in part due to the complicated relationship between these two groups at this time. On the one hand, the two groups were attempting to separate themselves by distinguishing between their beliefs. On the other hand, contact remained between the two groups and that is how some conversions occurred. By the end of the first century CE, Christianity was recognized as separate from Judaism.

---

29   Spaeth (1996, 17).

30   Rives (1995, 154–55).

31   Rives (1995, 47).

32   Heffernan (2012, 33).

It is also helpful to think in terms of elasticity when considering Christians and pagans in antiquity. To classify and separate individuals into rigid categories such as *Christian* and *pagan* from the start of the development of Christian communities denies us the opportunity to understand how and why Christianity developed and spread in antiquity until it became the official religion of the empire.[33] At the outset it is important to note that there is no homogeneous "Christian" opinion on what to make of various practices that we might label as "pagan" events, such as watching gladiatorial games or making animal sacrifices. Instead, what we find is a society shifting more toward a decline in certain beliefs and practices, but not eliminating them entirely. In addition to concerns about false idols and being corrupted by theater and gladiatorial performances, many Christians objected to the traditional practice of blood sacrifice. Some Christians mistakenly thought of pagans as focusing their religious practices on animal killings on behalf of their gods, whereas Christians prayed to God. Evidence suggests, however, that these rituals were not as important as the Christians made them out to be. Also, distinguishing between the eating of cooked animals at a banquet feast and animal sacrifices in which the animals were cooked and consumed became more and more complex as religious traditions changed and evolved.[34] Some Christians attended Christian rituals and participated in them without eliminating the possibility of joining in other non-Christian activities. Curse tablets, for example, were used by people of all faiths.

There is no evidence that there was one cohesive community of Christians who met to worship together in Carthage at the time of the events described in the *Passio*. The *Passio* describes a group of catechumens that included a leader, Saturus, and it tells of Perpetua and the other members of this group. It also mentions Perpetua's Christian brother and other family members, some of whom were likely Christian, as well as the Christian deacons who visit her in prison and the catechumen Rusticus who appears in the arena before her death. But there must have been other Christian groups that met in house churches in Carthage and the surrounding cities as well; they simply are not the subject of the *Passio* and therefore are not mentioned.

Members of the community in Carthage who identified as Christian gathered to worship in house churches. At the time, the Christian population, although gaining in popularity, was small, but that does not mean the

---

33 See the Preface for definitions of *Christianity*, *Christian*, and *pagan* and how they are used in this text.

34 Maxwell (2012, 854–56).

religion escaped the attention of the authorities.[35] As Christianity spread throughout Africa in the centuries following Perpetua's death, the bishop at Carthage was ranked first among the bishops in the territory and Carthage became the place where the plenary councils met and where bishops sent their delegates.

How could an individual living in Roman Carthage at this time know if someone was a Christian or not? Being a Christian was just one part of an individual's identity. In Perpetua's diary, for example, we see many distinct facets of her identity: she is a Christian, a mother, a daughter, a sibling, a friend, and possibly a slave owner. Although much of this work discusses how Perpetua rejected certain key beliefs of ancient Roman society— worship of the emperor, for example—that does not mean that she would not have thought of herself as a Roman woman. She could be both a Christian and a Roman, and she would have grown up in a world where an education in Greek and Roman authors and training in Roman values were a part of the culture. Certainly there is evidence from Perpetua's diary that the education she would have received before her conversion to Christianity, and the values that her father speaks with her about, including *pietas*, were a Roman part of her life before her conversion (see "Roman Education").

Individuals could not be identified as Christian solely through their outward appearance. There was no particular required clothing, for example, that could indicate to an observer that they were looking at a Christian, nor could Christians be detected by other outward indicators, such as "Christian" versus "non-Christian" names. But Christians did have communal practices, such as visiting the poor or martyrs who were in prison, and this could have helped observers identify people in their community who considered themselves Christians. Christians also met together to worship. In the house-churches of the wealthier residents, persons from all strata of society could come together.

Tertullian writes about the gatherings of early Christians and indicates that Christians could daily attend an early-morning meeting. An evening meal, the "love feast" or *agape*, occurred weekly (*Apology* 39). Christians greeted one another with a kiss when they met (this kiss of greeting occurs in several dreams in Perpetua's diary). Tertullian mentions that they made the symbol for a cross on their foreheads both in public and in private when going about their daily routines, so that is another possible way for individuals to identify their fellow community members as Christians (*de Corona* 3). Christians also distinguished themselves from other faiths by being baptized (see "Baptism").

---

35 Salisbury (1997, 59–61).

We do not know if Perpetua or Felicity attended daily meetings, but they and their fellow prisoners experienced the *agape* one last time before their death (17.1). Perpetua also mentions that two deacons who visited her in prison helped her and her fellow prisoners improve their conditions (3.7). These deacons may have brought Perpetua and the others food and other items for daily living. Although Perpetua's diary never specifies the exact offense that led to her being sentenced to death, it is interesting to note that when early Christians were arrested, taking on the title of Christian was sufficient to be considered a crime. They did not have to commit a particular act such as murder or stealing. Allowing themselves to be called "Christian" was enough, and by declaring their Christian faith, Perpetua and her fellow catechumens were setting themselves apart from others within the community of imperial Rome by rejecting the established religious practices.

The Christian population in Carthage at the time of Perpetua's martyrdom may have been around 2,000 persons, or four percent of the total population of about 500,000 persons.[36] Perpetua's diary gives modern readers evidence of the way in which people became Christian in Severus's time—through conversion. Since abortion and infanticide were forbidden for Christians, this increased their population, and because Christians raised their children to be Christian, the generations that followed adopted their family's religious traditions.

MAGIC AND RELIGION

The prison guard in the *Passio* grew suspicious of Perpetua and her fellow Christians because he thought they might be able to use magic to escape from the prison (16.2). This was a common belief among the Christians' opponents, that Christians participated in magical activities. But Christians accused their opponents of practicing magic as well.[37] Dio Cassius offers a historian's perspective on magic during the Severan period, warning that any divination not state-sanctioned was bound to be lies and might incur rebellion (Dio Cassius 52.36.1–2).[38] Roman officials were concerned about magic's potential interference with political affairs: both Dio Cassius (77.8.1) and the *Historia Augusta* (*Sev.* 15.5) report that Severus executed persons who attempted to predict the date of his death. Yet the *Historia*

---

36   Salisbury (1997, 61).

37   Ogden (2007, 460–61). See also Wypustek (1997, 284).

38   Ogden (2007) 458, suggests that the speech created for Augustus's advisor Agrippa reflects Severan attitudes towards magic (Dio Cassius 52.36.1–2).

Augusta also claims that Septimius Severus himself consulted astrologers, even going so far as to prevail upon one to tell him when his predecessor would die (*Sev.* 4.3).[39]

An individual's knowledge of magic was not enough for prosecution, however, since it was the display of powers or practice that was punishable. For example, Apuleius, a Latin prose writer from Numidia, was accused of using magic, as well as other crimes, to attract the attention of a wealthy widow.[40] He was prosecuted in a court near Tripoli and wrote a witty defense called *A Discourse on Magic* (known as the *Apologia*).

Magic was used in antiquity to inflict curses and to influence future events. Spells existed for everything from being freed from bonds or chains to giving birth at a particular time to causing someone's death. The exercise of prayers and rituals associated with the early church could appear to be similar to magical practices such as spells and curses. As a result, it was sometimes assumed that the Christians were practicing magic or had evil intent when they practiced their religion. Christians in the act of silent prayer, long prayers, or group prayer could also look suspicious to onlookers, who might assume that these were specific conditions required to perform magic.

In antiquity, it was often thought that predicting the future required a magical ability, so a Christian who claimed to receive visions that foretold the future appeared to be invoking magic prophecies to do so. When martyrs were being tortured and executed, and bore the pain bravely, observers could conclude that a seemingly high tolerance for pain was beyond the realm of human ability. If animals failed to perform as expected in the arena, it could be explained by the Christians' "magic" as well.

Christians also appeared suspect to their opponents when they prayed to a cult of martyrs, as some persons believed that the dead held special magic powers and could intervene in the affairs of the living. Christian ceremonies like exorcisms or healing ceremonies were also associated with magic. Thus, any objects employed in the ceremonies held the potential to possess magical powers as well. Rings, for example, were often used as magical tools in ancient rituals.[41] So, when some of the martyrs in the *Passio* were able to receive visions and died bravely and without seeming to experience great trauma or extreme pain, when the group prayed for Felicity to give birth before they went to the arena so she could join them and then she did give birth, and when Saturus gave the gift of a ring dipped in his blood to Rusticus, all of these events could be interpreted as evidence of the Christian catechumens practicing magic.

---

39   Ogden (2007, 459).

40   Wypustek (1997, 276).

41   Wypustek (1997, 281–83).

MONTANISM

As the early church evolved, disagreements about orthodoxy led to different religious movements developing as Christianity spread throughout the Roman Empire. One example includes Montanism, or "New Prophecy," as it was called. Montanism developed in the early second century and was founded in the second century CE by a man named Montanus who claimed the Holy Spirit prophesied through him.[42] Montanism placed a high value on martyrdom. Montanus and his two female prophets, Maximilla and Priscilla, presented something different from prior Christian religious movements: women in Montanism were given a far greater role in the church than the non-Montanist church fathers allowed. Montanism allowed women to assume leadership roles within the movement, including achieving ministerial status. Both women and men could be ordained prebyters and bishops and communicate messages from the Holy Spirit. Public declarations of Christian faith were encouraged as well.

While we cannot know for certain whether or not Perpetua was a Montanist, the religious movement was popular in Carthage at the time.[43] The beginning paragraphs of the diary, by the anonymous editor-narrator, allude to the Spirit continuing to speak and praise the martyrdom of the two women. This may suggest that the diary's first paragraphs could have been written from the viewpoint of a Montanist. The bishops in Saturus's vision assign significant power to the martyrs to settle disputes, which also would be compatible with Montanist beliefs that martyrs had authority above the hierarchy of the church. There is also evidence that Perpetua's training as a catechumen and her knowledge of Christian theology could have influenced the visions and other aspects of the *Passio* in a way that might be similar to a Montanist influence (see "The Visions of Perpetua and Saturus" and "Roman Education"). Thus, it would be impossible to dissect the *Passio* into sections consisting of the "Montanist" and the "not-Montanist" parts. In Carthage, it was still possible at this time to consider oneself a Montanist and to attend a house-church with other Christians who did not follow Montanist teachings. The lines between the various Christian communities were still fairly fluid.[44] Around 207 CE Tertullian began following the Montanist movement, and his later writings reflected this (see "Tertullian").

---

42   Salisbury (1997, 156).

43   Salisbury (1997, 158) suggests the *Passio*'s content may been an influence on the Montanist movement and even have served to "shape the rituals" for the Montanists. Heffernan (2012, 171) also finds a "proto-Montanist" element in the *Passio* when Perpetua's brother asks her for a prophecy, as she could be regarded as a "prophetess" in this scene.

44   LeMoine (1999, 202) suggests that the editor was a Montanist. Markschies (2012, 277–90) argues that there is little evidence for Montanism in the *Passio*.

CHRISTIAN PERSECUTION

Thus far, we have discussed beliefs, rituals, and activities in which Christians were known to participate. But would Christian faith have been made obvious by a lack of partaking in Roman religious observances? The community members living in Roman Carthage would have had many opportunities to be a part of religious observances sanctioned by the Roman state, including games in which sacrifices to the emperor would have likely been performed at the start. The celebratory games, or *ludi*, included races, the theater, and even the very gladiatorial shows in which Perpetua herself ended up as a participant. But there is no evidence that Roman officials in the time of the empire kept an exact record of who attended or that they punished anyone for a lack of attendance at these events. And there is no Christian scripture that explicitly forbade the followers of Christ from attending these events, although Tertullian cautioned against attending. One could be considered a Christian and choose to attend the *ludi* or not. Some, like Perpetua, would have refused to participate in what they considered to be rituals that were incompatible with Christian beliefs. Others may have attended the *ludi*, made sacrifices to the emperor, and even become involved in activities at Roman temples. So there is also evidence that some Christians participated in high-profile pagan activities that would have helped to conceal from the rest of the community the fact that they were Christian.

Roman religion placed a particular emphasis on action, not on belief. Individuals could believe what they wanted as long as their actions did not obstruct the performance of prescribed ritual. So, when it came to observing the proper rituals such as emperor worship, civic officials would be looking to see whether or not individual persons upheld the correct observance of rituals, rather than enforcing a communal or correct set of beliefs about the gods that united individuals across the empire.[45] The main reason Christianity posed such a threat to Rome was that the religion challenged Roman authority.

The Roman historian Tacitus gives us some insight into imperial Roman views on the Christians when he describes them as *invisos* or "detested" because their conduct is *atrocia*, or "horrible," and *pudenda*, or "shameful." He then relates a macabre scene in which the Roman emperor Nero, who blamed the Christians for the fire that burned Rome in 64 CE, orders a group of Christians to be punished: they are torn apart by dogs, crucified, or covered with pitch and used as torches while their bodies burned for a garden party that he hosted. In this instance, though, Tacitus tells us

---

45   Rives (2007, 49).

that the Christians were pitied by the community in Rome, since they felt that the Christians were not being executed as a matter of safety for the city, but due to the Emperor Nero's cruel streak (*Annales* 15.44).

We do not know exactly how it became known to the Roman authorities that Perpetua and her fellow martyrs were members of the Christian community. At this time, Christianity would have been regarded by the state as superstition, and some perceived it as a cult that was a troublesome rival to the state's authority.[46] During Perpetua's lifetime, the persecution of Christians was generally handled by local authorities. In the *Passio* we see a group of Christians, including Perpetua, arrested and tried by the local official Hilarianus. Hilarianus's decision to persecute Perpetua may have been reflective of his personal belief that Christianity was becoming a major problem for him as a local official in terms of maintaining his authority. It was not likely to have been out of a desire to please any officials who had authority over him and were opponents of the Christians.[47] Jewish persons did not experience the same kind of persecution because the Romans had respect for their ancient traditions and because they were not trying to convert the community the way the Christians were.[48] Official imperial legislation against Christians did not exist during this time, and some local governors decided not to persecute Christians under their authority.

The description of Perpetua's death in her diary suggests that she may have wished to die in the arena as a way of demonstrating her Christian faith. As a Roman citizen in Carthage, she did not have to die in such a public and brutal manner, and there are numerous times in the *Passio* when others, including her father and Hilarianus, attempted to convince her that she did not have to be martyred.[49] She chose instead to die with her companions. Her behavior—including her concern about putting her hair up so that she would not appear to be in mourning, and her bravery—may have been her way of transforming the pagan spectacle of a gladiatorial combat into a demonstration of her Christian faith. The crowd's response of shock when Felicity and Perpetua were first led out into the arena wearing only nets suggests that this was not the traditional ritual they were used to seeing.

---

46   Wypustek (1997, 277) notes that Cicero's *De divinatione* (I.132) connects superstition to insanity.

47   See Rives (1996, 2–18) for the evidence regarding Hilarianus and his beliefs.

48   See Orlin (2010, 182–85) for the expulsion of members of the Jewish community from the city of Rome.

49   See Heffernan (2012, 204).

SEVERUS AND CHRISTIAN PERSECUTIONS

Severus was generally not seen by historians as playing an active and aggressive role in the persecution of the Christians, and there is no evidence that the emperor directly ordered Perpetua's death. But some historical sources suggest that a decree issued by Septimius Severus may have influenced local officials to crack down on Christian sects, since Christianity presented a challenge to local civic and religious authority. The *Scriptores Historiae Augustae* mention Septimius Severus's edict in 202 CE prohibiting conversion to Judaism and/or Christianity (*Sev.* 17.1). But it is not known whether or not the account of the edict in the *HA* is fictional, since it is not mentioned elsewhere.[50] While a number of Christians were persecuted in 202 and 203 CE during Severus's reign, Tertullian reports that the emperor saved some Christians from persecution (*Ad Scapula* 4), so the issue remains controversial. Although Septimius Severus was a popular emperor in the African province and the birthday games for his son were likely celebrated throughout the empire, it is highly unlikely that the emperor and his family were in attendance at the games in Carthage when Perpetua was martyred, and there is no evidence to attest to their presence at the games.

Despite his use of a Christian physician, Severus was a pagan emperor. He adopted attributes of the Egyptian god Serapis in portraiture and was a patron of the cult of Mithras as well. He employed the title used by previous emperors of *dominus noster*,[51] or "Our Lord," which caused Tertullian to comment on the emperor's improper use of the title (*Apologeticum* 34.1). The cultural and religious associations of the word at this time meant that Severus was emphasizing his role as supreme ruler in a way that conflicted with Christian beliefs.[52]

CHRISTIANITY AFTER 203 CE

In 212, Septimius Severus's son Caracalla offered the benefit of citizenship to the entire free populace of the Roman Empire. This and other laws enacted during the Severan period, such as the restrictions set on practicing magic, placed emphasis on conformity. Thus, the laws were an attempt to unite divergent groups of peoples throughout the empire while providing a sense of

---

50 The edict is a matter of scholarly dispute. See Wypustek (1997, 285) for a discussion of the disagreement among scholars over Septimius Severus's edict and what impact it had on Christians. See also LeMoine (1996, 214).

51 This title was also used by the Roman emperors Caligula, Nero, and Domitian. See Rankin (1995, 23–24).

52 Rankin (1995, 24).

political and cultural unity. But when it came to religious conformity, Roman officials still struggled at this point to effect any control over the disparate religious groups under their authority, including Christians. The result was that eventually, Roman officials adapted Christian models of authority to help shape Christianity into the official religion of the Roman Empire.

While the lack of a collective religious identity had not been a problem for the Roman Empire in earlier times, Roman officials now recognized that the stability of the Roman Empire depended on maintaining conformity. Emperor worship had been one way to accomplish this. The interest in Christianity turned from persecution to adoption because the Christian church was able to enact a kind of authority over its community that the Roman officials recognized as a good model for maintaining the imperial government's structure and authority. The Christian faith, which Romans had previously regarded as making the Christian community antisocial in relation to the rest of the community, suddenly became the cohesive factor that could unite Rome's imperial community.

The process of Christianity becoming the state religion happened slowly. It did not occur immediately in the years after Perpetua's death and during Caracalla's brief reign. Rather, the Romans continued to persecute Christians and regard them as harmful to the empire. Few Christians were executed before 197 CE. There were, however, persecutions in 197–198, 202–203, and 212–213. Between the years 203 and 211, we do not know of any executions of Christians in Carthage. Tertullian writes a response to the death of one Christian soldier, but it is possible that this event took place in Rome (*De corona militis*). This does not mean that Christians were not persecuted, but that the accounts that have survived tell of Christians being released with mild or no punishments. In 212, however, there are accounts of Christians being tried and executed once again. It is possible the attitude toward Christians shifted after the murder of Septimius Severus's son Geta in Rome in 211.

In 249 or 250 the emperor Decius issued an order that all citizens had to sacrifice in public on behalf of the emperor by a set deadline. He ensured that each citizen had done this by having a board of local officials witness the event. Persons who refused were, after they had been put on trial, often exiled and sometimes had their property taken away. But this edict was not necessarily aimed at Christians, but rather at anyone who would not make the mandatory sacrifice. And it appears that the majority of citizens did make the required sacrifice.

Since it seems that many Christians did comply with Decius's order, how did Christians reconcile their belief against worship of false idols with the emperor's demands? At this time, there were other ways to appear to meet the demands of the emperor. For example, some Christians bribed officials to get out of the sacrifice, and some even sent another person as a proxy to make the sacrifice on their behalf. That way they could obtain a certificate to show to Roman officials that proved they had sacrificed on the emperor's behalf. And some Christians made the sacrifice themselves, probably out of fear, yet continued their habitual activities, such as attending meetings with other Christians afterward.

The Great Persecution took place from 303 to 311/313 CE, one hundred years after Perpetua's death, and began under the reign of the jointly ruling emperors Diocletian and Maximian. Many Christians died during this period. A few years after Diocletian's persecutions, tension within the Christian community led to a decline in martyrdom's appeal.[53]

In 257 CE, the African bishop Cyprian was summoned by the proconsul of Africa, Aspasius Paternus. Aspasius Paternus warned Cyprian that the Emperors Valerian and Gallienus were demanding compliance with Roman rites from all those who did not practice Roman religion. When Cyprian denied that he, as a Christian, could comply with the emperors' decree, he was exiled. When Cyprian returned to Carthage a year later, he set about rebuilding a Christian community that had been fragmented by lapses in faith. He changed the church's policy regarding Christians who had lapsed in the time of the persecutions. Whereas previously lay confessors could forgive lapsed Christians, now this authority was granted only to bishops and priests. Just fifty years after Perpetua's death, the hierarchy of the church was replacing a more informally structured Christian society. Cyprian was recalled by the proconsul, Galerius Maximus, and asked to participate in Roman rituals on behalf of the emperor's well-being due to an edict issued by the emperors.[54] When he refused, he was sentenced to death, as the proconsul was obligated to follow the decree.

MARTYRS IN ANTIQUITY

How did martyrdom differ in Perpetua's time from our modern concept of a martyr? She did not desire to seek revenge, nor did she wish to depart from the world while injuring or killing others in the process. And she did

---

53 See Rebillard (2012, 34–59), who traces the timeline of persecutions beginning in 180 CE and examines the Christian response to persecution through his reading of Tertullian's works *De corona militis, Ad Scapulam, Scorpiace, De fuga in persecutione*, and *Ad Martyras*.

54 The emperor Decius instituted a similar decree a few years earlier in 250 CE. See Rebillard (2012, 34), who notes there is now scholarly consensus that imperial legislation against Christians did not exist before the reign of Decius and "that Decius himself did not have Christians in mind when he issued this edict. Rather, persecution was a local matter, in the hands of the governors."

not appear to be self-centered in her motivation to die, since within the text she showed so much concern for her son and father. Her act was one of self-sacrifice and done out of a desire to leave the world for what she believed would be a better place.[55]

The martyrs were open and honest about who they were and what they believed. They were seeking to gain their heavenly reward, and the catechumens modeled for the arena audience how to depart from the earth: the martyrs chose to remain firm in their convictions and went to their deaths with as much dignity and control over their emotions and bodies as the situation allowed them.[56]

THE SPREAD OF CHRISTIANITY WITHIN THE ROMAN EMPIRE

It would be historically inaccurate to report that Perpetua and Felicity's deaths united the Christian community in Carthage and that conversions to the Christian community increased dramatically as a result of their martyrdom. What is more likely following the death of Perpetua is that the schisms that had always been present within the Christian community became more apparent as the church became more structured. Even within Saturus's final vision in the text this is hinted at: various factions are in disagreement until Perpetua comes to address them in Greek and the angels tell the bishop his flock is acting like rival parties at the races and to leave the martyrs out of it (13.1–6).[57] While the *Passio* does not tell us the source of their disagreement, differing points of view among Christians led to the development of groups such as the Montanists.

Perpetua's diary gives us insight into how and why Christianity spread throughout the Roman world. At the time the diary was written, Christianity had not yet become the official religion of the Roman Empire; yet its impact on the Roman imperial authority meant that some Roman officials were attempting to suppress the Christian "sect," because they feared the effect it had on their society and culture, especially when some of the sect's followers refused to make the sacrifice to the emperor. The Christian author Tertullian discouraged Christians from participating in many aspects of Roman life, including attending the games with their bloody

---

55   See van Henten (2012, 121–23) for a discussion of the martyr's death as one of self-sacrifice. See also Farina (2009, 217–20) and Bremmer (2012, 50–53).

56   See LeMoine (1996, 213).

57   Farina (2009, 187).

spectacles, due to the emotions they incited.[58] But to non-Christian Roman officials, the games were one of many ways in which the empire displayed its power and wealth. For Perpetua and the other catechumens to be sentenced to die in these very games was another way for the Roman officials to spread the idea that Christianity was condemned.

In the third century CE the majority of non-Christian officials within the Roman Empire were still trying to maintain a nonviolent and non-confrontational coexistence with the growing Christian population. And many Christians were trying to exist in a nonconfrontational way with non-Christians as well—they did not start revolts against the Romans the way Jewish populations did earlier in the empire. At this time in Roman history, for the most part Christians could obtain certificates that offered proof of their sacrifice and be left alone by Roman officials. Perpetua's persecution did not set off widespread persecutions throughout the empire or even within Roman Africa. So Christians continued to meet in private homes until later in the third century when churches began to be built. Rome did not have a Christian basilica until the fourth century.

History, politics, and religion were closely entwined in antiquity, just as they are today. As we have seen, there is no clear distinction between civic and religious life in Carthage. Although there is the separation of church and state in some societies, we see evidence that just like the ancient Roman society, the two intersect at times. When the pledge of allegiance ("One nation, under God") is recited in public schools in America, when "In God We Trust" appears on US currency, or when the president of the United States of America speaks at the National Prayer Breakfast, we see that the interconnections between government and religion are still being demonstrated in our time.

BAPTISM

While Perpetua mentions in her diary that she was baptized while under house arrest (3.5), she does not provide us with many details. Was it a full immersion baptism that was performed in a large body of water? How and where was the ritual carried out if she was under house arrest? How long was she a catechumen before she was baptized? Who performed the baptism for Perpetua and the other catechumens? The text itself does not provide enough information for us to know for certain the answers to any

---

58   Tertullian, in his work *De spectaculis*, or "On the games," warned Christians not to attend the gladiatorial contests, as in his mind they were religious events that promoted worship of false idols—but that did not mean that Christians necessarily stopped attending.

of the above questions. So Perpetua's baptism, as depicted in the graphic portion of this book, shows a close-up scene of her experiencing part of the ritual, but this essay will describe in more detail what the experience may have been like for some members of the early Christian community.

Many Christians, like Perpetua, desired to be baptized because in the African church, this sacrament was "crucial to salvation."[59] To undergo this religious rite represented purification for the individual involved, because experiencing the ritual meant forgiveness, as sins were washed away. Yet the ritual's most significant aspect was not the outward washing of the body, but the internal cleansing of the spirit; for after they had confessed their sins, they could leave behind past ways and embark on a new life. Rejection of former habits could include giving up some interests that were popular during the Roman Empire. In particular, Tertullian mentions renouncing immoral ways that were particularly Roman, such as watching gladiatorial combat and other blood sports (*De Spectaculis*). Perpetua and her fellow catechumens, therefore, end up being the very kind of entertainment that Christians such as themselves, according to Tertullian, were supposed to avoid watching.

There is no one prescribed ceremony for baptism in antiquity. The rituals for baptism varied within the early Christian church. At that time baptism could be performed anywhere. Even laypeople within the church could administer the ritual ceremony, if there was a need and they were authorized to do so. Baptism was traditionally supposed to take place at dawn, and a pre-baptism exorcism could take place the night before. Christians who were to be baptized took off their clothes before being immersed in water. Women wore their hair down and were required to remove their jewelry. After the immersion was finished, Christians sometimes donned white robes (which symbolized their new state of purity). In early baptismal ceremonies, rivers were often used, and the ceremony was performed outdoors, because running, or "living," water was preferred if possible.[60] During the first through third centuries CE, apart from one baptistery in a house that was converted to a house-church around 240 CE (in Dura Europos, which is located in modern-day Syria), we do not have any record of special buildings or places set aside just for baptisms.

Tertullian's *De baptismo* offers us a source of information on baptism in Carthage, but even his account is not complete enough for us to know every aspect of the ritual. Moreover, it is unlikely that Perpetua's baptism was as complex and included all of the rituals he describes in detail, given

---

59   Heffernan (2012, 155).

60   Brandt (2011, 1587–1609) offers a detailed description of baptism rituals for the early Christian church. See also Ekenberg (2011, 1011–1050) and Norderval (2011, 947–72).

that she was under house arrest. He describes the preparation for baptism as follows: the pre-ritual events could include fasting, confession, praying, and all-night vigils. Before the rite could begin, the catechumens would renounce the devil and all his powers. Then they could enter the water and profess their faith. Tertullian describes the immersion into water as taking place three times. Next, they would be anointed with oil and more prayers would be said. Afterward, those who were baptized would receive milk and honey before receiving the Eucharist. Following the baptism, the Christians went from being catechumens to full members of the Christian community and were allowed to receive the Eucharist at worship.

Tertullian mentions that baptism of children was becoming more common in his time in Carthage. But he indicates his personal belief that Christians should wait until they are adults, and preferably that they should be married before undergoing the rite. He also explains the hierarchy of the early church: the bishop had the primary right to perform the ritual, and following the bishop, the deacons and presbyters could also be authorized to perform baptism. In Perpetua's time, those who were preparing for the baptismal rite followed a specific course of action. Catechumens were expected to undergo pre-baptismal instruction, which taught them how to live as Christians. They readied themselves for baptism by demonstrating that they understood the moral requirement of leaving the old way of life and sins behind.

The catechumens' instruction placed emphasis on becoming part of a new Christian family, with new responsibilities and ties within that community, although it would be incorrect to say that failure to participate in these activities would jeopardize one's membership in the community.[61] The Christian community placed a high importance on caring for the needy. Christians were encouraged to prove their commitment to the faith by sharing their money and other resources with the less fortunate, from prisoners—just as the deacons cared for Perpetua and her companions—to the old, sick, orphaned, and anyone else needing help. They were supposed to cast off the desire for accumulating wealth and material things just for themselves.

Some Christians considered themselves to be distinct from the non-Christian community in their beliefs in part because their religion taught them to show love for all people. They rejected the Roman practice of deciding at a child's birth whether or not the infant would be abandoned or brought up within the family. Abandoning an infant would go against the Christian teaching that all members of the community should be cared for, so they adopted needy children. An example of this in found in the *Passio*, when a Christian woman was ready to take in Felicity's daughter after she was born, since Felicity would not be able to care for her (15.7).

---

61   Rebillard (2012) 12.

There was a strong connection between baptism and martyrdom in antiquity, since martyrdom was considered another kind of baptism. The diary mentions that the crowd recognized Saturus as being baptized in blood while in the amphitheater and even calls out "well washed" as a sort of a joke when he is covered in blood (21.2). Felicity also is mentioned as going from the blood of the birth to the blood of the arena (18.3). Since death came with martyrdom, baptism right before martyrdom does not signify the act of living a new life on earth. Instead, Christians acknowledged that there was no prospect for further acts of sin since the person being martyred had come to the end of his or her life. Christians believed that anyone who was martyred would automatically go on to Heaven after dying.

ROMAN EDUCATION

It is possible that Perpetua's family was wealthy enough for her to have received an advanced education: evidence indicates the name Vibia was associated with a prominent family in Roman North Africa.[62] The narrator also describes her as *honeste nata*, or "well born," which suggests that her family had enough wealth to have provided Perpetua with an education that went beyond basic instruction. In addition, her use of rhetoric in the diary suggests her father could have given her the education that children of wealthy families received. The privilege of education had other benefits as well. The more education one had in antiquity, the easier it was to be integrated into society and to gain power within it.

Education in the Roman Empire incorporated much more than book learning. It was a comprehensive approach to learning designed to discipline, teach, and guide children and to prepare them for the social and political responsibilities of being productive adults within society.[63] Defining the term *paideia*, or education, in antiquity offers a challenge, because not only did what constituted an education mean different things to different societies, but education also changed over time as the Roman world expanded and came into contact with other cultures. But for those who wished to educate their children, contact with Greek culture in particular influenced the instruction that the Romans offered to their children.

Education was not a uniform experience in space and time throughout the empire, nor did all peoples under Roman rule receive the education

---

62   Heffernan (2012, 21).

63   Too (2001, 13) offers an overview of the current understanding of ancient education as "a process of socialization."

described below: "we can no longer take it for granted that we know what ancient education was in each and every one of its manifestations."[64] Education was not required at this time. Schools were often makeshift operations, held in storefronts. Instruction began in the early morning hours and lasted all day, with only a short lunch break. There was no law that entitled everyone to a free education. This is especially true when talking about women's education, and it is important to note that we do not know as much about the education of females in antiquity as we do about education for males. Since women were often married around the age of fourteen, they might not have had an opportunity to continue their education outside the home. Also, while we can learn from ancient sources a great deal about the kinds of topics children studied, we have to acknowledge that there was diversity in the quality and quantity of the educational experience.

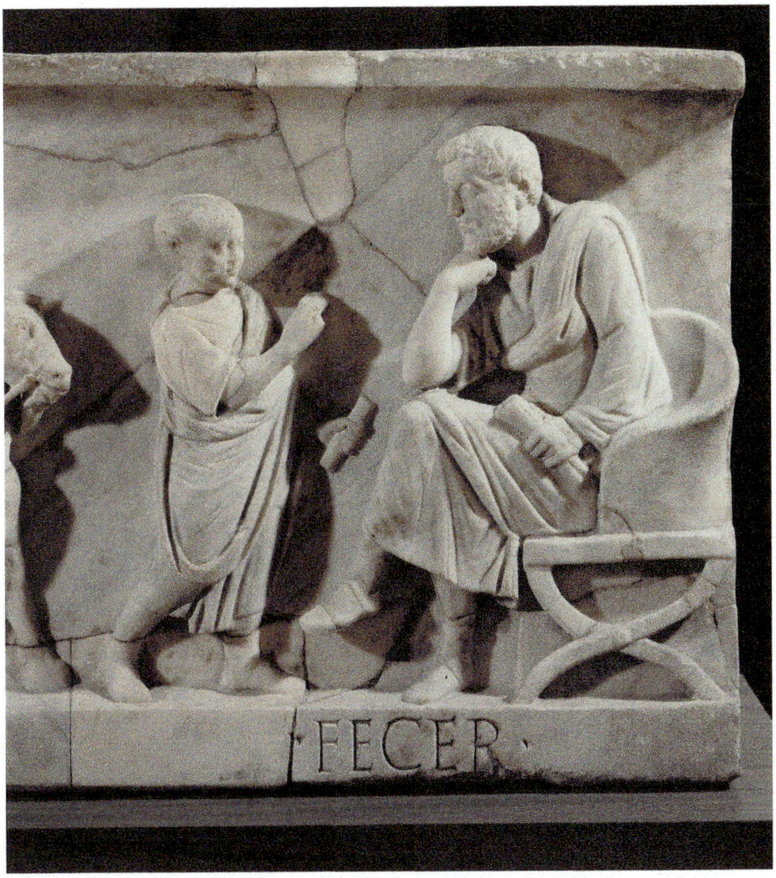
FECER

Figure 2.2 Detail of a child's sarcophagus from 150–160 BCE depicting a teacher and student [M. Cornelius Statius], Italy.

64 Too (2001, 11).

The Romans themselves did not idealize their educational process; and their literature, which sometimes satirized the school experience, offers plenty of complaints about poorly paid teachers, the intolerable demands parents placed on educators, and even critiques of how certain aspects of the curriculum became less practical over time.[65] Beating male students who were late to class or did not know their lessons was commonplace. The Roman poet Horace, for example, complained that his teacher Orbilius was *plagosus* or "full of blows" (*Epistles* 2.1.70). Moreover, the shift to an emphasis on learning more about style than substance was a particular complaint of the Roman historian Tacitus (*Annales* 4.61).

Education was an indicator of social status for families. Due to the fact that the *paterfamilias* was in charge of arranging for his children's education, the quality and levels of educational instruction offered to children varied throughout the empire. Education differed in antiquity in many ways from modern methods of instruction. There were no mandated grade levels of education students had to achieve, no standardization, and no government standards to meet. Young children from the poorest families could typically expect their education to be more limited and primarily vocational. Families could hire private tutors for their children, some children would be educated by their parents, some would attend private schools, and sometimes a combination of all three methods was employed. Despite this lack of consistency, it is possible, however, to surmise that children from wealthy families were likely to have received instruction in certain kinds of educational content and subject matter.

Education began at home when the children were very young, with their parents and/or tutors educating them in manners and moral concepts such as respect for past tradition (i.e., the *mos maiorum*); *gravitas*, or how to act dignified and responsibly; and *pietas*, or duty (see "Authority and Power").[66] Young girls could also be educated in domestic skills, and young boys could receive instruction in civics and other related topics. Parents could employ a private tutor who could teach them reading and writing. The literary texts used to teach reading were often poetry, which students would be required to memorize.

The *magister ludi*, who held a position similar to a modern-day elementary school teacher, taught children from age seven until roughly twelve. Instruction consisted of learning to read and write by copying the letters

---

65   Barrow (2011, 73–85) relates that the early Roman educational system placed an emphasis on learning values that would teach respect for the appropriate Roman way to live, but notes a decline in education over time.

66   See Morgan (1998, 271) for the argument that teaching literacy also gave students "cultural information and a repertoire of values that indicated they belonged to the ruling elite."

of the alphabet, and then copying words and sentences. There was often a second teacher at the school, known as the *calculator*, who taught basic math. Students would use a wax tablet and stylus to practice their writing, until they could write well enough to use parchment and a quill pen, and they employed an abacus for basic math. The school, or *ludus* as it was called in Latin, was conducted in a room with a chair for the teacher and stools for the pupils. Boys and girls set off in the early morning to school and, if their parents could afford it, were accompanied by a slave known as a *paedagogus*. This slave was generally Greek and would be responsible for teaching children the Greek language.

Between the ages of nine and twelve, male children from wealthy families were often sent to a type of teacher called a *grammaticus* who would teach them how to analyze poetry and polish their reading and writing skills. A *grammaticus* would also ensure that students understood the mythological and historical allusions and references contained within poems as well as the poem's grammatical structure.[67] In addition, students would begin more formal instruction in Greek. A bilingual approach to education meant that students could learn to speak and write both languages fluently. A lot of the training students did at this level was memory work. Practice in poetry recitation and poetic analysis meant that a student began learning about public speaking and literary analysis. Students could hone their oral skills for debate and cultivate their speaking and writing skills in general. By age fourteen or fifteen, children would have completed their instruction with the *grammaticus*.

The next phase of education—and one that was essential for those who wished to enter public life—was private instruction by a *rhetor*. The *rhetor* taught the students how to debate, or to argue for or against a cause. Emphasis was placed on constructing creative and sound arguments. This kind of training in how to formulate and effectively present an argument, along with honing persuasive speaking skills, meant that students who completed training with a *rhetor* had been prepared for careers in law and politics.

A final phase of education was philosophical training. This could include the study of essential questions about the nature of the world and how to think about humankind's place within it. Students often traveled abroad to Greece to study philosophy. This final phase of instruction, however, generally was for the Roman Empire's most wealthy and elite males.

Specific details about how and where women were being educated beyond what the *magister ludi* taught to pupils is lacking, but evidence

---

67   See Francese (2007, 42–43) for a comprehensive explanation of the *grammaticus*'s role in educating Roman youth.

suggests that it was possible for women from wealthy families to continue their education and that Perpetua was not necessarily the exception in her time. Her diary indicates that education in antiquity did not have to stop when one entered adulthood: her instruction as a catechumen was recent.

The Roman educational system encouraged Perpetua's father to instill in her and her brothers a strong sense of duty toward preserving and maintaining established Roman traditions and values. Perpetua seems to have had an especially close relationship with her father, who expressed his preference for her over her brothers (5.2). Thus, some scholars have suggested that Perpetua may have received some of her education at home from her father.[68] Since education in antiquity was meant to foster character development into adulthood, it is not surprising that Perpetua's father was so concerned about his daughter's actions. He attempted to "teach through example" by modeling the values he wished to instill in his children, and this may account for some of the frustration and sorrow he expressed when she chose a belief system and values incompatible with his own. When Perpetua's father asked her to consider what impact her actions would have on the rest of the family (5.4), he was very likely thinking of how he would be viewed as the *paterfamilias*, who was supposed to be responsible for the moral instruction of his children. He and Perpetua had no way of knowing before her death the extent to which her behavior would become a moral example for later generations of Christians, but this would not have offered him any comfort, as the church regarded her as a model in part for her rejection of the beliefs and traditions that men like her father upheld.

At the start of the diary the narrator describes her as *liberaliter instituta*, or "well educated," which suggests someone who has achieved at least the level of education that a *grammaticus* would teach. Perpetua's visions suggest that her education might have included Greek and Roman epic poetry. She demonstrated a familiarity with poetic rhythm and composition techniques as she composed her diary.[69] In particular, her vision of fighting the Egyptian implies familiarity with ancient athletic contests, including the wrestling and boxing matches commonly portrayed in epic poetry. And Saturus mentioned her conversing in Greek with a bishop and a presbyter in his vision (13.4).

She argued eloquently with the tribune when she refused the costumes for herself and her fellow prisoners, and also when she spoke with her father about how she could not be anything other than a Christian. The authority with which Perpetua spoke to her detractors indicated her confidence with

---

68   See, for example, McKechnie (1994, 284–85).

69   McKechnie (1994, 281–82).

rhetoric and her familiarity with the use of persuasive arguments of the kind that the Greek philosopher Plato used. She demonstrated her argumentative skill with her father:

> "Father," I said, "do you see that vase lying there, some little pitcher or other, for the sake of example?" And he said, "Yes." And I said to him, "Is it able to be called by any other name other than what it is?" "No," he said. "I too cannot call myself by any other name other than what I am, a Christian." (3.1–2)

In her Platonic-sounding dialogue, in which she used the concept of an object's identity as the basis for her argument, a little pitcher, or *urceolus*, was not able to be called by any other name, and neither is Perpetua to be called anything other than a Christian.[70] By her logic, if she could not call a vase by any other name (because it then it would be something else), then she could not be called anything other than a Christian, because then she would be someone else (i.e., not a Christian). When she confronted the tribune, she successfully argued for improved conditions in the prison. She shamed the tribune because she was authoritative in her argument:

> "Why don't you allow us, since we are certainly Caesar's most distinguished condemned prisoners who will fight on his birthday, to refresh ourselves? Is it not to your credit if we are led forth to that place a bit fatter?" (16.3)

Perpetua used dark humor to make a comparison between the condemned Christians and sacrificial animals. Her joke about animals being prepared for a ritual slaughter made the tribune uncomfortable. She gave him a reason to see her side of things, and she demonstrated that she was in charge of advocating on behalf of herself and her fellow prisoners. The tribune blushed at her comments, and she and her companions received better treatment after that.[71]

Finally, right before she entered the arena she argued eloquently to the tribune on behalf of herself and her fellow catechumens the reasons for not wanting to appear in costumes:

---

70   McKechnie (1994, 282) notes that Perpetua employs the Law of Identity in this passage. Gold (2011, 239) calls it a "Socratic question and answer sequence."

71   McKechnie (1994, 283) notes that she established control over the situation at once and then argued convincingly: "Rhetorically, it's a matter of *inventio*: finding a persuasive argument to put forward." See also LeMoine (1996, 217) for a discussion of Perpetua comparing the catechumens to sacrificial animals.

And when they were led to the gate and compelled to put on robes, the men were dressed as the priests of Saturn, and the women as the priestesses of Ceres, Perpetua, that noble woman, steadfastly resisted all the way up to the end. For she said, "We came here of our own free will precisely so that our freedom might not be obstructed. Likewise we surrendered our lives, so that we would not have to do any such thing. We made this pact with you." Injustice recognized justice. The tribune yielded and just as they were, they were led in without costumes. (18.4–6)

Perpetua directly challenged the authority of the tribune. She argued that the catechumens should not have to appear in pagan dress, and she once again showed off her rhetorical skill. The arguments she made in which she identified and labeled herself and her fellow catechumens as holding up their end of the bargain, and the tribune as not honoring his, suggest a familiarity with philosophical arguments and training in rhetoric.[72]

Classical training is not the only education she would have received. Perpetua was well informed about the Bible, as evidenced by her visions, which included many biblical allusions (see "The Visions of Perpetua and Saturus"). This familiarity was likely to have come from her training as a catechumen, which would have allowed for her to become familiar with the Scriptures. Although there were no fixed standards at this time for how long a catechumen attended instruction before baptism,[73] it is possible that she could have had several years' worth of Scripture study before the events described in the diary even began.

Although we do not have enough evidence to know exactly how common it was for girls to be educated beyond the school of the *ludi magister*, it is certainly possible for someone of "noble birth," as Perpetua is described, to be so, and it is quite possible that she was educated by a private tutor at home with her siblings.[74] Yet scholars dispute how much her diary can tell us about her education and even whether or not she had been acquainted with knowledge of classical authors.[75] It is conceivable, however, that her education was advanced beyond the training offered by the *ludi magister*'s school, and her diary suggests knowledge of Greek philosophy, Greek and Roman

---

72   McKechnie (1994, 283).

73   Rebillard (2012, 11).

74   See Ameling (2012, 85) for the evidence of educated women from wealthy families.

75   Ameling (2012, 87–98) for example, argues for a limited education for Perpetua based in part on very little evidence of direct allusions to classical authors in the texts. McKechnie (1994, 279–91) finds more direct evidence of Perpetua's knowledge of Greek philosophy and Greco-Roman epics by looking at the imagery she uses in her arguments and visions.

epic poetry, and rhetorical arguments, as well as familiarity with writing prose in Latin. She appeared poised and confident in her diary in scenes with authority figures such as the tribune, and she did not appear to be intimidated by the arguments of any authority figures, including her father.

SLAVES AND CHRISTIANITY

Why did slaves become involved in Christian activities such as house-church meetings? What were the reasons that Christianity appealed to slaves? Christianity could promise salvation to slaves that did not privilege the slave owners over their slaves. Yet slavery was an established and accepted part of Roman society and the early church did not change that. Christians and non-Christians alike owned slaves.

Two of the other martyrs mentioned in Perpetua's diary were slaves: Felicity and Revocatus. Christianity appealed to slaves and freedmen alike because it taught that all were equals in the Christian church. The cohesiveness of Christianity meant that slaves could attend meetings in house-churches along with their owners and the socioeconomic differences between them would not be emphasized in the religion.[76] All would be equal in death.

We do not have any first-person accounts from slaves or former slaves during the time of the Roman Empire that tell us in a straightforward manner what their lives were like from the slave's point of view or explain why they desired to become Christians.[77] The experiences of Felicity and her fellow slave Revocatus in the *Passio* are not told as first-person narratives, and most of our late antique sources that discuss the church's inclusion of slaves as a part of the Christian community come from a time after the early part of the third century CE. To attempt a history of the early church's stance on slavery or to attempt to reconstruct what a Roman slave might perceive as a sense of their religious identity versus another nonslave member of the population would not be possible due to our lack of historical information. While we do have material evidence in the form of literature, archaeological remains such as epitaphs, laws about slavery, and inscriptions, these provide only glimpses into the lives of slaves—collectively taken, "slave life" is a complex and varied experience.[78]

It is also not helpful to equate what we know about slavery in the modern world with slavery in antiquity, because although slaves were commodities in both times, many other aspects of slavery in the Roman

---

76   Brown (1971, 66).

77   For evidence of slaves' own words recorded in antiquity, see Joshel (2010, 109).

78   Joshel (2010, 27, 129–31).

Empire were different. In modern times and in advanced societies, slavery is defined as a law-breaking activity with the slaves as its victims, but the Romans did not regard enslaving others as an illegal activity. In their worldview, everyone who could afford it had slaves and slave ownership was a legal right. Many questions remain about cohesion and community among groups of slaves in antiquity. Slaves often lived together on larger properties, or estates, in antiquity, but the slaves would have come from very diverse areas geographically. Thus, there was no homogenous slave population in the Roman Empire.

Due to the disparate nature of the slave experience, slaves could work at skilled and unskilled labor and be treated quite differently by their owners as a result. Thus, there are no shared labor situations that were common, due to all the different kinds of jobs in which slaves could be employed. We have evidence of some rebellious slave activity that was a sign that slaves were capable of unified acts against the Roman Empire in late antiquity, including large groups of slaves raiding cities and slaves joining collective social movements to rebel against the Roman Empire,[79] but a large-scale slave revolt that would have suggested a cohesion within the entire slave population did not occur.

A history of slavery in the Roman Empire remains outside the purpose of this work; instead, we will focus on a brief discussion of the development of the slave system in the Roman world and how it intersected with the development of the early church. Slaves in Rome were often captives and following the Second Punic War, the slave system expanded as Rome expanded its territory and brought conquered peoples back to Italy and enslaved them. By the third century BCE, Rome had established the foundations of a slave system that would expand and develop until slavery became necessary for the Roman Empire to function. Yet the slave system was not merely the result of imperial expansion; it developed alongside the market economy, Rome's military expansion, and other factors as the empire extended its power.[80]

Slaves were not allowed to own property; instead, they were considered property. They were often poorly treated and there was no legal recourse they could seek against their owners. By the second century CE, however, treatment of slaves had begun to improve and there were more opportunities for slaves to be freed.

The accomplishments of the upper strata of Roman society could not have been possible without massive numbers of slaves who did agricultural

---

79   See Bradley (1987, 31) for more on slave wars and rebellion in Tacitus.

80   See Harper (2011, 276–79) for the relationship between slavery and Rome's market economy.

Figure 2.3 Two slaves turning a press, Roman, Imperial Period.

and domestic work, among other duties. Slaves who possessed a particular skill set would be put to work at their job, with any profits they earned going to the master. Eventually, as Roman conquests grew less frequent, slaves were purchased from dealers or internally produced through breeding, in order to sustain the social system and the economy. Thus, Roman society was a *slave society*, which is a distinct concept that sets it apart from "a society where people owned slaves." The difference between the two kinds of societies is that the economy of Rome was built on slavery, and in other societies, owning slaves signaled an individual's status to others, but the economy did not depend on slavery.[81] For the wealthiest Romans, the social aspects of Roman society were constructed around having slaves administer their property and take care of all matters related to the household. This kind of setup meant that there were vast numbers of slaves who did all kinds of labor for their owners.

---

81   Joshel (2010, 7–9). The antebellum South is another example of a "slave society."

We do not know what kind of slaves Revocatus and Felicity were, but we do know from sources in antiquity some details about what life was like for slaves during the Roman Empire. This presents another difficulty for us since the term *slave* in antiquity can be used to define a wide variety of experiences, both geographically and in terms of the labor required. A slave who was required to put forth harsh physical effort would have a vastly different experience compared to a slave who was given the task of being the hairdresser for a household. If Felicity, for example, was enslaved in Perpetua's household in Carthage, then her experience would have been very different from that of a slave who was acquired to work on a farm in Italy. Slaves were also tasked with accompanying wealthy women in public. Wealthy women were not encouraged to go out alone, and often remained at home, but a woman out in public who was accompanied by her household slaves would not be seen as indecent.

Often slaves were not treated well since they were considered to be property that increased their owner's status. One of our primary sources of information about slavery in ancient Rome comes from Roman drama. The plays of Plautus and Terence, for example, include characters that are slaves. These fictional characters enact elaborate plots against their masters, cower in fear of punishments, and in some instances even save the master and his family with their clever schemes. While the descriptions of slaves that come from the plays have to be put into the context of the comedic genre, we do learn how much the slave owners valued having dependable slaves. Slaves and their masters could appear to develop close relationships, especially if they had both lived in the same household for a long time.

There was a complex psychology behind the slave–owner relationship, and one of the values on which the relationship was constructed was fear. Fear was a great motivator for slaves to stay on task, and both the Roman comedies and early Christian writings mention this. No slave was free from fear of his or her owner. Beatings and other forms of punishment were considered acceptable if a slave failed to perform his or her duties. Keeping slaves in a constant psychological state of terror due to the power their owners wielded over them, and the violence that might be brought to bear against them, was used to great effect.

Slaves could also be rewarded for good behavior. Among other rewards, slaves could acquire property, even if they could not legally own it themselves, or they could earn private possessions that they were allowed to keep, such as clothing. There was no assigned slave uniform in the Roman Empire: sometimes slaves would wear their owner's cast-off clothing. And of course slaves could potentially earn their freedom if their owner permitted it.[82] But slaves' dependence on their owners meant that

---

82   Harper (2011, 219–49). See also Wiedemann (1987, 24–25) on the punishment of slaves.

even the promise of rewards was sometimes enough to motivate them. From the slave's perspective, though, the emphasis on servility might be more to avoid punishment or gain some kind of reward than to demonstrate their loyalty and industry. Varro in the *De Re Rustica* encourages slave owners to gift their slaves with an extra set of clothing or more food as an incentive to help maintain the peace in the household (1.17. 7). Columella in the *Res Rustica* tells us that the slaves who were in chains should be accommodated in cells that let in some light (1.6.3). But his approach to the humane treatment of slaves should also be understood in the context that slavery was an integral part of Roman society that allowed wealthy Romans to collect an income off a large agricultural estate without working the land themselves.

Not all owners provided medical care for their slaves, but owners who did not could risk punishment: the Roman historian Suetonius tells us that the emperor Claudius passed a law that if a slave owner abandoned a sick or dying slave at the temple of Aesculapius, he was not allowed to take the slave back home if the slave recovered. All slaves abandoned at the temple were freed instead. Slave owners who opted to kill their sick slaves rather than abandon them could be charged with murder (*Claudius* 25).[83]

Legal changes and other developments that affected the established slave system came slowly and did not begin in earnest until the fourth century CE, as the church continued to develop social reforms. We have already described how the early Christian church was still evolving at this time, especially during the third century CE. The community was moving from house-churches to more formalized meeting places, and leadership within the church was being restructured as well. As a consequence, the relationship between slavery and the Christian church was also developing as the community was experiencing growth and redefining itself.

In the early church teachings, obedience and the acceptance of servile status until the afterlife were emphasized. Since slaves were a central, rather than a peripheral, part of Roman society, as the Christian church became more an integral part of the Roman Empire, it began to have influence over the lives of slaves. But the Christian church was not making significant changes in the lives of slaves. Augustine of Hippo, for example, believed slavery was ordained by God and a punishment for sin (*City of God* XIX.15).

By the late empire, slaves could seek temporary refuge in Christian churches, although the church leaders could not declare them free and would still return them to their masters. Eventually, the church would have the authority to free slaves, although scholars argue that manumission was

---

83 Bradley (1987, 119–27).

not a main priority of the church.[84] Christianity offered everyone, both slave and free, instruction on how to endure the earthly life's trials in order to be better prepared for the afterlife.

FELICITY: PORTRAIT OF A SLAVE IN ROMAN AFRICA

The *Passio* is known as *The Passion of Perpetua and Felicity*, but Perpetua never mentioned Felicity in her part of the *Passio*. The way in which Felicity's story is told differs from Perpetua's as well, since the narrator relates the events in her life in a way that is designed to emphasize her transition from a pregnant woman who labors through a difficult birth to a martyr who was about to die a difficult death.[85] We know nothing about her personal life outside of what is mentioned by the narrator. The specific events in her life that led her to become a Christian and the particular reasons why she chose to die as a martyr also remain unknown to the *Passio*'s audience. We do not know why Perpetua does not talk about Felicity, either. But on the day of their martyrdom, the narrator tells us that Perpetua and Felicity faced the cow in the arena together.

Because we know very little about Felicity from the *Passio*, scholars rely on the few details mentioned by the narrator and the more general information we have on slaves and their reasons for converting to Christianity to piece together a more detailed narrative about her.[86] We know that she is young, since the diary describes her and the others as *adolescentes*. We are told at the start of the work that her name is Felicitas (translated as "Felicity" in English), which means "happiness" in Latin, and that she is a slave. Felicity is also close to her due date for giving birth, and she does so near the end of the narrative in her eighth month of pregnancy.

Some scholars have speculated that since Felicity and Revocatus are named together in the work, perhaps Revocatus is the father of her child.[87] She is referred to in the *Passio* immediately following the mention of Revocatus as *conserva eius*, which could translate as "his fellow slave," and the two names placed in proximity could suggest that they are a couple.

84　Bradley (1987, 114). See also Andreau and Descat (2011, 134–35).

85　Cobb (2008, 112–113) notes that the *Passio* emphasizes that "she chooses martyrdom over motherhood." See also Bremmer (2012, 35–53).

86　*The Acta Perpetuae et Felicitatis* offers more details about the life of Felicity, including the information that she had a husband and that he was plebeian and therefore free, not a slave. In the *Acta*, she was also asked to sacrifice to the emperor, just as Perpetua was, and just as Perpetua did, she refuses to make the sacrifice. See Bremmer (2012, 41), who cites the *Acta*'s mention of her as a married woman (I.5.2–8).

87　See also Bremmer (2012, 37) for a discussion of the Latin term *conserva* and the argument that she is Revocatus's fellow slave and not his spouse.

But that is speculation and we cannot know for certain. What we do know is that slaves were not allowed to be married at this time.[88] It is also possible that Perpetua and Felicity lived in the same household, and it is likely that they attended instruction as catechumens together, since Saturus is named as the catechumens' teacher.

Felicity is baptized along with the others later in the narrative (3.5). Since Christianity at this time appealed to both slaves and freed persons (see "Slaves and Christianity"), Felicity would have gained a new Christian family. In this family, she could have felt that she was among equals in a way that differed greatly from belonging to a Roman household as a slave, where the distinction between slave and free would have been markedly clear. It is also possible that she felt closer to her Christian family than any biological one that she may have known.

We find out later in the narrative that Felicity is relieved to have given birth before the day of the games, since this meant that she would be able to go along with her fellow catechumens to the arena and participate. She and her fellow Christians prayed together a few days before in the hope that that she would give birth in time to be executed along with them, and her prayers were answered (15.1–7).

At this time in the Roman Empire, it was illegal to execute a pregnant woman, and the catechumens feared Felicity would not give birth in time for the scheduled martyrdom. Also, since Felicity was a slave, she was therefore someone's property, and as a result, her child, once born, automatically became the property of her owner. The diary reveals that another Christian agreed to take her daughter to raise as a Christian following the birth. We do not know if the Christian person was Felicity's owner or someone else. But because slaves were a commodity in antiquity, this lack of information raises the question of whether a slave owner would have been willing to give up the rights to the child.[89] The *Passio* does not tell us any more about the situation.

We are told that Felicity rejoiced following the birth because she could go from "blood to blood"—that is, the blood of the birth to the blood of the arena. Her death equaled a second baptism (18.3), since early Christians believed martyrdom was a second baptism. She was transitioning from her role as mother to martyr when she gave up her child so she could die in the amphitheater. When Felicity was knocked down by the cow, Perpetua appeared by her side and helped her up. In her last scene in the narrative, she is walking out the amphitheater's Gate of Life with Perpetua at her side (20.7).

---

88   Heffernan (2012, 19).

89   Salisbury (1997, 115–16).

Following the martyrdom, Felicity was commemorated as one of the most celebrated martyrs of North Africa, along with Perpetua. Some examples of where she is mentioned following the *Passio* are in Augustine of Hippo's sermons on the two women, in the stories of the martyrs, in medieval legends, and in the liturgy of the Catholic Mass said in honor of both women.

PRISON LIFE

Perpetua was first incarcerated in someone's house rather than the jail in Carthage. She mentions that she and her fellow catechumens were under surveillance (3.1), but other than that, does not describe her experience as uncomfortable in any way. At that time individuals who were suspected of crimes were often held in custody in private homes, under house arrest, until they could be questioned by the authorities. The conditions she experienced in prison, however, were in sharp contrast to that. Following her baptism, Perpetua was moved to a prison to await her trial.[90] Following her trial, she was sent back to jail to await her death. In that way, her experience was typical of the times, because she was not given a jail sentence to serve as a punishment for what she had done: she was there waiting to die.

In antiquity, jail was not a place where prisoners were commonly held until they could be rehabilitated and returned to society. Rather, prisons served as a holding place for persons awaiting a trial or execution. This is not to say that some prisoners would not have been held in jail and then released afterward, perhaps as a result of being freed after a trial,[91] but since prison generally was not used as the end punishment for a crime and not designed for long-term stays, the cells used to hold people were quite cramped and very uncomfortable.

Perpetua depended on both family and her community of fellow Christians for support in prison. She revealed her alarm at the harsh environment. The darkness and crowded conditions she described indicate that she was most likely being held in an underground prison cell. The lack of light and close quarters scared her; the soldiers threatened and extorted the prisoners (3.6). It was a common experience for prisoners to be placed in chains and held in spaces underground, and Perpetua also mentioned being put in the stocks (8.1). Perpetua's jailers benefited when the deacons bribed them, but so did Perpetua: she was allowed to move about in the prison.

---

90 Perpetua never mentions an exact prison or a specific location in the *Passio*, but it is widely believed that the prison was located in Carthage (3.5).

91 McGowan (2003, 456).

She was then moved to a more pleasant part of the prison to interact with her visitors. When her young son was brought to her, she was overjoyed.[92]

It is likely that Perpetua was hungry and thirsty in prison, and the deacons, whom she would have considered part of her Christian family, along with her actual family members, could have brought her food when they came to visit. While some prisoners did get prison rations (known as *diaria*), most had to rely on visitors to bring them additional supplies. Prison officials welcomed this, since it meant that they did not have to spend money on maintaining the prisoners. In addition, the Christian community was committed to helping the needy, and visits from its members would have provided for the prisoners' physical and social needs.[93]

Following the trial, Perpetua mentioned being transferred from one prison to another, and this last place where she was held was a military prison (7.9). This is the setting where the catechumens were allowed to hold a final dinner, or *cena libera*. But there is no description in the *Passio* of what the prisoners ate at their last meal, which they transformed into an *agape*, or a Christian love feast. While fasting could also be considered part of a martyr's preparations for death, Perpetua made no mention of fasting while in jail, nor is there any indication that the other martyrs who died with her fasted.

While the prison experience was meant to be punishment, some Christians could also have seen their imprisonment as a sort of confined retreat (however unpleasant) and as a time for contemplative reflection. Written around 197 CE, Tertullian's *Ad Martyras* describes jail as a place where virtuous activities can be undertaken, such as uninterrupted prayer, and he mentions that prison can be seen as a refuge from worldly pagan activities like the public religious rituals and entertainments.

Part of the martyr's preparation for what lay ahead in the arena was demonstrating the stamina to endure the prison conditions.[94] Perpetua also saw her visions while imprisoned—in her vision of her brother Dinocrates, he suffered in the same way she did: he was hot, thirsty, and in a dark place (7.4).[95] Prison was also the place where she finally freed herself of all familial ties, including her relationship with her son. Felicity declared her distress at possibly not being able to die with her fellow catechumens

---

92   See Heffernan (2012, 151) for a discussion of the child's age. It is likely that her son was between one and two years of age. The second-century CE Greek physician Soranus tells us that infants were breastfed until two years of age (2.46–8). The Latin text of the *Passio* uses the term *infans*, which in antiquity meant a child who did not yet speak, not an *infant* in the modern sense of the word.

93   McGowan (2003, 459–60). See also Salisbury (1997, 86).

94   Hillner (2015, 266).

95   McGowan (2003, 466).

(15.2). This could indicate the Christians saw their prison experience as set apart and distinct from the other prisoners'.

Perpetua's prison experience tells the particular story of her and her fellow catechumens, but it is important to remember that the prisoner's experience could vary widely, especially because the prisoner's social status could be taken into account when determining the punishment.[96] Connections to community members and close family relations could also play an important role in the prison. As we see in the *Passio*, the deacons' bribery and Perpetua's own wit improved her prison experience slightly.

GLADIATORIAL COMBAT

Gladiatorial combat was originally associated with funerals. The earliest games, which were called *munus* in Latin, meaning a "duty" or "gift," first were performed as sacrificial honors for the dead. Although many gladiatorial fights were staged, a gladiator who chose to die would be expected to do so with honor—much as a Christian martyr was supposed to model and maintain decorum while willingly dying in the arena.[97] But over time the games came to represent much more than honorific sacrifices for dead, noble Romans. In the later empire, the games were presented in gladiatorial arenas throughout the empire to enormous crowds.

When Perpetua and her fellow catechumens were sentenced to die in the arena, their punishment fit their crime. The tribune Hilarianus made an example out of them in order to establish that their refusal to make a sacrifice on behalf of the emperor's well-being meant that they were then going to be sacrificed for the well-being of the state. The officials who governed the Roman Empire used the games' ritual violence to secure its stability and longevity, and as a way to safeguard against other forms of violence that could harm the state.[98] The audience that witnessed gladiatorial combat saw a form of violence that was regulated and contained within a designated physical space.

The earliest evidence for gladiatorial combat appears on tomb paintings in the fourth century BCE.[99] While at first the Romans held gladiatorial

---

96   McGowan (2003, 457).

97   Kitzler (2015, 50) notes that the gladiator represents masculinity since they were able "to face death voluntarily."

98   Salisbury (1997, 121–22).

99   Dunkle (2013, 7) notes that in addition to games held at funerals, there is evidence from the same time of banquets in Campania featuring gladiatorial contests as a form of dinner party entertainment.

fights as part of funerals to honor their fellow Romans,[100] eventually they became a form of popular entertainment. Birthday games for Roman rulers, such as the emperor or a member of his family, as we see in Perpetua's diary, have become commonplace by the time of early empire. While not all Romans loved the games, they were an established part of the Roman culture in the same way that organized sports are a part of our modern society. The amphitheater represented a place where the crowds could gather to watch a form of controlled violence, much as modern organized sports draw large crowds.

When gladiators fought in amphitheaters across Rome, events like this served to unify the community that lived within the borders of the empire. They could all experience the same entertainments, and, more important, both the lower and upper strata of society would attend. The community within the Roman Empire could see the games as a symbolic reenactment of Rome's military prowess. Exotic peoples and animals could be brought in from all over the empire, and the people could watch the gladiators conquer them.

Gladiatorial combat became a popular form of entertainment. But the actual gladiators themselves were looked down upon by society. They were often criminals, prisoners of war, or slaves, although some freedmen (and some women) also opted to become gladiators. If they were not slaves before, once they became the possession of a *lanista*, or trainer, they were his property. While they did not automatically die if they lost a match, they also were not guaranteed fame or a release from the lifestyle if they won a match, either. They underwent extensive training, so they were considered an investment by the *lanista* who owned them. They could achieve fame and fortune, and even Christian authors would praise them for their skill, but the profession itself was about selling the body for money.[101] Archaeological evidence shows that in some parts of the Roman world gladiators arranged for group burials similar to those of the highly respected colleges of priests, with similar tombstones and burial arrangements.[102] Thus, some gladiators achieved some dignity in death, even if they were not considered high-status persons in Roman society.

The games also offered an example of virtue in death. Martial virtue in particular was highly prized by the community, and the gladiators' combat came to exemplify this. Even though there is evidence that gladiators did not always die in combat, a gladiator who accepted that it was time to die

---

100   Dunkle (2013, 6). See Barton (1993, 25) for an account of Roman knights participating in gladiatorial combat in Caesar's games in 46 BCE.

101   Dunkle (2013, 35–40). See also Hope (2001, 184).

102   Hope (2001, 184–91).

was considered a courageous and virtuous person. Gladiators were held to high moral standards when it came to the arena. If they were no longer capable of fighting, they were expected to die bravely.

After Saturnus, Secundulus, and Revocatus displayed their courage in front of Hilarianus, the catechumens were whipped by the animal-hunters (18.7–9). The *venator*, or animal-hunter, wore only a tunic and no armor (presumably to make things more interesting), and his job was to hunt down animals in the arena. He did this with only either a hunting-spear (*venabulum*) or a light spear (*lancea*). These animal-hunters fought large and small game, and it was not uncommon to have *venatores* imported to Rome from places like North Africa and Spain to fight the larger animals until native Italian animal hunters were trained and became skilled in the task.

The *Passio* also mentions that Felicity would go from the midwife to the *retiarius*, a gladiator who fought with the net (18.3). Unlike many other types of gladiators, the *retiarius* did not fight wearing a helmet and did not carry a shield. Instead, he wore a special type of armor on his left shoulder called a *galerus*, which protected him from blows to the left side of his body. He carried a trident along with his net. He also wore protective armor, known as a *manica*, on his left arm and a loincloth along with a metal belt and greaves on his legs.[103]

Perpetua was sentenced to *damnatio ad bestias*, or "condemned to the beasts." This was the penalty given to lawbreakers and prisoners of war.[104] It meant she was sentenced to be torn apart by wild animals. This was a slow death, as the *Passio* illustrates, in which animals would maul the victims and tear them to pieces. The punishment was for Christians and non-Christians alike, although we may associate the Christian martyrs more with this kind of death because of all the accounts of the martyrs' lives that have been recorded for posterity. Slaves, whether Christian or not, could also be sentenced *ad bestias*. Since Christians refused to recognize the Romans' state gods, *ad bestias* was considered a suitable punishment for them. Their rejection of the state religion was seen as a threat to the empire's welfare. It was also routine to dress up criminals before execution. Plutarch describes this custom and the elaborate costumes criminals were often forced to wear (*Moralia* 554B). In Carthage, Saturn and Ceres were favorite deities, so the choice of the gods' attire for the catechumens is not surprising.

The portion of the games Perpetua died in was called the *venatio*. The *venatio* was a popular staged animal hunt in Roman times. It was expected

---

103   Dunkle (2013, 78–80, 107–11).

104   Welch (2007, 25–26).

to be an exotic spectacle, since the Romans enjoyed novelty and so care was taken to bring animals from the African province, among other places, and even elephant ballets were included among the entertainments. The condemnation of Perpetua to the wild animals was a different sort of *venatio* for the Romans. While they expected that the animals could die, and sometimes even the *venatores* and the variety of gladiators who worked with them in the arenas died as well, in this instance the pleasure at the spectacle may have come in part from watching criminals be humiliated. Perpetua and her fellow Christians, moreover, provided great entertainment when they resisted death.

The actual scenes from the *Passio* that took place in the amphitheater require some explanation. Perpetua and Felicity's punishment was to face a cow, not a bull. The narrator explains that this was against the usual practice (20.1).[105] The cow represented part of the way in which the authorities chose to shame the women. Male criminals were put before male beasts in the arena to represent aggression matched with aggression. When female prisoners were matched against a bull, it implied they were adulteresses. But to put a female prisoner before a cow indicated something entirely different.[106] The behavior of Perpetua and Felicity was perhaps not female enough for Roman officials, and therefore they were being shamed for not acting more like traditional Roman women. If the animals did not finish off the victims, then they could die by sword. Just as we see in the *Passio*, when the cow did not kill Perpetua, she guided the sword held by the novice gladiator to her throat.

By Perpetua's time, the *venatio* was combined together with gladiatorial combat. Perpetua, like a *venator*, wore no armor in the arena, but unlike the *venator*, she was given no weapons with which to fight. Since exotic animals were often imported from Africa for the fights in Rome, it is no surprise that the catechumens were put up against a number of beasts, including a boar, a bear, a bull, and a leopard. Some of them were even tied to platforms, as Saturus and Revocatus were (19.3), so the animals could attack them more easily.

Before the match, gladiators were given a dinner. It was called the *cena libera*. Gladiators, *damnati*, and the animal fighters would all dine together. This dinner was held outdoors, and the public could watch if they wished. The gladiators could also put their affairs in order in the event of their deaths. In Perpetua's diary, however, this last meal is described as a "love feast," or *agape*, where the Christians could be together one last

---

105   Dunkle (2013, 225) argues, however, that it was not unusual for a female criminal to meet her death at the hands of a female animal.

106   Shaw (1993, 7).

time. We do not have any information on the catechumens' menu, or exactly where it took place in the prison, but it must have been an area where they could be seen by others. When the Christians were heckled by the crowd, they shamed their onlookers by telling them of their forthcoming joy at being called at last to martyrdom and made it clear that those who judged them would be judged themselves (17.1–3).

THE AMPHITHEATER

While the diary does not name the particular amphitheater Perpetua perished in, it is possible it was the main one in Carthage, which could hold around 30,000 spectators (as opposed to another, smaller amphitheater used by the military).[107] This larger amphitheater, which was once beautifully decorated, was located below the Byrsa Hill. Very little of the above-ground structure of the amphitheater in Carthage remains today, as the stone was hauled away to be recycled for other uses, but the subterranean structure, where the some of the animals would have been contained before the fights, remains visible today.[108]

The amphitheater in Carthage had two gates that opened on to the arena from opposite ends of the minor axis, the Gate of Life (the *Porta Sanavivaria*) and the Gate of Death (the *Porta Libitinensis*, since Libitina was the goddess of funerals).[109] A contestant who won was led out through the Gate of Life. If anyone lost but remained alive, then being led out of the Gate of Death meant that the person was being taken to a chamber to be put to death out of the spectators' sight. Perpetua is led out the Gate of Life in the *Passio*, but then she is brought back in to die in front of the spectators.

The games took place throughout the day. Often in the morning mock fights would come before animal fights. Then at noon the criminals were executed. In the afternoon the gladiatorial combat began. It may have been customary in Rome for the higher strata of Roman society to skip the midday criminal executions. But in Carthage, the entire crowd would often stay to watch the executions; sometimes these criminals were the main event and the show was extended to last the entire day.[110] The crowd could delight in watching the punishment of those who had broken the law. In the eyes of the community, whoever threatened the stability and social

---

107   The Colosseum in Rome seated about 50,000 spectators.

108   See Bomgardner (1989, 94–103).

109   See Bomgardner (1989, 89) for the location of the gates.

110   Salisbury (1997, 133–34) argues that "educated Romans" skipped the noon show.

Figure 2.4 Roman amphitheater in Carthage.

fabric of their society by acting outside the law deserved the physical violence of the arena.

The audience for Perpetua's death would have been a diverse crowd. Why did audiences attend these events? For some, it was to see the "right" way to die—bravely. For others, Christians in particular, it was to learn how to be a martyr—both Christians and non-Christians alike observed the combat to see an example of how to face death courageously and faithfully. While Christianity did not promote gladiatorial combat as a suitable activity for its followers to watch or participate in, that did not mean Christians were not in attendance. So when Perpetua died in the amphitheater, she may have served as an example to some Christians watching from the audience. Some spectators would have come in particular for the sense of shared community or belonging provided by watching the spectacle in honor of Geta's birthday. Similar birthday celebrations would have taken place in amphitheaters around the Roman world. The audience assumed a participatory role in the action. Some persons would have cheered on their favorite gladiators. The element of surprise also appealed to them.

A few years after the birthday games in his honor, Septimius Severus's son Geta was dead and his brother Caracalla had his image erased from all imperial portraits and inscriptions. Yet the games of 203 CE in Carthage are remembered due to Perpetua's bravery. Perpetua, long after her death, remains a celebrated martyr.

CONSTRUCTING STATUS IN ANTIQUITY

In an essay about identity and status in antiquity, Valerie Hope summarizes the difficulties of establishing criteria in order to determine the status, or social ordering, of individuals in antiquity: "Status was multi-dimensional, and across the Roman Empire the language and symbols of status were not uniformly employed or uniformly evaluated."[111] The "multidimensional" aspect of status is particularly interesting in the *Passio*, as Perpetua seemed to be held in high regard in some situations more than in others. At the start of her diary, when she was thrown into prison, she complained about the deplorable conditions and having to rely on the deacons to make her experience tolerable (3.5–7). But later on, she described how Pudens, the military adjutant, recognizes "great power" in her and her fellow prisoners and he began to show respect for them (9.1) When she spoke to the tribune near the end of the *Passio* and argued for better treatment on behalf of herself and the other prisoners, she was successful (16.3). She was also given permission for herself and her fellow catechumens not to wear the dress of pagan gods when being put to death (18.5–6).

Much of Perpetua's diary raises significant questions about status in antiquity. Roman authors left behind a wealth of descriptive writings about status, but the surviving texts are primarily written by men. Some examples would include poems, legal documents, historical texts, correspondence, and inscriptions, which can all reveal much about who possessed power and who did not. These men tell us about how, from their perspective, they make distinctions between wealthy and nonwealthy persons, slave and free persons, male and female, soldiers and civilians, and tell us much about the legal distinctions that separate groups of people from one another in ancient society.

Status can change based on circumstances. Factors such as dress and appearance, social affiliations, and even location could all influence an onlooker's assessment of an individual's status. The crowd that appears throughout the story effected changes in Perpetua's status. Their view of Perpetua transformed from ridicule to respect. The immense crowd, no doubt curious, gathered to hear her trial (6.1). A crowd appeared at the final meal the prisoners were holding in prison and jeered until Saturus's words shamed them; the narrator tells the audience that many became believers as a result of what happened at the feast (17.1). The crowd looked down from Perpetua's gaze when she marched into the amphitheater, possibly as a sign of respect or in shame (18.2). The expectations for modesty

---

111   Hope (2000, 150).

from a Roman matron meant they would not have anticipated that a married woman would have stared back at them.[112]

Because of the crowd's reaction to Perpetua's dress and behavior when she was led in to fight the cow in the amphitheater, her status changed from that of a woman who was disobedient to the Roman state to that of a respected martyr (20.2–3). This was no ordinary day at the games where wild beasts tore nameless individuals to bits: the crowd was shocked at the treatment Perpetua and Felicity received. In fact, their horror when the two martyrs were led out dressed only in nets forced a change in attire. Removing their clothes stripped them of their decorum. But even when they were naked in nets before the cow, they gained the crowd's sympathy. They were then allowed enough modesty to put on loose-fitting outfits. The narrator described the crowd's shock—they shuddered in horror—at seeing a beautiful young girl and a young mother who had recently given birth about to die (20.2). Respect replaced the crowd's scorn.

AUTHORITY AND POWER IN THE *PASSIO*

Perpetua's relationship with her father, along with her mounting resistance against the Roman authorities, drives the action in her diary and plays a considerable role in what makes her story engaging even today. But in order to recognize why her father and the other authority figures reacted to her choices in the way they did, it is essential to know the context for Perpetua's interactions with authority figures. First, it is necessary to understand who possessed power in the Roman world and then to consider the relationship between power and gender in antiquity. Through an overview of the ways in which the Romans structured authority within their society and their families, and a close examination of expectations for male and female conduct, we can place Perpetua's story into a perspective that allows us to see her choices through not only her eyes, but also the eyes of the Roman authorities, her family, and the crowds who gathered at the prison and the arena.

Potestas, Latin for "power," played a critical role in Perpetua's story because in refusing to sacrifice on behalf of the emperor, Perpetua challenged the *potestas* of those who were in charge—and by extension, threatened the order of the very society in which she lived. Throughout the Roman Empire, this *potestas*, or authority, came from the gods as well as the emperor, who was venerated as a god. It also came from the magistrates, who were officials either elected or appointed by the emperor, and the *paterfamilias*, or male head of the Roman household.

---

112   Shaw (1993, 4). See also Perkins (1994, 844–45).

Roman-appointed officials were required to maintain order in the provinces. Since maintaining public order was his job, Hilarianus, the official at the trial of Perpetua and the other catechumens, had the authority to quash any threat to established civic order and religious traditions in Carthage, such as refusing to worship the emperor. Christians like Perpetua posed a threat to this order, since the well-being and longevity of the Roman state depended on the people's veneration of their emperor. But if the spread of Christianity did not take place until later in the empire, why did a small group of catechumens cause such a concern at this point in history? It may be that officials like Hilarianus thought that they could prevent a bigger problem by getting rid of the sect while it was still small. Public displays of deaths such as Perpetua's could be used as warnings and deterrents to anyone who dared to defy Roman civic and religious authority.

In many ways, the Roman family functioned like a smaller version of the Roman state, complete with its own rules about *potestas*. The family, or *familia*, was governed by a *paterfamilias*, or the oldest male, who was the head of the household. Men such as Perpetua's father were expected to have control over their own households, which included the family, consisting of his wife, children, and grandchildren, in addition to slaves. He was also responsible for making sure his household demonstrated support for the emperor and other government officials. This authority, known as *patria potestas*, was granted to the head of the household and gave the *paterfamilias* legal, social, and religious control over all of his household members. If a *paterfamilias* was not effective as head of the household, then his status as an upright Roman citizen could be placed in jeopardy.[113] When Perpetua's father begs her to consider the consequences of her actions and how it might affect her family, he is thinking of his status as well as her safety (5.2–4).

Officials had the right to investigate any activities they considered suspicious, such as a family member's refusal to make a sacrifice to the emperor. This is where having an established network of family and friends became important in Roman society: people relied on others to vow to officials that they supported the imperial authority. We do not know how often Roman officials investigated reports of Christian activities, but because Perpetua and her fellow catechumens were rounded up and arrested, it is possible that someone reported them to the authorities.

In antiquity, the concept of being an independent adult male or female who moved completely away from parental influence or control did not exist in the same way it does today. Although there were policies that allowed adult sons to gain some financial freedom in terms of setting up a

---

113 Heffernan (2012, 188) argues that Perpetua's actions require her father to either persuade her to change her mind or to reject her.

home and family of their own, even if they could gain a share of their father's estate to administer for themselves, their share and how it was used was still subject to their father's approval and could be withdrawn at any time.[114] Married women remained under the authority of either their husbands or fathers. There were two types of marriage in ancient Rome: *cum manu* and *sine manu*. In *cum manu* marriages, the husband obtained legal control over his wife when they got married. In the *sine manu* marriage, the father retained the legal authority over his daughter. Most marriages at this time were *sine manu*.[115] This could explain why Perpetua's father appeared at her trial and why he had the authority to decide that she could no longer see her baby while she was in prison.

In addition to *potestas*, another important value for the Romans was *pietas*. One way to define *pietas* would be to explain it as the duty an individual has toward others, including his or her country and the gods. In the Roman world this could also mean the duty toward family, and in Perpetua's case her duty to her father. To demonstrate *pietas* meant putting others before oneself. Romans also defined *pietas* as a kind of paternal love. Perpetua's father was talking about *pietas* when he told her that he put her before her brothers (5.2–4).

Perpetua's father was also thinking about his role as *paterfamilias* and how he would be viewed by his peers and the officials who had power over him if he did not maintain control over one of his family members. When Perpetua rejected his advice, she was not just rebuffing her father's efforts to keep her safe. She was rejecting the Roman value of *pietas* and, by extension, trading the entire value system of the Romans for a Christian belief that when she became a martyr, her Christian family would celebrate.[116] Following Perpetua's death, Augustine of Hippo remarked that Perpetua offered fitting and successful resistance to her father (*Serm.* 281.2), but from her father's perspective, her rebellion against the traditional ways of doing things was a violation of social norms that could lead to serious consequences for him and the rest of the family.

The scenes with authority figures raise significant questions. Perpetua describes a series of meetings she has with male authority figures in which she not only defies Roman authority, but she does it in a very public arena. Her encounters with her father and the magistrate Hilarianus, as well as other male authority figures in the prison and amphitheater, allow us to

---

114 Lassen (1997, 114–20).

115 Perpetua's husband is mentioned only once in the text, by the narrator, and we do not know why there are no subsequent references to him. For the argument that Saturus was Perpetua's husband see Osiek (2002).

116 Salisbury (1997, 89–90).

see how she conducted herself during her trial in the law court and in the gladiatorial arena, both of which were normally associated with masculine power and authority.

Christianity threatened the stability of a system in which the *paterfamilias* had authority over his family. It endangered the very structure of Roman society because its followers were encouraged to leave behind their familial attachments and form close bonds with their fellow Christians. Since the Roman officials' authority came from a political and social structure that assigned them power based on a social network that began with the Roman family and required everyone's participation, Christians who chose to no longer recognize the authority of the *paterfamilias* and broke their filial ties destabilized the cohesiveness of that very power structure.

PERPETUA AND THE LITTLE PITCHER: ENCOUNTER #1

In her diary, Perpetua's first encounter with a male authority figure took place between her and her father. She was being held under house arrest by the orders of the procurator Hilarianus. It was possible that she was detained at a wealthy person's home in the community, since this was one way a *paterfamilias* could demonstrate his loyalty to the government, by acting on behalf of the state. When Perpetua had her first meeting with her father, it is clear from her description of events that her father wanted her to be obedient to him and to recognize his authority over her as *paterfamilias*. But she was not willing to do this and instead engaged in a dialogue with him about her beliefs. She compared calling herself a Christian to naming a small vase that she claimed could not be called by any other name (3.1–2). The word Perpetua used, *urceolus*, is Latin for "little vase." She compared her body to something breakable: a container used as a burial urn. The vase was therefore associated with human mortality and was easily broken. Why would she do this? The female body in Perpetua's time was also considered fragile, and she was making a deliberate comparison between her body and that small container to emphasize her mortality.[117] She then assigned herself the new label of *Christian*. Perpetua notes that her father was so angry with her behavior that he moved toward her "as if to pluck [her] eyes out" before he left (3.3). The absence of her father for a few days following this episode gave her comfort. When Perpetua asserted her authority in this scene with her father, he was angered by her determination to call herself a Christian because he knew full well that it might result in her death. He may also have been angered by the fact that he was the *paterfamilias* and yet Perpetua did not subjugate herself to his will, as a good daughter was supposed to do (see "Roman Education").

---

117 LeMoine (1996, 216).

PERPETUA AND HILARIANUS: ENCOUNTER #2

Perpetua's next encounter with authorities occurred during her trial. Here we see a complete reversal of the expected roles of father and daughter. Perpetua spoke as her own legal advocate to the proconsul Hilarianus. Hilarianus questioned her about her beliefs in the Forum in Carthage. He tried to persuade her to make the sacrifice on behalf of the emperor, but she refused. In her diary she described what happened when she was taken to court for a hearing:

> On a different day, while we were at lunch, we were suddenly dragged away for the hearing. And we reached the forum. At once rumor ran through the nearby parts of the forum, and the crowd became immense. We climbed up onto the platform. The others confessed when interrogated. They came to me, and my father appeared there with my son. He pulled me down from the stair saying, "Make the sacrifice, have pity on your child." And the procurator Hilarianus, who at that time had accepted the right of the sword in place of the deceased proconsul Minucius Timinianus, said, "Have pity on the white hairs of your father, have pity on your young son. Make the sacrifice on behalf of the emperors' health." And I answered, "I won't do it." And Hilarianus said, "Are you a Christian?" And I answered, "I am a Christian." And when my father was determined to get me to reject my beliefs, he was ordered by Hilarianus to be thrown down, and beaten with a rod. And I grieved for my father's misfortune, as if I had been struck, thus I grieved on behalf of his miserable old age. Then the procurator sentenced all of us and condemned us to the beasts; and we went down to the prison cheerfully. (6.1–6)

Generally, it was considered a man's job in antiquity to plead a case before the court. While it was legal for Perpetua to advocate on her own behalf when she was questioned by Hilarianus, Perpetua disgraced her father. She refused to submit to his authority when he told her to make the sacrifice, and she did it in a very public forum. The head of the family had rights and responsibilities and should never appear to be incompetent at performing his duty publicly.

As we have seen earlier, Roman law was based in part on a system of assigning authority to the heads of households, and Perpetua's father failed in his obligation. He was therefore publicly censured in the law court. Perpetua tested the authority of both the judge and her father in the public forum of the law courts. She refused to obey either of them, and she maintained control of her emotions, appearing calm and rational (unlike her father), which belied any prevailing beliefs associating the female body with mental instability.[118] Yet her ability to assume male authority in this scene and act as her own legal advocate acted as a precursor to the role she would play as a legal advocate on behalf of her fellow prisoners.

PERPETUA AND THE TRIBUNE: ENCOUNTER #3

Perpetua's next encounter with legal authorities occurred when she confronted the tribune about the poor conditions she and her fellow prisoners were forced to endure. It was likely that the tribune did not fully understand Christianity, since he was frightened by false rumors that prisoners would somehow be able to use magic to get themselves out of prison. When he denied them the right to receive better treatment, it was in part because he assumed they could use incantations to free themselves from the chains and stocks.[119] Thus, his ignorance regarding Christianity probably contributed to their poor treatment. Perpetua pointed out that she and her friends were about to become the main amusement for a very large crowd, and that they would make a very pathetic sort of birthday party entertainment if they looked half-starved, wasting away in the arena. The tribune blushed at her remarks (16.2–4). His mortified reaction showed that Perpetua shamed him into better behavior through humor. She argued that the Christians who were about to be sacrificed to the animals have something in common with the emperor's son—they are both "the most noble" of all. The Latin word she used, *nobilissimus*, was an epithet of the emperor. It was also applied to his son Geta, who was the birthday boy in this story. But it was transformed by Perpetua into a word that described her and her fellow catechumens. She was joking, but her words were enough to shame the tribune. It is possible, after hearing Perpetua's words, to imagine the contrast between the lives of "the most noble" son of the emperor, Geta, and "the most noble" convicts who must die on his birthday as part of the celebration.[120] This encounter with the authorities differed from the previous two since she was advocating on behalf of not only herself, but also her fellow prisoners.

PERPETUA AND THE TRIBUNE: ENCOUNTER #4

Perpetua remained steadfast in her beliefs throughout her encounters with Roman authorities. She rejected traditional Roman *pietas* when she refused

---

118   LeMoine (1996, 213–16). See also Gold (2011, 243–44) and (2015, 483) for more on women's vices. The theme of the inferior woman, fit for men to rule, can be found, for example, in Aristotle's *Politics* 1.1254b13–14. See Smith (1983, 476) on Aristotle's explanation of why women are prone to possess unstable minds: "In short, women are too susceptible to being overcome by emotions and thus require the steadier rule of men."

119   See Wypustek (1997, 284).

120   LeMoine (1996, 217).

to submit to the will of her father, called herself a Christian in a court of law, and denied the crowd the opportunity to see her dressed as a priestess of Ceres. In her final confrontation with legal authorities, she is determined to once again advocate on behalf of herself and her fellow prisoners.

When the prisoners were led from the prison to the amphitheater, we learn that the prisoners were joyous, going off to their deaths. The crowd was subdued by Perpetua's demeanor, and when she looked at them, they lowered their eyes as if in shame at the sight of her (18.1–2). She established her authority by meeting their gaze rather than bowing her head in shame.

The authorities wished to dress Perpetua and the others in costumes instead of letting them go out and have the crowd see them for who they really were. A costume would, in part, have distracted the crowd from her reactions and her emotions:

> And when they were led to the gate and compelled to put on robes, the men were dressed as the priests of Saturn, and the women as the priestesses of Ceres. Perpetua, that noble woman, steadfastly resisted all the way up to the end. For she said, "We came here of our own free will precisely so that our freedom might not be obstructed. Likewise we surrendered our lives, so that we would not have to do any such thing. We made this pact with you." Injustice recognized justice. The tribune yielded and just as they were, they were led in without costumes. (18.2–4)

By participating in this ritual act with its distinctive dress, Perpetua and her companions would have stood out in the arena as being clearly designated as a sacrifice to the pagan gods, the way a sacrificial animal would, since sacrificial animals were clothed in woolen headbands the same way the priestesses of Ceres were.

Perpetua appealed to reason at this point and offered a rational explanation for not wanting to die dressed this way. She made a promise in court that was legally binding and if she upheld her end of the deal, then she expected the Roman officials to keep their promise to her as well. In the previous section of the *Passio*, where she encountered the prison guard, Perpetua set up a joke about being fattened up like animals being led to the slaughter, but now that she as being dressed up like a sacrificial animal, she objected to losing her respectability while going off to her death.[121] She wanted to die as a courageous and brave Christian martyr on her own terms, not be remembered merely as a participant in Roman ritual.

---

121   See LeMoine (1996, 218–19) for the headbands worn by priestesses and sacrificial animals.

A few minutes later, the crowd was shocked and horrified when Perpetua and Felicity were led out. The women were naked except for the nets that covered them. The narrator described the crowd's response to a young and pretty girl being led to her death along with another young woman who has obviously just given birth: they were too ashamed to look upon them naked in this context. The women were allowed to put on tunics before they began to fight to the death. The narrator has established that Perpetua asserted her right to die with honor and decorum. After she was knocked to the ground by the cow brought out to fight her and she tore her tunic, she covered her thighs and asked for a pin with which to put up her hair. She was concerned with maintaining self-control at all times, and at no time does she appear to lose control of her mind or body, contrary to what the crowd might have expected from a female in that time and place. The shock, the blushing, and even the crying were all responses that we may have expected from Perpetua at one point or another in the narrative but instead are the reactions of her father and the tribune, who were the male authorities who were supposed to be in charge. Perpetua succeeded in her attempt to create a "public test of authority," and she continued to retain as much power as possible over herself and her circumstances until the end of her life.[122] Her final act demonstrated this. She remained in control of her mind and body long enough to guide the hand of the novice gladiator to her throat so he could kill her.

Perpetua assumed many roles in the *Passio*: her father described her as *filia* (daughter), she was a mother to her son, and then both her father and her brother called her *domina* (lady). She described herself as *Christiana* (a Christian woman) and finally she told her audience *facta sum masculus* (I became a man). But her last moments in the arena marked her as feminine; she pinned up her hair so that she would not look like a woman in mourning and covered her thighs for the sake of modesty. At the end, we are watching the actions of a brave female martyr. This emphasis on her feminine behavior may be because a narrator has taken over the diary again at this point.[123] But with his final words, he reminded the audience that she remained in charge of her own death as she guided the hand of the inexperienced gladiator to her throat; he referred to her as "such a woman" (21.10).

Certain behaviors in antiquity were associated with men, and certain behaviors were associated with women. An audience reading Perpetua's diary in antiquity would perceive her behaviors and those of other persons in the text as more feminine or masculine ways depending on how they

---

122   LeMoine (1996, 217).

123   Cooper (2013, 129). See also Vierow (1999, 610), who argues that women receive attention for "youth, beauty or offspring, men impress crowds with their character or ability as teachers."

were acting. For example, when Perpetua appears to possess control of her body and emotions, her behavior is regarded as masculine. She also behaves the way a man would be expected to at that time when she responds calmly in answer to those around her who are trying to persuade her to do something she does not want to do, like make the sacrifice to the emperor, or stop being a Christian.

Thus, the Romans saw an individual's conduct as part of the means for determining whether or not one was perceived of as female or male in a given situation. Other factors that could determine gender included appearance, such as clothing (or lack of it), and mannerisms. In her fourth vision, Perpetua is transformed into a man and stripped naked (men sometimes fought naked in athletic contests) and she engages in a confident and aggressive wrestling match with her opponent—confidence and aggression in antiquity are behaviors associated with men. At this point in the narrative, with her change in gender from female to male, Perpetua shatters the expectations society has placed on her as a woman (see "The Visions of Perpetua and Saturus").[124] When she is experiencing emotions such as fear (in the darkness in prison and for her son whom she has not seen in a few days) or feeling pity for her father, then the diary's audience would perceive her as acting in a feminine way. And when she is nursing her son, this is feminine behavior as well.

During the course of the narrative, Perpetua and her companion Felicity both have demonstrated that they are strong women who are capable of enduring pain: Felicity while giving birth, and Perpetua while enduring prison conditions—while in the stocks and when she misses her child. Perpetua's ability to endure pain and torment bravely and to intercede on behalf of others is associated with her having power in the text.[125] After she intercedes with prayers on behalf of her brother Dinocrates and he no longer appears to be suffering, Perpetua observes that the prison guard Pudens recognizes her "great power" and allows her and her companions to receive visitors and have better condition in prison as a result (9.1). Power, suffering, and gender are all linked in this text.

Are Perpetua's authority-challenging behaviors to be seen in the religious context, as part of her devotion to Christianity, or in the civic context, as an act of defiance against the authority of the Roman Empire? Or are her behaviors indicative of the way in which both worlds were colliding at this time? If we assign Perpetua's behaviors solely to the categories of either "actions of a Christian martyr" or "individualistic acts of rebellion against the higher authority of Rome," then we miss out on a deeper understanding of how the categories of *civic* and *religious* overlapped in antiquity.

---

124 See Perkins (1994, 844) for the ways in which Perpetua refuses to be seen as the victim in her last vision.

125 Perkins (1994, 847).

Instead, we have examined how power and authority functioned in the public arena at this time and put Perpetua's behavior into this context.

In ancient times, men were considered physically and morally superior to women. In the Bible, the Christian as male athlete was upheld as a model of restraint and discipline (I Cor. 9:24–7). Women were considered weaker, both in strength and in moral character. So it is not surprising that Perpetua transforms from the female sex to the male sex before her fight with the Egyptian in her final vision (see "The Visions of Perpetua and Saturus"). Throughout the narrative, she has indicated that she will not act dependent, passive, or submissive in any way to any authority figure. Thus, not only does she defy the expectations society had for women in her own time, but her diary also challenges her audience to think about where power and authority came from in the Roman world, and how the definitions of who can have power and where it comes from may be changing at the start of the second century CE.[126]

THE VISIONS OF PERPETUA AND SATURUS

Perpetua's visions give us insight into her spiritual life as a catechumen as well as demonstrate her knowledge of classical texts. Because of the allusions to Scripture and classical texts that appear within them, this series of dream-visions suggests that she was an educated person: the classical references reflect her earlier education before she became a catechumen. After each vision, she briefly explains its meaning to her audience and the audience can see the progression from (1) knowledge of her suffering due to her impending martyrdom to (2) her newfound confidence that she can intercede on behalf of her dead brother to (3) her final determination that she will be fighting the devil himself.[127] Perpetua's dreams combine prophecy with a representation of her desires. When she leaves behind the prison walls and escapes her captivity by means of her visions, those visions reveal a self-assurance that she will receive salvation from the Lord.

This section of the commentary will offer an introductory guide to some of the interpretative ideas that various scholars have presented regarding the *Passio*'s visions.[128] It must be acknowledged, however, that individuals reading the text, whether scholars or students, will bring their

---

126 The Montanist movement gave women leadership roles within the church (see "Roman Religion and Early Christianity"). See also Gold (2011, 243).

127 See Miller (1994, 148–83) for a discussion of Perpetua's visions within the context of the genre of martyr texts.

128 Heffernan (2012) provides a detailed guide to the biblical references within the visions in his commentary. See also Salisbury (1997, 98–115), who offers critical analysis as well.

own point of view and assign a context to Perpetua and Saturus's visions. Therefore, this part of the commentary is not an attempt to find or recover one specific reading, definition, or meaning for the visions to pass on to the reader. Rather, this discussion endeavors to show a range of interpretations and possibilities within each vision and demonstrate that the imagery is drawn from multiple sources.

THE OLD MAN IN THE GARDEN: VISION ONE (4.3–9)

In antiquity, it was common for persons to believe that some dreams (or visions) were true and could predict the future. When Perpetua's brother comes to her and asks for a vision, he is placing great faith in her that she can communicate with the Lord, since she is a Christian. He says to her, "Lady Sister, already you possess great worth, so much that you might request a vision and it would be shown to you, whether there will be suffering or escape." Her brother uses the term *domina*, or "lady" in Latin, to address her, and this is a sign of great respect shown to martyrs because they are allowed to ask for God's favor.[129] Perpetua writes in response to his request: "And I, who knew that I could converse with God, whose great blessings I had experienced, made a promise confidently to him [her brother], saying, 'I will tell you tomorrow.'" Perpetua then records in her diary, "And I asked and this is what was shown to me" (4.1–2). Thus, in this part of the *Passio*, before her first vision, the audience learns that Perpetua is confident that she can talk with God and receive a response (4.3–9).

One way in which scholars have interpreted Perpetua's visions is to argue that this was Perpetua's way of preparing herself for her upcoming martyrdom. This first vision, for example, can be read as representing her journey from a material world in which she would be subjected to torments, before her arrival in paradise. The ladder, an image taken from the Bible, and in particular Jacob's dream at *Genesis* 28:12–16,[130] is covered in a variety of sharp weapons, and in Perpetua's vision has a serpent at the base. It is possible that these weapons, which could "cut to pieces" anyone who was not climbing carefully, could foreshadow what she knows will be a bloody death in the amphitheater.[131] After persisting through a cautious climb up the ladder, she arrives at the top to find herself in a vast garden with an old man who feeds her a milky morsel of cheese. She has arrived at the Good Shepherd's garden at last.

The key features of this vision—the ladder, the serpent, and the old man who is a shepherd—suggest a strong biblical influence. Her dream

---

129   Shaw (1993, 7). Her father will also address her as *domina* later on in the *Passio* at 5.5.

130   Frend (1993, 172); see also 172–74 for a discussion of allusions to late Jewish and New Testament apocalyptic texts in the visions). Waldner (2012, 203) locates the *Passio* "in the experimental field between prophecy and divination."

131   Perkins (1994, 840).

may also draw from her life experiences as a Christian in Roman Africa. In particular, many of the references come from Revelation, along with other books of the Bible. The serpent may be the *draco magnus* from Revelation 12:3. The old, white-haired man (Rev. 1:13–14) and the others clothed in white (Rev. 7:13–14) also recall Scripture passages, and the white-haired man evokes images of the Good Shepherd. The sweet taste in her mouth may recall the baptism ritual she and her fellow catechumens would have recently experienced, where they could have been fed honey, along with bread and milk. White was a color that was associated with martyrs; it symbolized purity, joy, and innocence as well.[132]

Perpetua and Saturus appear together in this vision, and this is the first mention of him in her diary. She states that he is waiting for her, and it is within this vision that the audience learns that he turned himself in after the initial arrest of the catechumens:

> Yet Saturus climbed first. (At that time when we had been led away, he had not been there. Afterward, he had voluntarily surrendered himself on our account, because he had instructed us.) And he arrived at the top of the ladder and he turned and said to me, "Perpetua, I am waiting for you, but take care that the serpent does not bite you." And I said, "In the name of Jesus Christ, he will not harm me." (4.5–6)

Perpetua's self-confidence at this point, when she climbs to the garden to meet the old man and is not afraid of the snake, foreshadows her poise during her entrance into the amphitheater right before she dies at the end of the *Passio*. First, she marches into the amphitheater as though she were "the bride of Christ, as the beloved of God, casting down the gaze of all by the strength of her eyes" (18.2). Then she steps boldly in front of the crowd: "Perpetua was singing a psalm, already stepping on the head of the Egyptian" (18.7). This portrait of her stepping bravely also foreshadows her final vision, in which she steps on the head of an Egyptian man. Thus, her first and last visions both convey the same sense of her confidence.

It is curious to note that she is nourished by the cheese given to her by an old man with white hair who has been milking sheep. This is in direct contrast to how she is treated by her white-haired father, who does not support her and will not allow her to supply her own child with her breast milk as nourishment after a certain point in the text.[133] When she awakens from this encounter with the old man, the contrast is stark between the comfort the

132   LeMoine (1999, 202–3). See also Miller (1994, 157)

133   Bal (2012, 141).

vision offers and the uncomfortable prison conditions. [134] The description of the vision is immediately followed by another encounter with her father, where he cries at the thought of what is going to happen to her. He cannot support her religious views, but he laments the fact that she was always his favorite and now he will have to face the fact that she will die (5.2–6).

Further influences on her dream may come from other, nonscriptural sources. When Perpetua envisions stepping on the serpent's head, she may be recalling the Greek author Artemidorus, who wrote a work called *The Interpretation of Dreams*. His interpretation of venom-bearing animals as symbolizing men's power and the heads of these animals as parents may signify that the serpent represents her father and that she stamps out his authority under her feet as she crushes the serpent's head. According to Artemidorus, a ladder could symbolize travel. Her vision could also recall Vergil's *Aeneid* as themes of prophecy, bravery, and the struggle to find one's way are present in both. *The Shepherd of Hermas*, another early Christian text from either the first or second century, is also a likely influence, since a shepherd figure appears as a guide in this text as well.[135]

DINOCRATES: VISIONS TWO (7.3–9) AND THREE (8.1–4)

Perpetua's next two visions come to her after, much to her surprise, she calls out the name of her brother Dinocrates, whom she had not thought about in a long time. Before the start of her second vision, she indicates her ability to help him through prayer: "And I knew at once that I was worthy and ought to intercede on his behalf" (7.2). She then began to pray and call out to God. It is possible that others in the prison witnessed her having this vision, since she was at group prayer when she called out Dinocrates's name. The second and third visions establish Perpetua's ability to act as an advocate on behalf of others. This theme of advocacy predates the time when Perpetua and Felicity will be celebrated in the Mass as intercessors on behalf of sinners' souls.[136]

During the second vision, when she sees her brother Dinocrates, he is suffering. This is because he died at the age of seven due to a cancerous wound on his face, and when he appears, he is trapped in a dark, crowded place without access to water. He is dirty, hot, and thirsty, and she can still see evidence of cancer. A great divide separates them, and they are unable to approach each other as a result. He wants to drink from a pool of water, but since the pool's rim is just out of his reach, he is unable to do so. When

---

134   McGowan (2003, 460) points out each vision "includes a prize of food or drink won" and that this could have been in part influenced by the hunger and thirst experienced by the prisoner.

135   Salisbury (1997, 100–102). See also Farina (2009, 24).

136   LeMoine (1999, 204).

she wakes up, she realizes he is suffering, and she decides to intervene for him through her prayers.

When Perpetua sees her brother again in her third vision, he is clean and healed, except for a scar on his face, and now he can drink the water from the basin, since the rim has been lowered and a golden cup appears above it. He can consume his fill of water, as the cup appears to never run out, and then he runs off and plays, splashing in the water. Perpetua awakens positive that her prayers on his behalf have been beneficial. Thus the theme in the second and third visions is one of redemption.

Both the pool of water and the golden cup signify that a new life is being granted to Dinocrates. He will no longer suffer in purgatory-like conditions since he has reached a kind of paradise. The golden cup in Greek myth represented safety, and the one drinking from it was granted immortality.[137] Apart from suggesting a baptism, the pool of water also recalls the fact that public bath complexes, fountains, and other water features were a fixture of cities within the Roman Empire. In particular, Perpetua would have been familiar with the Antonine Baths, the largest bath complex in the African provinces.[138] The public baths in Carthage would have been a popular site for the community to go to refresh themselves and cool off in the heat of the day.

Dinocrates's suffering may be reminiscent of the myth of Tantalus from Homer's *Odyssey*. The idea of an underworld in which there is suffering is not only a Christian concept, but also is contained within classical works. In the Greek version of the afterlife, Tantalus stood in a pool of water with fruit hanging above his head. His eternal punishment was that the water always receded before he could drink it and the fruit was always just out of his reach. Dinocrates's locale, described as a dark place, populated with other persons, could allude to Tartarus, which is underneath the Greek underworld. Pale faces and thirsty crowds are a common part of the descriptions of the underworld in Greek and Roman texts.[139] Aeneas, the hero of Vergil's *Aeneid*, visits the underworld with his father, Anchises, in Book VI and learns that good souls can be reborn. The images of suffering and separation are replaced by ones of restoration and redemption in Perpetua's third vision.

THE EGYPTIAN: VISION FOUR (10.1–10.14)

Her fourth and final vision is also her last entry in the prison diary. She has this vision on the day before she is to fight in the amphitheater. She sees Pomponius the deacon coming to the prison's entrance. He is dressed

---

137   Heffernan (2012, 235) and Salisbury (1997, 106).

138   Heffernan (2012, 221). See also Cooper (2011, 699).

139   Heffernan (2012, 214–18). See also Farina (2009, 22) and Salisbury (1997, 105).

in a white garment and elaborate sandals. He knocks on the door and takes her on a journey through rugged terrain to an amphitheater where she transforms into a man and fights an Egyptian. She is surrounded by handsome men whom she refers to as her assistants. They rub her with oil before she fights. She is victorious, and a giant man tells her, "Peace be with you, daughter." Then he gives her a golden bough with apples. She walks toward the Gate of Life at the end of the amphitheater. One of the last things she records in the diary is that now she knows it is not beasts that she will fight, but the devil. Thus she predicts her martyrdom after this vision as well as after her first one, even though she departs through the Gate of Life at the end of this final vision. This vision also establishes that she is confident her conversion to Christianity will be rewarded. While there are many ways to interpret this vision, one possibility would be to consider this intersection of pagan and Christian symbolism as foreshadowing the diary's final scene in which she transforms a pagan event—the games in the amphitheater—into a celebration of her death as a Christian.

Just as the Good Shepherd–like figure was paternal toward her in the first vision, now Pomponius has replaced her father in this final vision. Pomponius is dressed in a white robe, like the white-robed figures that occur in prior visions and in Revelation. He can function as a Christlike figure who guides her on a difficult journey. The intricate sandals he wears could allude to Mercury, the Roman messenger god and guide to the underworld.[140] Perpetua is rubbed with oil, which recalls baptism as well as athletes preparing for a match. The athletic competition takes place in an amphitheater, reminiscent of the gladiatorial contests in Rome, yet the athlete-martyr who sacrifices everything for God is a Christian symbol (1 Cor 9.24).[141] She fights in a style that is similar to *pankration*, a type of sport in antiquity that resembles wrestling, but the moves in the fight scene cannot fit neatly into any category of ancient sport, especially since there is a part where she is levitating so she can kick the Egyptian in the head (10.11). The golden apples the giant man offers her can suggest the apple tree in Genesis or can recall Hercules's labors (the golden apples of the Hesperides).[142] Golden apples represented eternal life in antiquity. The Gate of Life she walks through at the end is a feature of Roman amphitheaters, used for gladiators who have been spared being put to death.

---

140   Heffernan (2012, 254–58).

141   1 Corinthians 9.24–25 mentions the eternal crown martyrs receive, unlike the temporary crown of athletes. Gold (2011, 243) notes "she *must* prevail because she is fighting for God."

142   Miller (1994, 163–64). See also Heffernan (2012, 268). Shaw (2003, 537) describes how the match between Perpetua and the gladiator is not quite *pankration* and not quite a gladiatorial contest either.

Perpetua's final dream is filled with evidence that she is recognized as a member of a Christian community and has transitioned successfully from the family she was born into to her new Christian one. From the deacon who leads her to the amphitheater and says that he will be with her, to her male attendants in the amphitheater who sing hymns, and finally, to the kiss and wish for peace from the giant, she is never without sympathetic companions in the arena.[143] The Roman and Christian worlds have intersected throughout the *Passio*, and this vision in particular demonstrates how impossible it would be to read the diary without acknowledging these multiple influences on Perpetua's dream-visions. Finally, the audience can see that she will no longer be concerned with Roman laws or her family: now all she has left to do is be victorious in martyrdom. She has achieved the ultimate transformation from her father's daughter and son's mother to a Christian martyr.

TO PREVAIL IS TO BE MALE? GENDER IN PERPETUA'S FINAL VISION

What does Perpetua's victory in the vision have to do with her becoming male? To answer this question, it is necessary to look at how the terms *sex* and *gender* could be applied to persons in antiquity.[144] The Romans did not have a word for gender because gender is a modern construct; in any case, the words would not have been synonyms. Sex in antiquity was biologically determined, but determining gender was a different matter entirely. Gender in antiquity was seen as a changing or moving category, and determining an individual's gender in any given situation depended on a number of factors, including dress, mannerisms, and behavior: "For [the Romans], gender is produced at the place where anatomical sex is intersected by social relations, especially power relations."[145] Perpetua behaved according to the expectations for a male fighter when she fought in the arena, which was traditionally considered a space in the Roman world where men could acquire power and status.

In Perpetua's time, this idea of transitioning from one gender to another in a dream would not have been seen as unusual. Also, she could maintain her sense of modesty if she were male and stripped naked to be rubbed down with oil. The fact that she has a male body during the fight with the Egyptian signified to her audience in antiquity that she had moral superiority in the arena, since men in antiquity were considered morally superior to

---

143   Salisbury (1997, 108–109).

144   Montserrat (2000, 154) details the ways in which gender was a mutable and elastic category for the Romans. See also Williams (2012, 54–77) for a discussion of the roles that sex and gender play in the *Passio*.

145   Montserrat (2000, 153–55) discusses the significance of changing gender in dreams. Cf. Robert (1982, 256).

women.[146] Perpetua remained calm and rational throughout the fight with the Egyptian, and she continued to remain in charge of what happens to her after the fight. Once she had achieved her victory, she could become female again, and the giant man recognized this, calling her "daughter."

There are many possibilities when it comes to interpreting the significance of Perpetua's Egyptian opponent in the amphitheater.[147] The association of Satan with an Egyptian and negative associations with Egypt occur in Revelation 11.8, and Ezekiel 29.3.[148] Positive attributes can be assigned as well: he may be Egyptian to serve an example of a superb athlete and worthy opponent. Or he may be described as "foul in appearance" because he is from Egypt, since the Romans stereotyped the Egyptians as being barbarians, or it may be because of influences on Rome from the East. The Egyptian man as her opponent may symbolize the competing religious influences of the time in the Roman world.[149] The wrestling match with the Egyptian could also be inspired by Perpetua's knowledge of ancient novels, which contain themes of fighting and wrestling. The ancient novel *Aethopica*, for example, contains a fight scene in which the main character defeats an Ethiopian. There is also possible influence from the late-second-century author Apuleius's novel, *The Golden Ass*,[150] which features the Egyptian cult of Isis, a hero who fights in an arena, and the hero's transformation into a donkey and back into himself.

This vision, like the others in the *Passio*, is about transcending limits. Just as the giant man cannot be contained within the boundaries of the amphitheater, neither can Perpetua remain within the established set of behaviors for young Roman matrons. Perpetua assigns herself roles throughout the diary that defy society's expectations for her, and these are reflected within her visions as well as by events outside the visions in the diary. She defies her father's expectations for her and tells him, *Christiana sum*, or "I am a Christian," before she has the visions of Dinocrates and prays on his behalf. Then she reveals in the dream-vision that she is *masculus* before she assumes the role of legal advocate on behalf of others in the prison, an act that would be forbidden for a woman at this time but permitted for men. In her final vision, she has greatly exceeded the limits set on her by society but, most of all, the societal expectations for her gender.

---

146   See Gold (2011, 243): "Perpetua's sudden and brief transformation in *Passio* 10.7 into a *masculus* is both necessary in order to explain her victory over the large Egyptian man and a sign of her confidence in her ability to win." See also Gold (2015, 486).

147   The emperor Septimius Severus associated himself with the Egyptian god Serapis.

148   LeMoine (1999, 203). See also Heffernan (2012, 261).

149   See Gold (2011, 241–43) for a summary of the various scholarly interpretations of what the Egyptian in the vision represents.

150   Farina (2009, 23–26).

THE VISION OF SATURUS (11.1–13.8)

Saturus records his own vision, which is included in the *Passio*. His account, like Perpetua's second and third visions, includes Perpetua acting as an advocate on behalf of others, and in this instance, she is being called on to mediate a disagreement between two church members. The faith that her fellow Christians have in Perpetua to alleviate their suffering has been firmly established by the end of this vision. Tertullian speaks of the peace Christians are able to find when they seek out imprisoned martyrs (*Ad Martyras* 1.6).

Saturus describes how he and Perpetua had already faced martyrdom at the start of the vision. Thus, his vision predicts what happens to their souls in the afterlife. They were carried by four angels to a beautiful garden, where they were set down on the ground and they began to go across a park where they saw some other martyrs that they knew, including one who died while in prison. The four angels recall a passage in the Bible: Ezekiel's vision of four angels who carried the throne of God while flying (Ez 1.5).[151] The angels then encourage them to go meet God.

Just as in Perpetua's first vision, this vision also alludes to Revelation. When they arrive at a location where the walls are made of light, they see four angels standing there (Rev 7.1).[152] White-robed persons sing "Holy, Holy, Holy" before them while they look at a white-haired man with a young-looking face on a throne (Rev 4.8, 1.14). They offer the kiss of peace to the old man. When they leave the area, they see two high-ranking members of the church standing in front of the gates of heaven. The gates, the angels, and the chanting also recall Revelation.[153] Both Perpetua and Saturus envision Heaven as a kind of garden where a Good Shepherd–like figure resides. Their descriptions of vast gardens suggest the Garden of Eden,[154] and their visions of the afterlife offer insight into what the martyrs thought that they would gain from dying. The elders advise Perpetua and Saturus to "go and play," and the two converse briefly, during which time Perpetua informs Saturus that she is "even happier" to be in the garden following her martyrdom than she was "in the flesh" (12.7).

Reconciliation also features prominently in this vision. Saturus relates that the two men standing in front of the gates were the bishop Optatus and the elder Aspasius. They are outside of the gates of Heaven and coming to ask Perpetua to settle a dispute between them. Just as Perpetua had interceded on behalf of her brother following her vision of him, the appeal to

---

151 Heffernan (2012, 276) cites Ezekiel 1.5 and notes "The image of the four angels is likely derived from Scripture."

152 Heffernan (2012, 276–78, 286). Heffernan also points out that the imagery of the light can suggest Revelation 4.6 as well: "God's throne is depicted as one saturated with images of radiance" (284).

153 LeMoine (1999, 203). See also Salisbury (1997, 114).

154 See Heffernan (2012, 276).

Perpetua in this vision is also suggestive of how martyrs could act as intermediaries and grant forgiveness and peace to their peers. In addition, it is significant to note that the bishop and priest have granted Perpetua the authority and the leading role in resolving their argument.[155] Perpetua speaks to them in Greek (see "Roman Education"), and then the angels rebuke the two church members and remind them that they are to offer each other forgiveness. They also chide Optatus for letting his people argue as if they were coming back from the chariot races and fighting among themselves regarding the chariot-racing teams. (Just as amphitheater events were pagan entertainment Christians were supposed to avoid, they were also discouraged from watching the chariot races.)[156] Saturus notices that the angels want to close the gates of Heaven and sees many more martyrs standing there. He awakens to an indescribable scent that leaves him rejoicing over his vision.

Saturus's vision offers a look at the promise of the afterlife for Christians and is meant to be a delight for the senses.[157] The white robes of purity worn by those who stand near the old man contrast with the garden's bright colors and the sounds of the heavenly music, and the sweet fragrance also add to the sensory experience. Like the garden in Perpetua's vision, Saturus' pleasure-garden would offer visual appeal to his fellow Christians and offer them a glimpse of the paradise that awaits them, with its beautiful roses and every other type of flower. He reveals that their fellow martyrs who died earlier are in Heaven waiting for them, thus indicating that in his vision, martyrdom is rewarded. But the vision was also a reminder of the duties the earthly Christian community had, including to help mediate between disagreeing factions and establish peace while waiting for their heavenly kingdom.[158]

PRISON DREAMS: SOME CONCLUSIONS

The Christian community in Carthage placed a high value on visions like the ones documented by Perpetua and Saturus. After Perpetua and Saturus record their visions, they are preserved by the Christian community, and then later on Perpetua's visions are read at services in the early church. Augustine of Hippo mentions the ladder she ascended to God in her first vision (*Sermones* 280.1), and Tertullian also speaks of the martyrs she sees in her

---

155   McGowan (2003, 467). See also Kitzler (2015, 52–55) and Heffernan (2012, 292–95).

156   Beard, North, and Price (1998, 262).

157   LeMoine (1999, 202) also describes the senses as offering "testimony" to the visions' credibility

158   For the martyr as "Christian hero," see Heffernan (2012, 291): ". . . the presence of the martyrs in prison was a source of conflict resolution as well as a source of pride for the community. The martyrs may have been the most zealous of the Christians living in the community, and hence the foundation of the faithful. As long as there were martyrs in prison, the Christians could walk proudly in the midst of pagan scorn."

first vision (*De anima* 55.3–4). Following Perpetua and Felicity's death, the audience for these visions could, therefore, continue to experience the martyr's message. In Perpetua's case, the message in the text is one of "freedom and fulfillment" for those who are waiting for the end of time.[159]

Perpetua and Saturus's visions can also be placed into the context of the Roman cultural interest in prophecy in early-third-century Carthage. The concept of visions that can offer prophecy was not only validated by Christian authors such as Tertullian, but it was also accepted in the popular literature and culture of the time. Septimius Severus was known for his interest in oracles and prophecies because of the connection the ancients made between prophetic dreams and political power.[160]

The symbolism in the visions in the *Passio* comes from a combination of texts in addition to the Bible: additional sources include her education, which would have included ancient Greek and Roman epic, the catechesis of African Christianity, and even pagan influences. The ladder in the first vision, for example, is featured in Roman African culture both as a symbol attributed to the god Saturn and as a warning to members of the church that not all may ascend it successfully. Both Perpetua's and Saturus's visions also allude to other Christian literature such as *The Shepherd of Hermas* and the *Apocalypse of St. Peter*,[161] texts that were written in the middle of the second century CE. The pleasant garden she ascends to may be reminiscent of the *locus amoenus*, or "pleasant space," that one can read about in Greco-Roman literature.[162] Her exposure to the diverse cultural and social milieu in Roman Africa, along with the fact that she was well educated, would surely have inspired the imagery contained in her depictions of the visions. But the recording of the visions is based on Perpetua's *memory* of what happened, since she has written each vision down at some point in time after the dream occurred. Her visions do not exist outside her "narrative recreation" of them. This sets the events in the visions apart from other events in her diary.[163]

Perpetua is surrounded by male figures of authority throughout the diary and her visions are no exception to this. Rather, they reveal her concerns about her departure from her worldly life. Throughout the *Passio*, the figure of the old man in the garden, the deacon Pomponius, Saturus, and her father all appear with her in scenes that draw attention to the choices

---

159   LeMoine (1999, 204).

160   Waldner (2012, 219).

161   See Salisbury (1997, 96–115) for a discussion of other Christian texts (apart from the Bible) that can be seen as influences on the visions in the *Passio*.

162   Miller (1994, 156).

163   Heffernan (2012, 168).

she will make. But she is shown stamping out male authority, whether it is crushing the serpent under her feet in the first vision or on the head of the Egyptian in the last.[164] Her ability to conquer these trials empowers her, and that sense of confidence carries over into the remainder of the diary, as evidenced when she marches into the amphitheater as though she were stepping on the head of the Egyptian.

In addition to preparing herself for martyrdom, Perpetua's visions can also highlight her newfound realization that she can help her family through intercessory prayer, even if she is leaving the material world behind. Perpetua's release from breastfeeding occurs right before her vision of Dinocrates being relieved from his suffering, thus she is freed from earthly concerns for her son and has moved on to more spiritual concerns for others in her family.[165] The visions locate her outside of her familial obligations due to the *patria potestas* and the authority of the Roman law courts.

PERPETUA'S DEATH

Resisting death through physical means was the norm for gladiatorial fights and fights with animals. But Perpetua's fight was a moral one. She was twenty-two years old and looking for a better existence, even if it meant leaving behind everything familiar and her ties to her blood family. She did not just talk about being a good Christian; she stood up for her beliefs, even if it led to suffering and eventually death. Perpetua and her fellow catechumens believed that they would soon face the Judgment Day before God—that the "end days" mentioned at the start of the *Passio* were at hand (1.1). She died not only for what she believed in, but also because she believed others would benefit from her death.

Perpetua did not fit the stereotype of what some persons within the community of imperial Rome might have thought of Christians: that they were an illiterate and uneducated population, often poor and easily persuaded by their leaders to abandon religious practices that Roman officials had established. Perpetua was an educated and articulate person who acted as the catechumens' unofficial leader: in Saturus's vision, Perpetua was the one who demonstrated authority and solved disputes.[166] Although rumors about Christians persisted—that they were prone to debauchery and had magical powers—she and her fellow martyrs defied the stereotypes and expectations and achieved a dignified death.

---

164   Miller (1994, 180). Cf. Lefkowitz (1976, 419).

165   Dronke (1984, 11).

166   Kitzler (2015, 39).

PART III
PERPETUA'S PRISON DIARY

ABOUT THE TRANSLATION OF THE *PASSIO*

The following text of the *Passio* has been translated from Latin.[1] The story is told through multiple voices of people who appear within the text; a narrator; Perpetua; and her teacher, Saturus. In the first two chapters, an anonymous narrator praises the value of reading this text and acts as an editor, describing the text's purpose. In chapter 1, the narrator explains that this work offers an example of faith from the holy martyrs. In chapter 2, the narrator gives the diary a context by providing details about the martyrs, Perpetua and her fellow catechumens: the two slaves, Felicity and Revocatus; and two other men, Saturninus and Secundulus. Finally, the narrator ends chapter 2 by explaining that Perpetua and her fellow catechumens were arrested and that Perpetua wrote her own account of her martyrdom.

The narrator functions as a commentator who has chosen to add to the text, in order to present its audience with the "right" way to understand the events and the text's "purpose," and to prepare the audience for what follows in Perpetua's own words. The narrator emphasizes key details about Perpetua at the start: her social status, her role as a wife and mother, and the fact that she was well educated. Much of this comes out in the diary: her articulate voice and mention of her son allow the audience to learn some details of her background, but it appears as if the editor-narrator wants the audience to be assured of her socially acceptable credentials to be a hero-martyr.[2]

Chapters 3 through 10, authored by Perpetua, encourage the reader to see how she experienced life as a Christian in the third century CE. The audience learns about her relationships with her son and father and discovers

---

1   I consulted the Latin texts found in Heffernan (2012) and Halporn (1984) when preparing my translation of the *Passio*. In the very first paragraph of the *Passio*, there are a few parts of the text where the narrator employs words or phrases from the Bible and this is indicated in italics in the translation.

2   Kitzler (2015, 56–80) provides a more detailed discussion of textual interpretation and editorial staging of Perpetua's diary. Kitzler also offers a comprehensive look at the *nachleben* of the *Passio* until the end of the fifth century. See also Cotter-Lynch (2016), who traces the textual genealogy of Perpetua's story from the third to the thirteenth century.

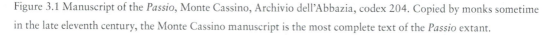

Figure 3.1 Manuscript of the *Passio*, Monte Cassino, Archivio dell'Abbazia, codex 204. Copied by monks sometime in the late eleventh century, the Monte Cassino manuscript is the most complete text of the *Passio* extant.

the family ties she gave up to gain new ones with members of the Christian faith. Her narrative voice differs from the earlier narrator's voice.

In chapters 11 through 13, Saturus, who is the catechumens' leader, describes his vision of martyrdom, in which Perpetua appears.[3] Although the narrator does not mention Saturus at the beginning of the *Passio*, Perpetua explains in chapter 4 that he was not present at the time of the group's arrest and so he voluntarily joined them later in prison. Finally, the narrator returns in chapters 14 through 21 to describe the martyrs' deaths and to end the work by declaring that the account of the martyrs' courageous acts should be read. Although Perpetua is the central figure of the story, note that the text is actually called *The Passion of Perpetua and Felicity*. Perpetua never mentions the slave Felicity in her part of the text. Instead, the narrator tells Felicity's story in chapter 15.

At the end of the text, the narrator focuses on Perpetua's desire to demonstrate her strength and bravery while dying. She does not appear afraid,

---

3   Sometime between 203 and 210 CE, while acting as an editor, the narrator combined the narratives of Saturus and Perpetua.

nor does she waver in her steadfast faith. The narrator concludes that the martyrs' model deaths serve as an example for future Christians.

A BRIEF HISTORY OF THE TEXT

Most scholars of the *Passio* now consider it to be an authentic text, even though there is still some debate over certain details. What makes Perpetua's *Passio* different from other accounts? The *Passio* includes her first-person experience, which is framed by an eyewitness account of the martyrs' deaths and editorial commentary. While the text is not considered primarily to be a historical document (although historical figures are mentioned within it), there are certain aspects that have come to be of interest, including the parts that relate to gender roles and to social hierarchies. According to the conventions of the time, only after her death as a martyr should Perpetua have had authority as someone to whom the living could pray and ask for assistance, yet before her death she appears to be the martyrs' unofficial leader and seems to be able to influence authority figures.

Perpetua's story is not the oldest extant Christian text in Latin. It is the second oldest, following the *Acta Martyrum Scillitanorum*, which describes the martyrdom of twelve Christians in 180 CE. While numerous accounts of martyrdom in early Christian literature exist, we will briefly focus on two types: the *acta* and the *passiones*. *Acta* were brief reports recorded when Christians were brought into Roman law courts and appeared before the Roman magistrate. They detail the court proceedings, including the names of those involved, the interrogation and subsequent sentencing, and the execution of those who professed their Christian faith. *Passiones*—which were sometimes also referred to as *martyria*—provided much more detail than *acta* about the martyrs. *Passiones* were often eyewitness accounts and could include descriptions of the arrests, accounts of miracles performed by martyrs, and other details besides just the names, sentencing, and the martyrs' execution.

Multiple versions of Perpetua's story exist. In addition to the *Passio*, there is a briefer account in Latin known as the *Acta Perpetuae*, and there is also a version in Greek. Both appear to have been derived from the longer *Passio*. Scholars date the events in the *Passio* to 203 CE for the following reasons: the text itself mentions the birthday celebrations of Caesar Geta (7.9); historical documents that discuss the Severan Dynasty provide the dates in Geta's life that validate Perpetua's account; and Tertullian's *De Anima* 55.4 , which can be dated between 203 and 209/210 CE, also mentions Perpetua.[4]

---

4   See Kitzler (2015, 13–17) for the dating of the *Passio*. See also Heffernan (2012, 66).

THE PASSION OF PERPETUA AND FELICITY

1.1 If ancient examples of the faith, which attest to God's grace and work to instruct man, were collected in writing for this purpose, so that God is honored and man is comforted by their reading, as if through a revisiting of those acts, why shouldn't even new examples be collected to serve either objective? **2.** Indeed, because these examples also will one day be old and considered necessary for future generations, even if in their present time, these new acts are regarded as having a lesser authority, due to the usual respect given to the past. **3.** But let those who believe that there is one power of one Holy Spirit for all the ages of time perceive this: newer things ought to be considered as greater, as they are the closest to the end days, in accordance with the abundance of grace decreed in the end time. **4.** *In the final days, God says, I shall pour out my Spirit on all flesh, and their sons and daughters will prophesize, and I shall pour out my Spirit on my servants and my handmaidens, and the young shall see visions and the old shall dream dreams.* **5.** And so we also, who both acknowledge and honor those prophecies and the recent visions equally pledged, and who consider the other powers of the Holy Spirit as an aid for the Church (to which also it was sent the same Spirit in order to distribute gifts among all, *just as the Lord has distributed to each one*) out of necessity both collect and celebrate the new by reading for the glory of God, lest anyone weak or disheartened in the faith may think divine grace dwelled only among the ancients in granting the honor either of martyrdom or of revelations, since God always achieves what he has promised, as evidence to the nonbelievers and as a blessing to the believers. **6.** And so, *what we have heard and what we have touched, we announce to you* brothers and little sons, *so you* who were involved might remember the glory of God, *and you* who learn about it now through hearing it *may have communion* with the holy martyrs, and through those martyrs *with our Lord Jesus Christ*, to whom is glory and honor for all time. Amen.

2.1 The young catechumens, Revocatus and his fellow slave Felicity, Saturninus and Secundulus, were taken into custody. Among them also was Vibia Perpetua, well born, well educated, and married lawfully. **2.** She had a father and mother and two brothers, one of whom was her fellow catechumen, and a young son at her breast. **3.** She herself, moreover, was about twenty-two years old. From this point on she herself narrates the whole account of her martyrdom, as she left it written in her own hand and according to her own mind.

3.1 "While we were still under observation," she said, "and my father wanted to destroy my faith with his arguments, he kept trying to dislodge me from my beliefs because of his affection. 'Father,' I said, 'do you see that vase lying there, some little pitcher or other, for the sake of example?' And he said, 'Yes.' 2. And I said to him, 'Is it able to be called by any other name other than what it is?' 'No,' he said. 'I too cannot call myself by any other name other than what I am, a Christian.'" 3. Then my father, disturbed by this word, hurled himself at me as if he would pluck my eyes out. But he only scared me and he left in defeat, along with the devil's arguments. 4. Then for a few days, when I was separated from my father, I thanked the Lord because he was not there. 5. During that time we were baptized and the Holy Spirit told me to seek nothing else from the water of baptism except the endurance of the flesh. After a few days we were taken into prison; and I was very afraid, since I had never experienced such a dark place. 6. Oh what a harsh day! The intense heat thanks to the crowds. The terrifying threats of the soldiers. And most of all, I was tormented by worry over my child there. 7. Then Tertius and Pomponius, the blessed deacons who took care of us, established by bribe that we were let out for a few hours to refresh ourselves in a more pleasant place in the prison. 8. Then going out from the prison all of us were at leisure: I was nursing my child who was already faint from hunger; worried on his behalf, I talked with my mother and I comforted my brother. To them I entrusted my son; I was suffering greatly because I could see their concern for my well-being. 9. I suffered many days occupied with such concerns, and I gained permission for my child to remain in prison with me. And at once I regained my health and was freed from suffering and anxiety regarding my child. And the prison suddenly became a palace for me, so that I would prefer to be there than any other place.

4.1 Then my brother spoke to me: "Lady Sister, already you possess great worth, so much that you might request a vision and it would be shown to you, whether there will be suffering or escape." 2. And I, who knew that I could converse with God, whose great blessings I had experienced, made a promise confidently to him, saying, "I will tell you tomorrow." And I asked and this is what was shown to me. 3. I saw a bronze ladder of amazing length reaching all the way up to heaven, and it was narrow, so that it was only possible to climb it one by one, and on the ladder's sides, every type of iron tool was attached. There were swords, lances, hooks, knives, and darts, so that anyone who would climb negligently, or not looking up, would be cut to pieces, and his flesh would stick to the iron. 4. And there was a serpent of amazing size lying under this ladder ready to ambush the climbers, and he frightened people from climbing. 5. Yet Saturus climbed first. (At that time when we had been led away, he had not been there. Afterward, he had voluntarily surrendered himself on our account, because he had instructed us.) 6. And he arrived at the top of the ladder and he turned and said to me, "Perpetua, I am waiting for you, but take care that the serpent does not bite you." And I said, "In the name of Jesus Christ, he will not harm me." 7. From below the ladder, as if fearing me, the serpent slowly stuck out its head. As if I was stamping on the first step, I stepped on its head, and I climbed up. 8. And I saw the vast space of a garden and sitting in the middle a white-haired old man dressed as a shepherd, a great man, milking sheep, and many thousands standing around dressed in white. 9. And he lifted his head and looked at me and said to me, "You are welcome, child." And he called me and from the cheese that he was milking, gave to me about a mouthful; and I took it in clasped hands and I chewed it. And everyone standing around said, "Amen." 10. And at the sound of their voice I awakened. And I was still chewing something sweet. And at once I related my vision to my brother and we understood that there would be suffering ahead of us, and we no longer had any hope in this world.

5.1 After a few days, a rumor spread quickly that we would be granted a hearing. My father arrived abruptly from the city, consumed by worry, and he came up to me in order to dislodge me from my beliefs, saying: 2. "Daughter, have mercy on my white hairs, have mercy on your father, if I am worthy to be called father by you. If with these hands I have brought you to the prime of your age, if I have put you first before all of your brothers, don't dishonor me publicly. 3. Consider your brothers, consider your mother, think of your maternal aunt, think of your son, who will not be able to live without you. 4. Bury your pride, do not destroy us all: for none of us will speak freely if you suffer punishment." 5. He was saying these things because of a father's piety, kissing my hands and throwing himself down before my feet. Crying, he no longer called me his daughter, but called me lady. 6. And I was sad for my father's downfall, because he was the only one from my whole family who would be unhappy at my suffering. And I consoled him by saying these words: "What happens on that criminal's scaffold will be what God wills. For know that we will not be under our own control, but in God's hands." And overcome with grief, he departed from me.

6.1 On a different day, while we were at lunch, we were suddenly dragged away for the hearing. And we reached the forum. At once rumor ran through the nearby parts of the forum, and the crowd became immense. 2. We climbed up onto the platform. The others confessed when interrogated. They came to me, and my father appeared there with my son. He pulled me down from the stair saying, "Make the sacrifice, have pity on your child." 3. And the procurator Hilarianus, who at that time had accepted the right of the sword in place of the deceased proconsul Minucius Timinianus, said, "Have pity on the white hairs of your father, have pity on your young son. Make the sacrifice on behalf of the emperors' health." 4. And I answered, "I won't do it." And Hilarianus said, "Are you a Christian?" And I answered, "I am a Christian." 5. And since my father was determined to get me to reject my beliefs, he was ordered by Hilarianus to be thrown down, and beaten with a rod. And I grieved for my father's misfortune, as if I had been struck, thus I grieved on behalf of his miserable old age. 6. Then the procurator sentenced all of us and condemned us to the beasts; and we went down to the prison cheerfully. 7. Then since my child was accustomed to nurse from me and to remain in prison with me, I immediately sent the deacon, Pomponius, to my father, demanding the child. 8. But my father was unwilling to give him back. And as God willed it, he did not wish to nurse anymore, and my breasts did not become inflamed, and I was not tormented by breast pain or by concern for my child.

7.1 After a few days while we were all praying, suddenly in the middle of our prayer, a voice came from me and I said the name Dinocrates. And I was shocked because he had never come into my mind before this time, and I grieved, remembering his misfortune. 2. And I knew at once that I was worthy and that I ought to intercede on his behalf. And I began to pray for a long time for him and to cry out to God. 3. This was shown to me at once on that night: 4. I saw Dinocrates going out from a dark place where there were also many others. He was very hot and thirsty, with a dirty face and a pale complexion, and with the wound in his face which he had when he died. 5. This Dinocrates had been my brother in the flesh, seven years old, whose skin cancer on his face led to his painful demise, so the manner of his death was hateful to all. 6. So I prayed for him. But a great divide existed between him and me, so that we were unable to approach each other. 7. There was a pool full of water in that place where Dinocrates was and it had a rim higher than the boy's height. And Dinocrates stretched himself up like he was trying to drink. 8. I was sad, because although the pool held water, due to the height of the rim, he would not be able to drink. 9. And I woke up, and I realized that my brother was in trouble. But I had faith that I was going to help him. And I was praying on behalf of him all the days until we were transferred into the military prison. For we were going to fight in the military games, on Geta Caesar's birthday . 10. And I prayed day and night for him, groaning and crying, so that my prayer might be granted.

8.1 On the day we were spending time in the stocks, this vision was shown to me: I saw that place I had seen before, and Dinocrates was clean, well dressed, and looked refreshed. Where he had been wounded, I saw a scar. 2. And I saw that pool I had seen before, with its rim now lowered to the boy's belly button, and he drew water from it without stopping. 3. And there was a golden cup full of water above the rim. And Dinocrates approached and began to drink from it; and the cup did not run out.

4. When he quenched his thirst, he began to play, rejoicing as small children do. And I woke up. Then I realized that he was freed from his pain.

9.1 Then after a few days Pudens, the military adjutant, who was the overseer of the prison, realizing that there was great power in us, began to hold us in high regard. He admitted many visitors to see us so that we could take comfort in one another. 2. When the day of the games approached, however, my father, worn out by grief, came to me and began to pluck out his beard and throw it onto the ground, and he threw himself face down, and cursed his old age, and he said such words as might move all creation. 3. And I pitied him because of his unhappy old age.

10.1 On the day before we were to fight, I saw this in a vision: the deacon Pomponius had come to the prison's entrance and was beating on it loudly. 2. I went out and I opened the door for him. He was dressed in an unbelted white tunic and his shoes had elaborate straps. 3. And he said to me, "Perpetua, we are waiting for you; come." He held my hand and we began to go through terrain that was rough and winding. 4. We had just arrived all out of breath at the amphitheater, when he led me into the middle of the arena, and he said to me: "Don't be afraid, for I am here with you and I suffer with you." And then he left. 5. I caught sight of the huge, stunned crowd. Since I knew that I had been condemned to the beasts, I was amazed because the beasts were not being unleashed upon me. 6. A certain Egyptian, who was horrible in appearance and determined to fight with me, came out along with his assistants. Handsome young men came to me as well; they were my supporters and assistants. 7. I was undressed and I became a man. My supporters began to rub me with oil, just as they usually do for an athletic contest. In turn I saw that Egyptian was rolling in the sand. 8. Then a man came out of such great size that he even rose above the highest point of the amphitheater. He was dressed in an unbelted tunic, a purple one with two stripes extending down the middle of his chest, and intricate sandals decorated with gold and silver. He was carrying a rod as if he were a gladiatorial trainer and a green branch on which there were golden apples. 9. And he called for silence and said, "If the Egyptian is victorious over her, he will kill her with a sword; if she is victorious over him, she will receive this branch." Then he left. 10. We approached one another and we began to throw punches. He wanted to grab my feet; but I began kicking him in the face with my heels. 11. And I was raised up into the air and I began to kick him as if I was not treading on the ground. But when I saw him hesitate, I joined hands so that I interlocked my fingers and I seized hold of his head. Then he fell on his face and I trampled on his head. 12. And the crowd began to shout and my supporters began to sing psalms. And I approached the gladiatorial trainer and I received the branch. 13. He kissed me and he spoke to me: "Daughter, peace be with you." And I began to go with glory to the Gate of Life. **14.** And I awakened. Then I realized that I was not going to fight against wild beasts but the devil; and I knew that the victory was mine. **15.** This is what I did all the way up to the day before the games; if anyone wishes to write about the final act of the games, however, let him write about it.

11.1 But blessed Saturus also described a vision of his own, which he wrote down himself. **2.** We had experienced martyrdom, he said, and we withdrew from the flesh, and we began to be carried off toward the east by four angels, whose hands did not touch us. **3.** But we were going, not lying on our backs facing upward, but as if we were climbing a gently sloping hill. **4.** And when we were first set free from this world, we saw an immense light, and I said to Perpetua—for she was by my side — "This is what God has promised to us: we have received His promise." **5.** And while we were being carried by the four angels, a great promenade appeared before us. It was a sort of pleasure-garden containing rose trees and flowers of every kind. **6.** The trees were as tall as cypress trees and their leaves were falling without stopping. **7.** But there in the garden were four other angels, brighter than the others, who, when they saw us, gave us honor, and they said to the other angels, "Here they are! Here they are!" with admiration. And the four angels who were carrying us were very frightened and they put us down. **8.** And we went on foot across the park. **9.** There we found Iocundus and Saturninus and Artaxius, who were burned alive in the same persecution as us, and Quintus, a martyr who himself had departed from life while in prison. And we asked them where the others were. 10. The angels said to us, "Come first, enter, and greet the Lord."

12.1 And we came near a place whose walls appeared to be built from light, and before the entrance of that place, four angels were standing, and they dressed those who entered in white robes. **2.** We came in and we heard a chorus say in unison, "Holy, holy, holy," and they did not stop. **3.** And we saw someone sitting in that same place who looked as if he were an old man: he had snow-white hair but his face appeared youthful. We did not see his feet. **4.** On his right and on his left there were four elders, and many other elders were standing behind them. **5.** We came in and we stood before the throne in admiration, and the four angels raised us up and we kissed him. And with his hand he touched us lightly on our faces. **6.** And the other elders said to us, "Let us stand." And we stood, and gave the kiss of peace. And the elders said to us, "Go and play." **7.** And I said to Perpetua, "You have what you want!" And she said to me, "I give thanks to God that just as I was happy in the flesh, now I am even happier here."

13.1 We went out, and we saw before the gates the bishop Optatus to the right and on the left the learned elder Aspasius, and they were sad and set apart. **2.** And they prostrated themselves at our feet and said to us:

"Make peace between us, since you have departed and left us behind in this way." **3.** We said to them: "Surely you, our bishop and priest, are not the sort to throw yourselves at our feet?" We were moved and we embraced them. **4.** Perpetua began to speak to them in Greek, and we led them aside in the pleasure-garden under a rose tree. **5.** And while we were talking with them, the angels said to them: "Allow them to rest, and if you have any disagreements between yourselves, forgive one another." **6.** And the angels rebuked them and said to Optatus: "Restore order among your people, since they have come to you as if returning from the races and arguing about the teams." **7.** Thus it seemed to us as if they wished to close the gates. **8.** And we began to recognize many brothers there, also martyrs. We were all nurtured and left satisfied by an indescribable scent. Then I woke up rejoicing.

14.1 These are the glorious visions of the very martyrs, most blessed Saturus and Perpetua, which they themselves have written. **2.** But God called for Secundulus's departure from this world earlier while still in prison, for it was not without God's grace that he was spared the beasts. **3.** Yet he certainly knew the sword in his flesh, even if not in his soul.

15.1 Now, regarding Felicity, God's grace touched her in this way. **2.** When she was in her eighth month (for she was pregnant when she was arrested), she was in great sorrow as the date of the games was becoming imminent, since she feared her death would be postponed because of her pregnancy (since it is not permitted for pregnant women to be presented for execution), and that she might spill her holy and innocent blood later on, among the other, actual criminals. **3.** But her fellow martyrs were grievously saddened that they might leave behind so good a companion as a lonely comrade on the path to the same hope (of salvation). **4.** And so they poured out abundant prayer to God, with a continuous cry in unison, two days before the games. **5.** Immediately after their prayer, her labor began. And when, because of the natural difficulties of being in labor during the eighth month, she suffered while giving birth, one of the assistant prison wardens said to her, "How much do you suffer at this moment? What will you do when you are thrown before the beasts, which you were not afraid of, when you were unwilling to make the sacrifice?" **6.** And she answered, "At this moment, I suffer what I suffer; in that place, however, there will be another in me who suffers on behalf of me, since now I am going to suffer on His behalf." **7.** So she delivered a baby girl, whom a sister raised for her as her own daughter.

16.1 Since therefore the Holy Spirit has given permission, and by granting permission has willed the account of the contest to be written down, although we are undeserving to add to such glorious descriptions, nevertheless as if we are at the command of the most holy Perpetua, we carry out the obligation, adding one proof regarding her perseverance and sublimity of spirit. **2.** When the tribune harshly chastised them, because he feared the warnings of the most deluded men, that the prisoners might be able to be removed from prison by some magical spells, Perpetua spoke to him face to face: **3.** "Why don't you allow us, since we are certainly Caesar's most distinguished condemned prisoners who will fight on his birthday, to refresh ourselves? Is it not to your credit if we are led forth to that place a bit fatter?" **4.** The tribune shuddered in horror and blushed; and so he ordered them to be treated more humanely and he allowed her brothers and the others to enter the prison and be refreshed with them; now the military adjutant himself had become a believer.

17.1 On the day before the games when there was the last meal, which they call "free," as much as it was possible they dined not as if at a "free meal," but as if at a "love feast." They spoke as fearlessly to the people as they were accustomed to, warning the crowd of the judgment of God. They were calling to witness their happiness at their own suffering, and making fun of the curiosity of those who rushed to see them, when Saturus spoke: **2.** "Is tomorrow not enough for you? Why do you look gladly at what you hate? Today we are friends, tomorrow we will be enemies. Yet take careful note of our faces, that you may recognize us on that day." **3.** So all went away astonished from that prison, and many from the crowd began to believe.

18.1 The day of their victory dawned, and they marched from the prison into the amphitheater as if into heaven, joyful with radiant faces, and if they happened to tremble, it was with joy, not fear. **2.** Perpetua was following with a luminous face and calm step as the bride of Christ, as the beloved of God, casting down the gaze of all by the strength of her eyes. **3.** Likewise Felicity, rejoicing that she had delivered her child safely so that she might fight the beasts, was passing from blood to blood, from the midwife to the net-carrying gladiator, as she was about to be washed after childbirth in a second baptism. **4.** And when they were led to the gate and compelled to put on robes, the men were dressed as the priests of Saturn, and the women as the priestesses of Ceres. Perpetua, that noble woman, steadfastly resisted all the way up to the end. **5.** For she said, "We came here of our own free will precisely so that our freedom might not be obstructed. Likewise we surrendered our lives, so that we would not have to do any such thing. We made this pact with you." **6.** Injustice recognized justice. The tribune yielded and just as they were, they were led in without costumes. **7.** Perpetua was singing a psalm, already stepping on the head of the Egyptian. Revocatus and Saturninus and Saturus were threatening the crowds who had come to watch. **8.** Then when they reached the gaze of Hilarianus, by nod and gesture they began to say to Hilarianus: "You condemn us," they said; "God, however, condemns you." **9.** The crowd, which was provoked by this, demanded that they be driven with whips along a line of beast-fighting gladiators; and for their part they were rejoicing because they had obtained some part of Christ's sufferings.

19.1 But the one who had said: "Ask and you shall receive" to those asking had given the death that each had desired. **2.** For whenever they talked among themselves, about the hope of their martyrdom, Saturninus said that he wished he would be thrown to all types of beasts, as certainly he would wear the more glorious crown. **3.** And so at the start of the spectacle, he and Revocatus fought with a leopard and while they were on the platform, they were also harassed by a bear. **4.** Saturus, however, hated nothing more than the bear, but he assumed that he would perish now by one bite of the leopard. **5.** And so, when he was given to a wild boar, it was the hunter who had tied him to the wild boar who was instead gored by that very beast. He passed away a few days after the games; Saturus was only dragged. **6.** And when he was tied on the bridge for the bear, the bear was unwilling to leave its cage. And so Saturus, uninjured, was called back for the second time.

20.1 For the young women, however, the devil prepared, contrary to customary practice, a very fierce cow as he sought to imitate their sex by means of the beast. **2.** And so the women were led out naked and covered in nets. The crowd shuddered at the sight of the one, a charming young girl, and the other, who had recently given birth and whose breasts were dripping with milk. **3.** And so they were called back and clad in unbelted robes. First Perpetua was thrown down and she landed on her back. **4.** And when she sat up, her tunic was torn on the side and she pulled it together to cover her thigh, more mindful of modesty than pain. **5.** Then she asked for a hairpin and pinned up her disheveled hair; for it is not fitting for a martyr to suffer with loosened hair, since she be might appear to be mourning in her glory. **6.** And so she got up and when she saw Felicity had been thrown to the ground, she approached her and pulled her hand and got her up. And they both stood side by side. **7.** And after they had won over the heartless crowd, they were called back to the Gate of Life. **8.** There Perpetua was met by a certain catechumen named Rusticus who clung to her. And as if she awakened from a deep sleep (she was so completely caught up in the spirit and in ecstasy), she began to look around and said to all the astonished onlookers: "When," she asked, "are we to be brought before that cow, or whatever?" **9.** And when she heard what had already happened, at first she did not believe it, until she recognized certain marks of distress on her body and on her clothing. **10.** Then she called over her brother and that catechumen and she said to them, "All of you stand strong in faith and love one another, and do not lose your belief because of our sufferings."

21.1 Meanwhile, Saturus was at another gate encouraging Pudens the soldier while saying, "It is certainly," he said, "just as I presumed and I predicted. I have not felt any beast yet. And now, believe with all of your heart: I will go out there and be finished off by one bite from a leopard." 2. And all at once at the end of the game, he was thrown in front of a leopard and covered in blood from one bite, so that the crowd cried out, as a witness to the second baptism of blood, "Washed and saved! Washed and saved!" 3. For truly the one who was washed in this manner was saved. 4. Then he said to Pudens the soldier, "Farewell," and "remember both the faith and me. And do not let these things upset you, but let them strengthen you." 5. And at once he demanded the ring from his finger, and dipping it in his wound, he returned it to Pudens as an inheritance, a token he is leaving behind for him as a memory of his blood. 6. Then, since he was now half-dead, he was thrown on the ground with the others in the usual place to have his throat cut. 7. And when the crowd demanded them in the middle of the amphitheater, so that their eyes could be accomplices to murder as the sword pierced the martyrs' bodies, the martyrs rose unassisted and they arranged themselves as the crowd wished. First they kissed one another, and through this solemn ritual of peace, they brought their martyrdom to an ideal end. 8. The others, however, received the sword in silence and did not move. Saturus in particular, who had been the first to go up before, was the first to surrender his spirit, for he awaited Perpetua. 9. Perpetua, however, so that she would taste some pain, cried out as she was stabbed between the bones, and she guided the hesitant right hand of the inexperienced gladiator to her throat. 10. Perhaps such a woman, who was feared by the unclean spirit, would not have been able to be killed, except that she herself wished it. 11. O you most brave and blessed martyrs! O you truly called and chosen in the glory of our Lord Jesus Christ! The one who exalts, honors, and adores this glory, by all means ought to read these examples of the faith, which are no less worthy than the old ones to instruct the Church, so that also these new examples of bravery bear witness that the one and the same Holy Spirit is still active, and the all-powerful God, the Father and his son, our Lord Jesus Christ, to whom there is glory and boundless power for all time. Amen.

PART IV

CONCLUSION

FURTHER INTERPRETATIONS OF THE TEXT

There are many different ways to interpret the events in the diary and various ways to explain Perpetua's actions. One question this diary raises is, "What was Perpetua's place in society?" One scholar has suggested that Perpetua appeared so captivated by Saturus's teachings that she became a fanatical devotee. Therefore, she would no longer feel she had to listen to the "reasonable pleas" from her father or Roman officials to show proper piety to Rome and the emperor: "Perpetua was obviously an adored only daughter who grew up into a spoilt and willful young woman, but in her case, her frustrations drove her into fanatical adherence to an apocalyptic form of Christianity and hostility to the society in which she had been reared."[1] This interpretation of Perpetua's behavior is based, in part, on the reactions of her father and the other male authority figures who responded to her desire to throw away her family's reputation and her own life because they perceived her actions as threatening to the *mos maiorum*.

Another interpretation portrays a determined young woman who eloquently defended herself and her fellow prisoners and freely chose to go to her death: "To fulfill duties with appropriate decorum and to control personal destiny by courageous action are the attributes and actions of an honorable man of authority. These are also the attributes and actions of two young mothers, the slave Felicity and the matron Perpetua."[2] Here, too, this interpretation of Perpetua's behavior is based, in part, on the reactions of others in the text, but it also takes into account the role of the amphitheater's crowd in assigning her authority and giving her power. In particular, the crowd validated her right to die with honor and decorum by being shocked when she and Felicity appeared in front of them wrapped only in nets. When they demanded that the women be clothed before they returned to the arena, they were recognizing them as the heroes, not the villains, of this story.

1   Frend (1993, 175).

2   LeMoine (1996, 218).

We cannot, of course, know what Perpetua was thinking when she refused to make the sacrifice to the emperor. Both scholars assume that Perpetua liked to challenge authority, although the scholars reach very different conclusions about how to describe her character as a result of these tendencies. But we cannot deny that she experienced a transformation in the diary: from mother and daughter to Christian martyr.

The persons mentioned in the *Passio* do not always behave according to societal expectations for their gender or status at the time—but should we expect them to, given the circumstances? Rather than look for one particular way to interpret the text, this work has explored women's changing roles in society at that time through an examination of why Christianity appealed to the martyrs and why Perpetua rejected civic and familial authority.

THE *PASSIO* AFTER 203 CE

On feast days and at Christian worship, stories about the lives of the saints were told. Christians valued accounts written by martyrs since the testimonies established a record of the injustices committed against their community and the martyrs' brave deeds encouraged the faithful. These stories also aided Christians in distinguishing their beliefs from non-Christian beliefs.[3] For historians, these accounts are useful because they offer a record of the ways in which the Roman law courts prosecuted individuals.[4]

A liturgical reading of the *Passio* offered a Christian congregation the chance to relive the events. Perpetua's words were read aloud to congregations in North African churches, and Augustine preached sermons on her martyrdom and the visions (*Sermones* 280–82). In Augustine's eyes, the women attained remarkable achievements, but their deeds glorified God. Kitzler argues that Augustine emphasizes the women as married to Christ (281.1) and offers an explanation for their sometimes masculine behavior: Christ was acting through them (*Serm.* 280.4). Thus, Perpetua and Felicity were transformed into icons with a new emphasis on their status as married woman.[5]

Commentators took passages from the *Passio* out of context and altered them to become "a 'correct' interpretation for the benefit of the contemporary public."[6] Tertullian refers to Perpetua as *fortissima martyr*, or

---

3 Kitzler (2015, 36).

4 Shaw (2003, 553).

5 See Kitzler (2015, 90).

6 Kitzler (2015, 55). See also Salisbury (1997, 171–72).

"the bravest of martyrs" (*De anima* 55.4), indicating the high regard in which her story was held. Immediately following in *De anima*, he also comments on her visions and adds his interpretation to them: she mentions the martyrs she sees in paradise and Tertullian grants her observation the authority to suggest that all martyrs go directly to Heaven. This part of her vision, taken out of the *Passio*'s context and given this emphasis in Tertullian's writing, provides yet another example of the way in which editors and commentators have shaped the perception and understanding of Perpetua's words.

There is evidence within the early church that women and men worshipped together and that women were regarded as equals within the congregation. As the structure of the church became more formal, however, women were excluded from leadership roles. Eventually, the goal became to suggest that equality would be available for women in the afterlife. But even though both Perpetua and Felicity were praised for their conduct, these women were not figures of authority within the early church except in the ways in which the church granted them a role of official capacity, such as when church leaders read passages from the *Passio* on special feast days.

Perpetua's diary and the memory of her deeds remain a part of the Roman Catholic Church today. She and Felicity are among the women mentioned in the Roman Canon of the Catholic Mass. Just as the narrator of the *Passio* framed Perpetua's account with his own commentary and gave her words a context, later there became a designated day upon which to commemorate the women. The obligatory memorial of Perpetua and Felicity is still celebrated annually on March 7 in the Roman Catholic Church.

Thus, after Perpetua's death, the *Passio* rapidly became a popular and authoritative text in the early church. But it soon became clear that the church held the power to be an intercessory force between Christians and Christ. The social structure of the church shifted from the focus on the martyrs and placed more emphasis on the religious leaders' roles in celebrating the liturgy. And as time went on, the *Passio* became a text used to recall the martyrs' heroic deeds similar to the way the first narrator talks about the heroic deeds of the ancestors serving as an example to the people.

In the *Passio*, Perpetua is not a perfect heroine; instead, she comes off as relatable and her behavior seems human, not saintly. She fights with her father, she is terrified in prison, and she leaves her child behind. Her narrative conveys a sense of urgency to her story, and she portrays herself in the *Passio* not as an extremist who is eager for death, but as a Christian who faces assignment to the arena and subsequent martyrdom with bravery. She is the one who bravely grabs the blade from the gladiator assigned to kill her and guides it into her throat. Within the diary, she appeals to the

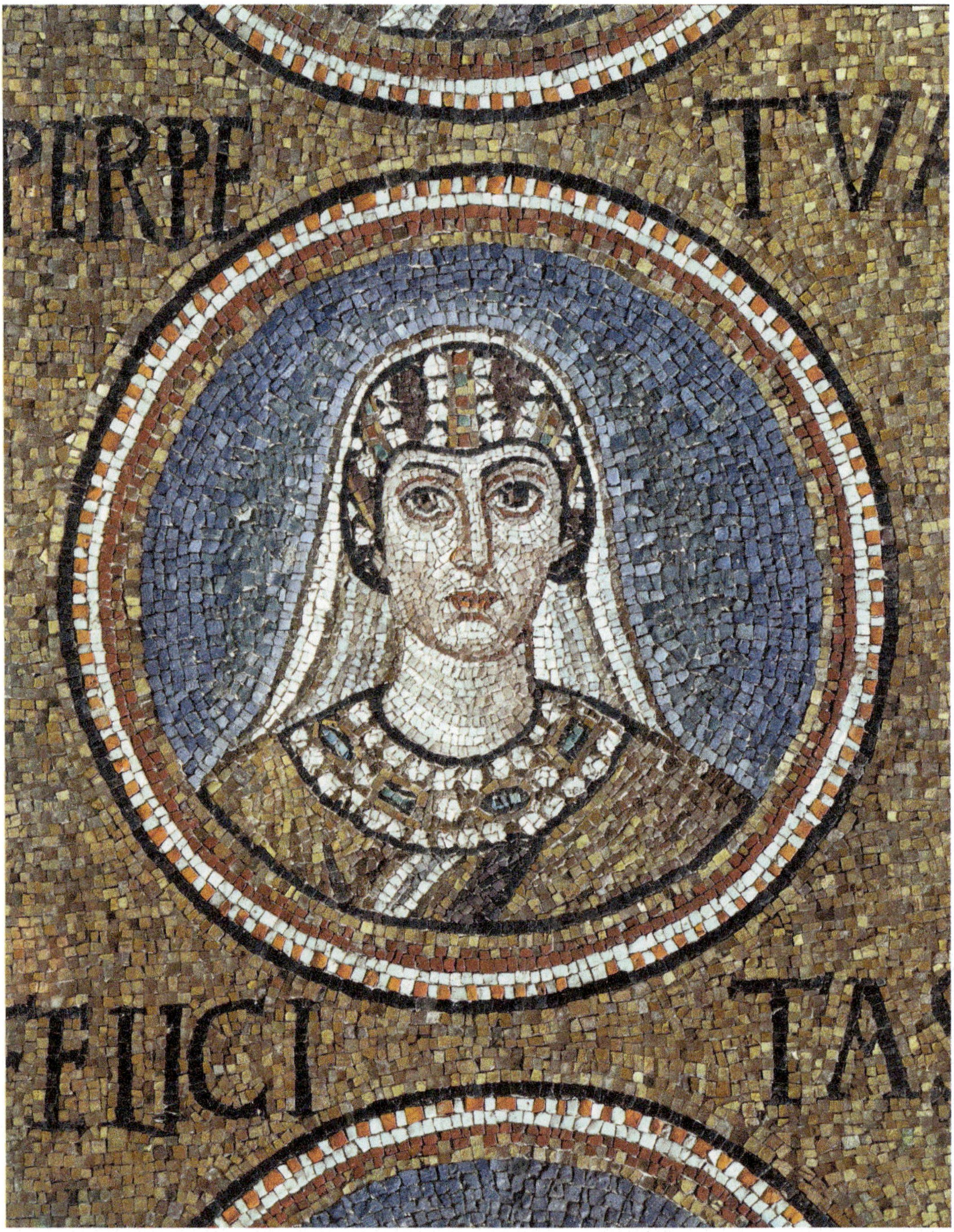
PERPE
TVA
FELICI
TAS

Figure 4.1 Mosaic of Perpetua from Ravenna, Italy, Fifth Century.

audience, who find her a sympathetic figure at the end of her life, and in the course of the catechumens' final days, there are several indications that others have become believers, such as Pudens and members of the crowd who gather to see the martyrs' last prison meal.

FURTHER READING

This work depicts Christianity in the early third century CE, and, more generally, life in Roman Africa during the reign of Septimius Severus. Many subject areas addressed in the book—including Christianity, the daily life and material culture of the Roman Empire, and, in particular, Roman Africa—are vast, and by extension, the scholarly resources on these topics are considerable. The following list offers recommended reading for this book's more general audience. But it is by no means an exhaustive list. For an additional and more specialized list of works consulted, see the Bibliography.

THE *PASSIO PERPETUAE ET FELICITATIS*

Numerous volumes have been written on the saints' lives and women in the early church, but I will restrict my mention here to works that focus on Perpetua. Recent scholarly interest in Perpetua has meant that there are several critical works published or forthcoming from Oxford University Press: Jan M. Bremmer and Marco Formisano's *Perpetua's Passions: Multidisciplinary Approaches to the* Passio Perpetuae et Felicitatis (2012) contains many critical essays about various aspects of the *Passio* along with a translation of the text. Thomas Heffernan's *The Passion of Perpetua and Felicity* (2012) provides a translation and commentary on the text. And forthcoming from Oxford University Press is Barbara Gold's *Perpetua: A Martyr's Tale.*

Other works include Joyce Salisbury's *Perpetua's Passion: The Death and Memory of a Young Roman Woman* (New York: Routledge, 1997), which also provides many details about life in Roman Africa in the early third century CE, and William Farina's *Perpetua of Carthage: Portrait of a Third-Century Martyr* (Jefferson, NC, and London: McFarland, 2009).

SEQUENTIAL ART AND COMICS

Scott McCloud's *Understanding Comics: The Invisible Art* (New York: William Morrow Publishing, 1994) offers a detailed look at how and why graphic art forms are able to convey significant shared human experiences in a way that differs from printed media. McCloud's work also offers a brief overview of material evidence of sequential art that conveys narratives before the invention of the printing press, such as the Bayeux Tapestry. Will Eisner's *Comics and Sequential Art*: *Principles and Practices from the Legendary Cartoonist* (New York: W. W. Norton, 2008) provides audiences who are not as familiar with the medium an excellent introduction to how comics are structured and how the various elements come together to create a meaningful and engaging narrative. Lan Dong's edited collection *Teaching Comics and Graphic Narratives*: *Essays on Theory, Strategy and Practice* (Jefferson, NC, and London: McFarland, 2012) also makes a compelling case for why graphic narratives are now taking their place beside more traditional reading assignments in college and university classrooms. Finally, Thierry Groensteen's *Comics and Narration* (Jackson: University Press of Mississippi, 2015) delves into theories regarding the cognitive processes that readers experience when looking at sequential art.

THE MAKING OF THE GRAPHIC PORTION OF THE TEXT

Every scholar who studies this text faces significant challenges. Key questions need to be asked and answered about the *Passio*. How was Perpetua's baptism performed? How did Felicity give birth while in prison? Questions such as these also had to be considered when creating a visual representation of the *Passio*. This section will discuss the methodology behind the making of the text's sequential art and offer a few examples of the critical thought process that went into the making of the graphic art.

The first decision Liz and I had to make when we integrated images and text together was how we would portray Perpetua and the other characters. Because we have no physical evidence that could tell us *exactly* what Perpetua and Felicity looked like, we decided to make composite character sketches that reflected the various races and ethnicities living in Roman Carthage at the time.[7] In the early third century CE, the city would have been quite cosmopolitan because of Carthage's location and would have contained a diversity of peoples, religions, and cultures. The civilizations that had influenced the city's development, including Berber, Roman, and Hellenic, also enriched the ethnic diversity of the city.

Liz considered Greek, Roman/Italian, Berber, and Arab influences when drawing Perpetua and Felicity. This respect for acknowledging what we know and what we do not know about peoples' appearances in antiquity

---

7   While we do have sculptures, paintings, and mosaics that can offer us some idea of hairstyles and facial features of the times, this kind of material evidence was used as a guide, but not as an exact model, in the creation of this work's characters. In the end, Liz and I felt that the composite portraits would be the best way to acknowledge the diversity of Roman Africa.

is important.[8] We did not want to make Perpetua and Felicity appear to be somehow familiar looking to the audience in a way that would seem anachronistic.

We had to make significant choices regarding how to depict the material and cultural details within the scenes described in in the text. One example would be the scene where Felicity gives birth in prison. Roman women often used a special birthing chair when giving birth, but since prisons were not equipped for long-term occupation, we chose not to put Felicity on a birthing chair since we could not be certain that she would have had access to one while in prison. Instead, she is shown being propped upright, which would be in keeping with the Roman practice of being upright while in labor.

The final two pages of the graphic version of the *Passio* depict a speaker saying the text's final words to a large and diverse crowd. Liz and I deliberately chose to depict the ending in this way to remind readers that when we talk about the Christian church in the early third century CE, we are talking not about a specific building, or a particular locale in Roman Africa, but a community of believers that was growing and spreading throughout the Roman Empire. That is why we did not attempt to tie the *Passio*'s conclusion to a particular space or a particular person's sermon. For example, we could have placed the final scene in the Basilica Restituta in Carthage, which was where Augustine was known to have preached and which was considered to be Carthage's main cathedral, but instead we set the scene outdoors to make it more universal.

SETTINGS AND LOCATIONS

The role of place in the *Passio* is an important one. Perpetua is rarely specific about the exact location of events taking place, which provided some challenges for depicting the graphic text's visual backgrounds. Where is the prison that she is sent to? When she says she is "under observation," does that mean she is under house arrest, and, if so, where? What about the amphitheater? Was it the military amphitheater or the city's amphitheater? What was the more pleasant area of the prison like? Without more concrete details in the text, we cannot know.

Liz and I used the material evidence in situ from Roman Africa to reconstruct Carthage's material culture. We looked extensively and thoroughly at the archaeological remains to design everything from the size of the

---

8   An example of a greatly stylized version of Perpetua's looks appears in the 1956 *Girl Annual* comic "Lady without Fear: The True Story of St. Perpetua, Martyr." The British artist Gerald Haylock's depiction of Perpetua—her ingénue look recalls a '50s starlet—tells us about the standards for beauty in Haylock's time but not what the population looked like in Roman Africa in the third century CE.

bricks in buildings to the interior decoration of the private home in which Perpetua is possibly kept under house arrest. In addition to the archaeological evidence for Roman Africa's homes, the remains of the forum still exist today in modern-day Tunisia and so do the remains of the civic amphitheater. Since structures in Roman Carthage that exist today as remains have been meticulously researched by scholars, we read archaeologists' descriptions of their field excavations as well. Likewise, many examples of the public and domestic artwork, along with reconstructed models of various buildings, can be found in museums such as Tunisia's Bardo Museum.

Close study of material evidence from museum collections in Rome and the Roman mosaics of the Bardo National Museum in Tunisia offered a greater understanding of the details of daily life in Imperial Rome at the start of the third century. Material evidence—clothing, shoes, jewelry, coins, homes, paintings, sculptures, basilicas, amphitheaters, and monuments from around the Roman Empire—provided the context for what Perpetua's world would have looked like. In order for Liz to be able to draw Perpetua's hairstyle, jewelry, shoes, and clothing, for example, I sent her photos of sculptures, mosaics, wall paintings, and photos of actual earrings and necklaces that were the fashion during that time period. For the scenes in which Perpetua is under house arrest, I sent Liz pictures of ruins of houses from Roman Africa. Trips to the catacombs of ancient Rome helped to put early Christianity into context and define what the lives of the early Christians were like.

CLOTHING IN ANTIQUITY

Dress conveys one's identity—slave, Roman military, Roman religious official, male, female, young, old, and so forth—and can reveal one's socioeconomic position in society and suggest boundaries and divisions between groups. Outfits for the text's graphic portion needed to be intentionally designed to distinguish the different persons. Dress also needed to be as consistent as possible, to help the audience identify individuals from scene to scene.

Clothing and adornment serves as a way to set oneself apart from other individuals within a community or to indicate belonging to a particular subculture, and, as we have seen in the *Passio*, dress can function as a form of resistance. When Perpetua objects to being dressed as a priestess of Ceres before her execution (18.5), she is insisting that as a catechumen she will maintain her identity as a Christian and reject any visual expression of pagan beliefs. When her clothing tears and her hair becomes disheveled, she covers herself up and pins up her locks in order to not look as though she is in mourning (20.4–5). Thus, at critical points in the narrative, Perpetua claims authority, autonomy, and power over her own image through dress and appearance. She was dressed in a long white tunic as part of Saturus's vision—this clothing shows the martyr choosing to express Christian identity through dress, as the white tunic represents purity.[9]

The question of how to dress Perpetua and the others in the diary proved to be a challenging one. Although this story is about events that took place during the Roman Empire, it takes place in Carthage in Africa. The question scholars ask is: How did Roman citizens in the provinces dress? Did they adhere more to local customs of dress, or did they adopt the kind of dress one was more likely to find in the city of Rome?[10] The time period proved to be a bit challenging for determining clothing styles because fashions were changing at the turn of the century and various types of dress can go in and out of style.

The fact that Perpetua's story is set not in Rome but in Roman Africa meant that the question of how "Roman" the characters' clothing would look had to be a factor. Just as the characters in the graphic portion of the text are drawn as composites to reflect the ethnicity of that part of the world, their clothing has to reflect multiple factors: the climate, the fashions of the times, and the influence of Roman styles of dress in Carthage. Equally, we cannot assume that Roman clothing in Carthage would look identical to what was worn in the city of Rome at the start of the third century. Thus, how much Roman citizens in North Africa would have resembled their Roman-citizen-in-Rome counterparts in dress had to be taken into consideration. Liz and I looked at evidence from mosaics and wall paintings (including some from the Bardo National Museum in Tunisia) that showed the styles and customs of dress in Roman Africa. In addition, we consulted the works of scholars whose research focused on ancient dress, including that of soldiers, to determine how we should depict the persons in the diary.

Roman dress in antiquity as seen in Hollywood movies does not often reflect reality. The stereotype of the stern, toga-wearing Roman is just that—a typecast image taken from sculptures. This is not to say that there were not times and places that the toga was worn. When Perpetua appears in court, for example, the Roman official Hilarianus will appear in his toga (6.3). The toga is not everyday wear, however, so the characters only appear in it in specific times and places when official business demands this kind of formal dress. It is possible to consider that the Roman freedmen whose families were well established in Carthage would want their dress to reflect their identity and their connection to imperial Rome. Perpetua is dressed like a Roman matron since she is a Roman citizen and because

---

9   Heffernan (2012, 286).

10   See Charles-Picard (1959, 229–30) and Vout (1996, 204–20).

there is no official dress code for Christians. The articles of Roman dress she and other members of her family wear helps convey the presence of Roman values and ideals in the community of Carthage and the sense that there were certain times and places that the family identified with that community.

It would be incorrect to assume that there was a uniformity of dress for any of the groups with which the characters are affiliated. There was no required dress for slaves in imperial Rome. Although we know that in some instances slaves could be given their owner's castoff clothing, some slaves appear in the graphic section dressed in tunics, to help set them apart as having a different identity and affiliation to a different social group. Soldiers also lack a standard military uniform. There is no compulsory outfit that we can say that all Roman military persons wore no matter where they were stationed and no one uniform style of clothing for Christians, Judeans, or pagans at this time, either.

For the clothing of the military adjutant, Pudens, I consulted with Michael Alexander Speidel at the University of Bern, who is an expert on Roman military dress. He cautioned that there was no dress code for the Roman military. But he did point out that the soldiers' dress and the weapons they carried conveyed authority—and it was possible, although not required, for Pudens to carry his *hastile*, or spear, within the jail. Thus, Pudens carries the weapon to his meeting with Perpetua to communicate to her his authority and his position within the Roman military.

QUESTIONS

IDENTITY

1. What roles do Christianity, the Roman Empire, family, individual, and community play in shaping Perpetua's identity? What role does gender play in her story?

2. How did Christians and non-Christians relate to one another in Roman Africa? How did her father, who was not a Christian, react to Perpetua's decision to die as a Christian martyr?

3. Does being a twenty-two-year-old woman mean the same thing in antiquity as it does today? What was it like to be a Christian woman in Roman Africa?

4. What steps did Roman officials take to ensure that the community of imperial Rome remained cohesive in the third century CE?

5. Did Emperor Septimius Severus play a significant role in Perpetua's death, or was the decision to put Christians to death being handled at the local level in the provinces? What visual symbols of the emperor's authority appear in the text?

6. What was life like for slaves at this time? When the narrative suddenly shifts to Felicity, what role does she, as a pregnant woman who gives birth right before she goes to her death, play in this narrative?

7. How much of the commentary added by someone other than Perpetua is designed to make her narrative conform to later expectations about sainthood and martyrdom? How has the definition of a martyr changed over time?

MAKING THE GRAPHIC HISTORY

1. How does seeing graphic representation of resistance to social norms differ from reading about it?

2. What visual symbols represent early Christianity? How is this imagery used in the graphic portion of the text and in the diary?

3. At the end of the text, do you think the focus should be on how Perpetua lived or how she died? Does she become a hero? If yes, is it before or after she dies?

4. What emotions does the crowd in the *Passio* show at each event?

VALUES

1. Does Perpetua appear to be thinking for herself, or does it seem as though she has swapped one form of authority for another when she defies her father to become Christian?

2. Is she perceived as inflexible due to her religious convictions once her martyrdom becomes public? Is she transformed into a brave martyr by her circumstances?

3. Why won't Perpetua sacrifice to the emperor, even though her decision can lead only to her death? Why does she decide to leave her young son behind?

4. How do the male authority figures in the *Passio* react when she stands up for her beliefs?

5. What role do violence and intolerance play in Perpetua's story?

6. Does the crowd make the martyrs seem like criminales at the love feast and then heroes in death? How does the crowd's behavior change from the feast to the amphitheater?

7. When Perpetua receives public recognition of her acts through her audience's response, is she getting their approval? What is the most positive response from the crowd?

8. How does she earn honor and respect from the officials in charge who are acknowledging her requests and granting them?

9. What Roman value does Perpetua's father think she is rejecting by becoming Christian? Why is it so important to him that she uphold Roman values?

10. Does Perpetua ever appear to regret her decision to deny her father's authority?

THE PRIMARY SOURCE

1. What is the narrator-editor trying to accomplish at the start of the text? What details does this person tell you about Perpetua that she does not reveal herself?

2. What is the narrator telling you at the end of the story about Perpetua's life and death? Did she seem heroic to you before his eyewitness account?

TIMELINE FOR ROME AND CARTHAGE

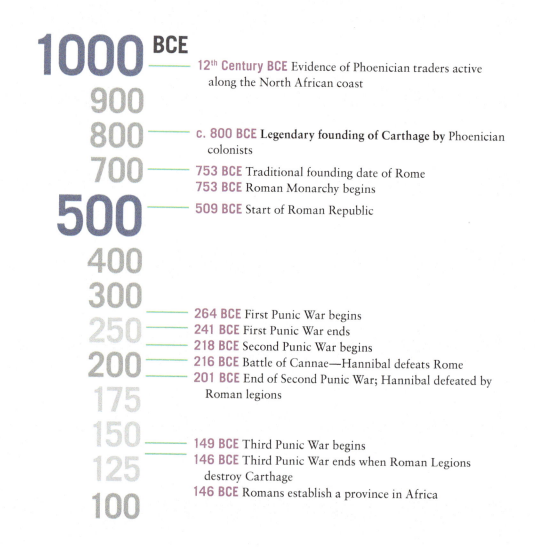

1000 BCE
900
800
700
500
400
300
250
200
175
150
125
100

12th Century BCE Evidence of Phoenician traders active along the North African coast

c. 800 BCE Legendary founding of Carthage by Phoenician colonists

753 BCE Traditional founding date of Rome
753 BCE Roman Monarchy begins
509 BCE Start of Roman Republic

264 BCE First Punic War begins
241 BCE First Punic War ends
218 BCE Second Punic War begins
216 BCE Battle of Cannae—Hannibal defeats Rome
201 BCE End of Second Punic War; Hannibal defeated by Roman legions

149 BCE Third Punic War begins
146 BCE Third Punic War ends when Roman Legions destroy Carthage
146 BCE Romans establish a province in Africa

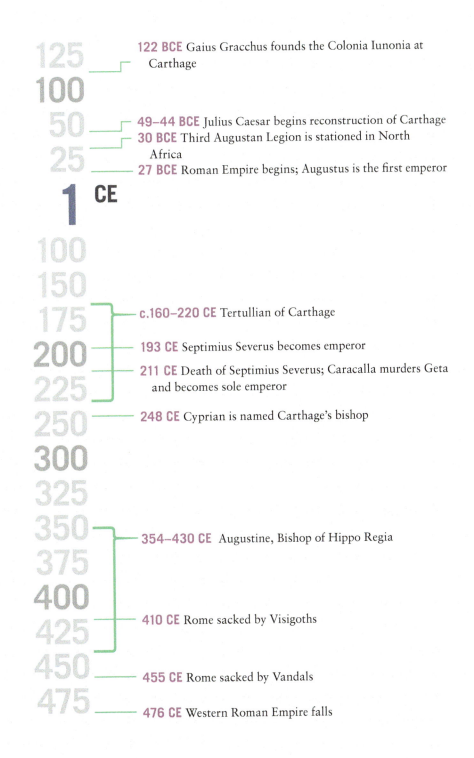

125

100

122 BCE Gaius Gracchus founds the Colonia Iunonia at
Carthage

50

25

49–44 BCE Julius Caesar begins reconstruction of Carthage

30 BCE Third Augustan Legion is stationed in North
Africa

27 BCE Roman Empire begins; Augustus is the first emperor

1 CE

100

150

175

c.160–220 CE Tertullian of Carthage

200

193 CE Septimius Severus becomes emperor

211 CE Death of Septimius Severus; Caracalla murders Geta
and becomes sole emperor

225

250

248 CE Cyprian is named Carthage's bishop

300

325

350

354–430 CE Augustine, Bishop of Hippo Regia

375

400

410 CE Rome sacked by Visigoths

425

450

455 CE Rome sacked by Vandals

475

476 CE Western Roman Empire falls

TIMELINE OF CHRISTIAN PERSECUTIONS

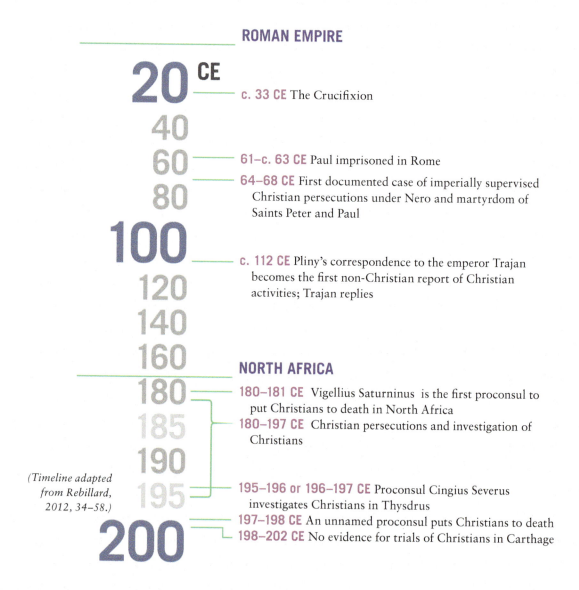

ROMAN EMPIRE

20 CE

c. 33 CE The Crucifixion

40

60 — **61–c. 63 CE** Paul imprisoned in Rome

64–68 CE First documented case of imperially supervised Christian persecutions under Nero and martyrdom of Saints Peter and Paul

80

100 — **c. 112 CE** Pliny's correspondence to the emperor Trajan becomes the first non-Christian report of Christian activities; Trajan replies

120

140

160

NORTH AFRICA

180 — **180–181 CE** Vigellius Saturninus is the first proconsul to put Christians to death in North Africa

180–197 CE Christian persecutions and investigation of Christians

185

190

(Timeline adapted from Rebillard, 2012, 34–58.)

195 — **195–196 or 196–197 CE** Proconsul Cingius Severus investigates Christians in Thysdrus

197–198 CE An unnamed proconsul puts Christians to death

198–202 CE No evidence for trials of Christians in Carthage

200

205

210

215

220

225

230

235

240

245

250

255

260

265

270

275

280

290

300

310

March 7, 203 CE Date given in the *Passio* for Perpetua's martyrdom

203–211 CE Period of relative peace for Christians in North Africa

209–210 CE C. Julius Asper gives a slight punishment to a Christian but does not order his death

210–211 or 211–212 CE C. Valeris Pudens releases a Christian since he did not have an accuser

212 CE Executions occur at the hands of C. Julius (Scapula) Lepidus Tertullus; additional executions take place in Numidia and Mauretania

250 CE Edit of Decius requires all citizens to sacrifice on behalf of the emperor

257-260 CE Valerian persecutions

258 CE Martyrdom of Cyprian

303 CE Edict of Diocletian orders the destruction of Christian churches and the burning of the Scriptures, and forbids Christian assemblies

313 CE The so-called Edict of Milan by the Emperors Constantine and Licinius legalizes Christianity (it is debatable whether or not there was a formal edict)

BIBLIOGRAPHY

PRIMARY SOURCES

Halporn, J. W. "Passio Sanctarum Perpetuae et Felicitatis." In *Bryn Mawr Latin Commentaries*. Bryn Mawr, PA: Bryn Mawr College, 1984.

Heffernan, T. *The Passion of Perpetua and Felicity*. New York and Oxford: Oxford University Press, 2012.

SECONDARY SOURCES

Ameling, W., "*Femina Liberaliter Instituta*—Some Thoughts on a Martyr's Liberal Education." In *Perpetua's Passions*: *Multidisciplinary Approaches to the Passio Perpetuae et Felicitatis*, edited by J. Bremmer and M. Formisano, 78–102. New York and Oxford: Oxford University Press, 2012.

Andreau, J., and R. Descat. *The Slave in Greece and Rome*. Translated by Marion Leopold. Madison: University of Wisconsin Press, 2011.

Bal, M. "Perpetual Contest." In *Perpetua's Passions*: *Multidisciplinary Approaches to the Passio Perpetuae et Felicitatis*, edited by J. Bremmer and M. Formisano, 134–49. New York and Oxford: Oxford University Press, 2012.

Barrow, R. *Greek and Roman Education*. London: Bristol Classical Press, 2011.

Barton, C. *The Sorrows of the Ancient Romans*: *The Gladiator and the Monster*. Princeton, NJ: Princeton University Press, 1993.

Beard, M., J. North, and S. Price, eds. *Religions of Rome. Volume 1*: *A History*. Cambridge: Cambridge University Press, 1998.

Binder, S. "Jewish-Christian Contacts in the Second and Third Centuries C.E.? The Case of Carthage; Tertullian and the Mishnah's Views on Idolatry." In *Studies in Rabbinic Judaism and Early Christianity: Text and Context*, edited by D. Jaffé, 187–230. Leiden, The Netherlands: Brill, 2010.

Birley, A. *Septimius Severus: The African Emperor*, 2nd ed. London and New York: Routledge, 1999.

Bomgardner, D. "The Carthage Amphitheater: A Reappraisal." *American Journal of Archaeology* 93, no. 1 (1989): 85–103.

Bradley, K. R. *Slaves and Masters in the Roman Empire*: *A Study in Social Control*. Oxford: Oxford University Press, 1987.

Brandt, O. "Understanding the Structures in Early Christian Baptisteries." In *Ablution, Initiation and Baptism*: *Late Antiquity, Early Judaism, and Early Christianity*, edited by D. Hellholm, T. Vegge, Ø. Norderval, and C. Hellholm, 1587–1609. Berlin: De Gruyter, 2011.

Bremmer, J. N. "The Motivation of Martyrs: Perpetua and the Palestinians." In *Religion im kulturellen Diskurs. Festschrift für Hans G. Kippenberg zu seinem 65. Geburtstag/ Religion in Cultural Discourse. Essays in Honor of Hans G. Kippenberg on Occasion of His 65th Birthday*, edited by B. Luchesi and K. von Stuckrad, 535–54. Berlin and New York: De Gruyter, 2004.

———. "Felicitas: The Martyrdom of a Young African Woman." In *Perpetua's Passions: Multidisciplinary Approaches to the Passio Perpetuae et Felicitatis*, edited by J. N. Bremmer and M. Formisano, 35–53. New York and Oxford: Oxford University Press, 2012.

Brown, P. *The World of Late Antiquity: AD 150–750*. New York and London: W. W. Norton and Company, 1971.

Bullard, R. "The Berbers of the Maghreb and Ancient Carthage." In *Africa and Africans in Antiquity*, edited by E. M. Yamauchi, 180–209. East Lansing: Michigan State University Press, 2001.

Charles-Picard, G. *La civilisation de l'Afrique romaine*. Paris: Collection des Études augustiniennes, Série Antiquité, 1990.

Cobb, L. S. *Dying to Be Men: Gender and Language in Early Christian Martyr Texts*. New York: Columbia University Press, 2008.

Coleman, K. "Fatal Charades: Roman Executions Staged as Mythological Enactments." *Journal of Roman Studies* 80 (1990): 44–73.

Cooley, A. "Septimius Severus: The Augustan Emperor." In *Severan Culture*, edited by S. Swain, S. Harrison and J. Elsner, 385–97. Cambridge: Cambridge University Press, 2007.

Cooper, K. "A Father, a Daughter, and a Procurator: Authority and Resistance in the Prison Memoir of Perpetua of Carthage." *Gender and History* 23, no. 3 (2011): 685–702.

———. *Band of Angels: The Forgotten World of Early Christian Women*. New York: Overlook Press, 2013.

Cotter-Lynch, M. Saint Perpetua across the Middle Ages: Mother, Gladiator, Saint. New York: Palgrave Macmillan, 2016.

Daniel-Hughes, C. *The Salvation of the Flesh in Tertullian of Carthage: Dressing for the Resurrection*. New York: Palgrave Macmillan, 2011.

———. "The Perils of Idolatrous Garb: Tertullian and Christian Belonging in Roman Carthage." In *Religious Competition in the Greco-Roman World*, edited by N. P. DesRosiers and L. C. Vuong, 15–26. Atlanta: SBL Press, 2016.

Davies, J. *Rome's Religious History: Livy, Tacitus and Ammianus on Their Gods*. Cambridge: Cambridge University Press, 2004.

Desmond, M. *Reading Dido: Gender, Textuality and the Medieval* Aeneid. Medieval Cultures 8. Minneapolis: University of Minnesota Press, 1994.

Dronke, P. *Women Writers of the Middle Ages: A Critical Study of Texts from Perpetua (†203) to Marguerite Porete (†1310)*. Cambridge: Cambridge University Press, 1984.

Duncan, R., and M. Smith. *The Power of Comics: History, Form and Culture*. London and New York: Bloomsbury, 2009.

Dunkle, R. *Gladiators: Violence and Spectacle in Ancient Rome*. London and New York: Routledge, 2013.

Ekenberg, A. "Initiation in the *Apostolic Tradition*." In *Ablution, Initiation and Baptism: Late Antiquity, Early Judaism, and Early Christianity*, edited by D. Hellholm, T. Vegge, Ø. Norderval, and C. Hellholm, 1011–50. Berlin: De Gruyter, 2011.

Farina, W. *Perpetua of Carthage: Portrait of a Third-Century Martyr*. Jefferson, NC, and London: McFarland, 2009.

Feeney, D. *Literature and Religion at Rome: Cultures, Contexts, and Beliefs*. Cambridge: Cambridge University Press, 1998.

Fishwick, D. "On the Origins of Africa Proconsularis, I: [The Amalgamation of Africa Vetus and Africa Nova]." *Antiquités africaines* 29 (1993): 53–62.

Francese, C. *Ancient Rome in So Many Words*. New York: Hippocrene Books, 2007.

Frend, W. "Blandina and Perpetua: Two Early Christian Heroines." In *Women and Early Christianity*, edited by D. M. Scholer,, 87–97. New York: Garland Press, 1993.

Galinsky, K. *Augustan Culture: An Interpretive Introduction*. Princeton, NJ: Princeton University Press, 1996.

Gold, B. "Gender Fluidity and Closure in Perpetua's Prison Diary." *Eugesta* 1 (2011): 237–51.

———. "Remaking Perpetua: A Female Martyr Reconstructed." In *Sex in Antiquity: Exploring Gender and Sexuality in the Ancient World*, edited by Mark Masterson, Nancy Sorkin Rabinowitz, and James Robson, 482–99. London and New York: Routledge, 2015.

Gros, P. "Le forum de la haute ville dans la Carthage romaine d'après les textes et l'archéologie." *Comptes rendus des séances de l'Académie des Inscriptions et Belles-Lettres* 126, no. 3 (1982): 636–58.

Harper, K. *Slavery in the Late Roman World, AD 275–425*. Cambridge: Cambridge University Press, 2011.

Henten, J. W., van. "The *Passio Perpetuae* and Jewish Martyrdom: The Motif of Motherly Love." In *Perpetua's Passions: Multidisciplinary Approaches to the Passio Perpetuae et Felicitatis*, edited by J. Bremmer and M. Formisano, 118–33. New York and Oxford: Oxford University Press, 2012.

Hillner, J. *Prison, Punishment and Penance in Late Antiquity*. Cambridge: Cambridge University Press, 2015.

Hope, V. "Status and Identity in the Roman World." In *Experiencing Rome: Culture, Identity and Power in the Roman Empire*, edited by J. Huskinson, 125–52. London and New York: Routledge, 2000.

———. "Negotiating Identity and Status: The Gladiators of Roman Nîmes." In *Cultural Identity in the Roman Empire*, edited by R. Laurence and J. Berry, 179–95. London and New York: Routledge, 2001.

Joshel, S. *Slavery in the Roman World*. Cambridge: Cambridge University Press, 2010.

Kitzler, P. *From* Passio Perpetuae *to* Acta Perpetuae: *Recontextualizing a Martyr Story in the Literature of the Early Church*. Berlin: De Gruyter, 2015.

Lassen, E. "The Roman Family: Ideal and Metaphor." In *Constructing Early Christian Families: Family as Social Reality and Metaphor*, edited by H. Moxnes, 103–20. London and New York: Routledge, 1997.

Lefkowitz M. "The Motivations for St. Perpetua's Martyrdom." *Journal of the American Academy of Religion* 44 (1976): 417–21.

LeMoine, F. "Authority in the Public Arena: Perpetua's Trial in Roman Law and Civic Spectacle." *Graven Images* 3 (1996): 213–22.

———. "Apocalyptic Experience and the Conversion of Women in Early Christianity." In *Fearful Hope: Approaching the New Millennium*, edited by Christopher Kleinhenz and Fannie J. LeMoine, 201–6. Madison: University of Wisconsin Press, 1999.

Markschies, C. "The 'Passio Sanctarum Perpetuae et Felicitatis' and Montanism?" In *Perpetua's Passions: Multidisciplinary Approaches to the Passio Perpetuae et Felicitatis*, edited by Jan Bremmer and M. Formisano, 277–90. New York and Oxford: Oxford University Press, 2012.

Maxwell, J. "Paganism and Christianization." In *The Oxford Handbook of Late Antiquity*, edited by S. Johnson, 849–75. Oxford: Oxford University Press, 2012.

McGowan, A. "Discipline and Diet: Feeding the Martyrs in Roman Carthage." *Harvard Theological Review* 96, no. 4 (2003): 455–76.

McKechnie, P. "St. Perpetua and Roman Education in AD 200." *L'antiquité classique* 63 (1994): 279–91.

Miles, R. "Rivalling Rome: Carthage." In *Rome the Cosmopolis*, edited by Catharine Edwards and Greg Woolf, 123–46. Cambridge: Cambridge University Press, 2003.

Miller, P. *Dreams in Late Antiquity: Studies in the Imagination of a Culture*. Princeton, NJ: Princeton University Press, 1994.

Montserrat, D. "Reading Gender in the Roman World." In *Experiencing Rome: Culture, Identity and Power in the Roman Empire*, edited by J. Huskinson, 153–81. London and New York: Routledge, 2000.

Morgan, T. *Literate Education in the Hellenistic and Roman Worlds*. Cambridge: Cambridge University Press, 1998.

Norderval, Ø. "Simplicity and Power: Tertullian's *De Baptismo*." In *Ablution, Initiation and Baptism: Late Antiquity, Early Judaism, and Early Christianity*, edited by D. Hellholm, T. Vegge, Ø. Norderval, and C. Hellholm, 947–72. Berlin: De Gruyter, 2011.

Norris, H. *Ancient European Costume and Fashion*. New York: Dover Publications, 2013.

Ogden, D. "Magic in the Severan Period." In *Severan Culture*, edited by S. Swain, S. Harrison, and J. Elsner, 458–69. Cambridge: Cambridge University Press, 2007.

Olson, K. *Dress and the Roman Woman: Self-Presentation and Society*. London and New York: Routledge, 2008.

Orlin, E. *Foreign Cults in Rome: Creating a Roman Empire*. Oxford: Oxford University Press, 2010.

Osiek, C. "Perpetua's Husband." The Journal of Early Christian Studies 10.2 (2002): 287–90.

Perkins, J. "'The Passion of Perpetua': A Narrative of Empowerment." *Latomus* 53, no. 4 (1994): 837–47.

———. "The Rhetoric of the Maternal Body in the Passion of Perpetua." In *Mapping Gender in Ancient Religious Discourses*, edited by T. Penner and C. V. Stichele, 313–32. Leiden, The Netherlands: Brill, 2007.

Quinn, J. C. "Roman Africa?" *Digressus* Supplement 1 (2003): 7–34.

Rankin, D. *Tertullian and the Church*. Cambridge: Cambridge University Press, 1995.

Raven, S. *Rome in Africa*. London and New York: Longman, 1984.

Rebillard, É. *Christians and Their Many Identities in Late Antiquity, North Africa, 200–450 CE*. Ithaca, NY, and London: Cornell University Press, 2012.

Reis, D. "Peripatetic Pedagogy: Travel and Transgression in the *Apocryphal Acts of the Apostles*." *Studia Patristica* 13 (2013): 263–75.

Rives, J. *Religion and Authority in Roman Carthage from Augustus to Constantine*. Oxford: Clarendon Press, 1995.

———. "The Piety of a Persecutor." *Journal of Early Christian Studies* 4, no. 1 (1996): 1–25.

———. "Religion in the Roman World." In *Experiencing Rome: Culture, Identity and Power in the Roman Empire*, edited by J. Huskinson, 245–75. London and New York: Routledge, 2000.

———. *Religion in the Roman Empire*. Malden, MA, and Oxford, UK: Blackwell, 2007.

Robert, L. "Une vision de Perpétue martyre à Carthage en 203." *Comptes rendus des séances de l'Académie des inscriptions et Belles-Lettres* 126, no. 2 (1982): 228–76.

Ros, K. "The Roman Theater at Carthage." *American Journal of Archaeology* 100, no. 3 (1996): 449–89.

Ross, C. F. "The Reconstruction of the Later Toga." *American Journal of Archaeology* 15, no. 1 (1911): 24–31.

Rüpke, J. *Die Religion Der Römer: Eine Einführung*. Munich: Beck, 2006.

———. *From Jupiter to Christ: On the History of Religion in the Roman Imperial Period*. Translated by David M. B. Richardson. Oxford: Oxford University Press, 2014.

Salisbury, J. *Perpetua's Passion: The Death and Memory of a Young Roman Woman*. New York and London: Routledge, 1997.

Shaw, B. D. "The Passion of Perpetua." *Past and Present* 139 (1993): 3–45.

———. "Body/Power/Identity: Passions of the Martyrs." *Journal of Early Christian Studies* 4, no. 3 (1996): 269–312.

———. "Judicial Nightmares and Christian Memory." *Journal of Early Christian Studies* 11, no. 4 (2003): 533–63.

Sigismund-Nielsen, H. "Vibia Perpetua: An Indecent Woman." In *Perpetua's Passions: Multidisciplinary Approaches to the Passio Perpetuae et Felicitatis*, edited by Jan Bremmer and M. Formisano, 103–17. New York and Oxford: Oxford University Press, 2012.

Smith, N. D. "Plato and Aristotle on the Nature of Women." *Journal of the History of Philosophy* 21, no. 4 (1983): 467–78.

Spaeth, B. *The Roman Goddess Ceres*. Austin: University of Texas Press, 1996.

Speidel, M. A. "Dressed for Occasion: Clothes and Context in the Roman Army." In *Wearing the Cloak: Dressing the Soldier in Roman Times*, edited by M.-L. Nosch, 1–12. Oxford: Oxbow Books, 2012.

Too, Y. L. "Introduction: Writing the History of Ancient Education." In *Education in Greek and Roman Antiquity*, edited by Y. L. Too, 1–21. Leiden, The Netherlands: Brill, 2001.

Vierow, H. "Feminine and Masculine Voices in the *Passion of Saints Perpetua and Felicitas*." *Latomus* 58, no. 3 (1999): 600–19.

Vout, C. "The Myth of the Toga: Understanding the History of Roman Dress." *Greece and Rome* 43, no. 2 (1996): 204–20.

Waldner, K., "Visions, Prophecy and Authority in the *Passio Perpetuae*." In *Perpetua's Passions: Multidisciplinary Approaches to the Passio Perpetuae et Felicitatis*, edited by J. N. Bremmer and M. Formisano, 201–19. Oxford: Oxford University Press, 2012.

Welch, K. *The Roman Amphitheater: From Its Origins to the Colosseum*. Cambridge: Cambridge University Press, 2007.

Wiedemann, T. *Slavery*. Oxford: Oxford University Press, 1987.

———. *Greek and Roman Slavery*. London: Routledge, 1988.

Williams, C. "Perpetua's Gender: A Latinist Reads the *Passio Perpetuae et Felicitatis*." In *Perpetua's Passions: Multidisciplinary Approaches to the Passio Perpetuae et Felicitatis*, edited by Jan Bremmer and M. Formisano, 54–77. New York and Oxford: Oxford University Press, 2012.

Wypustek, A. "Magic, Montanism, Perpetua, and the Severan Persecution." *Vigiliae Christianae* 51, no. 3 (1997): 276–97.

GLOSSARY

AGAPE "Love feast," or communal meal, where Christians would come together to eat.

CATECHUMEN Christian convert who was preparing for the baptismal rite through instruction.

CENA LIBERA Banquet that took place in a public area which served as a gladiator's last meal.

CUM MANU A Latin phrase that can be translated as "with legal control" that refers to a wife being placed under the *potestas* of her husband when she married.

DIARIA Daily ration of food for prisoners or slaves.

MONOTHEISM Belief in one God.

MONTANISM Also known as New Prophecy, this was a Christian sect popular in the late second century CE that placed a high value on martyrdom.

MOS MAIORUM Translated from the Latin as "the ancestral custom," the term represents the unwritten social norms for public and private life.

PATERFAMILIAS Male head of the Roman family.

PATRIA POTESTAS Power the Roman male head of the family exercises over his children.

PIETAS Roman virtue that corresponds to duty to one's country and/or parents.

POLYTHEISM Belief in multiple gods.

POTESTAS Roman word that corresponds to power and is used in a legal sense.

RELIGIO Demonstrating proper care for the Roman gods; appropriate religious behavior.

ROMANIZATION The expansion of Roman law, language and culture.

SINE MANU A Latin phrase that can be translated as "without legal control" that refers to a father retaining *potestas* over his daughter even after she is married instead of *potestas* transferring to her husband.

SUPERSTITIO Demonstrating excessive devotion or zeal for *religio*; inappropriate religious behavior.